THE MAYAN FACTOR:
PATH BEYOND TECHNOLOGY

THE
MAYAN FACTOR
Path Beyond Technology

José Argüelles, Ph.D.

BEAR & COMPANY, SANTA FE, NEW MEXICO

Library of Congress Cataloging-in-Publication Data

Argüelles, José, 1939-
    The Mayan factor.

    Bibliography: p.
    1. Mayas—Chronology—Miscellanea. 2. Indians of Mexico—Chronology—Miscellanea.
3. Indians of Central America—Chronology—Miscellanea. I. Title.
BF1999.A6395 1987   001.9'4   87-960

ISBN 0-939680-38-6

Bear & Company
P.O. Drawer 2860
Santa Fe, NM 87504

Art: José Argüelles

Design: Angela C. Werneke

Typography: Copygraphics, Santa Fe &
            Casa Sin Nombre, Ltd., Santa Fe

Printed in the United States of America by BookCrafters

Dedicated to my teacher, the incomparable C.T. Mukpo

TABLE OF CONTENTS

 ACKNOWLEDGMENTS

The writing and production of *The Mayan Factor* would not have been possible without the love so totally infused into it.

First and foremost to be credited is my mother-in-law, Maya, who read the manuscript as it came out, chapter by chapter, cheering me on when few were doing so. Naturally, the daughter of Maya, my wife Lloydine, must be thanked for radiating continuously the source connecting me to the Earth as the Earth is connected to the stars. The children in my life, too—Josh, Tara, Heidi, Paul, and Yvonne—and the circles they make with all of their friends, must also be mentioned for the truth of the love they offer so unconditionally. Finally, in this domestic vein, it would not be fair if I did not mention those psychic nodes of inter-dimensional warmth, the dog, Genji, and the cats, Sponsor and Onyx, living proof that we are not alone.

In addition to the people mentioned in the first chapter who offered me clues, information, and insight in the piecing together of *The Mayan Factor*, a few other individuals stand out who, during the fermentation and production process, were beacons of light. Their belief in me and the work were a profoundly sustaining nourishment. These include: Stan Padilla, quiet seer whose artistry and prayers are circles of protection purifying the channel of vision; Brooke Medicine Eagle, whose sisterhood is the twinkling essence of human regeneration; Don Eduardo Calderon, trickster of the dream body, who assisted in opening conduits of terrestrial memory; His Eminence Tai Situ Rinpoche, for bridging the worlds; Rupert Sheldrake, for engaging the field; and Ted and J. J., co-practitioners of cosmonogamous loyalty.

Of course, *The Mayan Factor* would be but another manuscript sitting in a file were it not for the genius of Barbara Clow of Bear & Company, who, upon receiving this text, promptly saw the need to give it to the world. Her husband, Gerry, also deserves mention for his steadfastness and humor in this whole process, as well as Angela Werneke for the care she has taken with visual presentation.

Lastly, in this regard, are the beings of the spirit world whose guidance has been of enduring compassion, seeding my wisdom-wonder rapturously as I have exhausted my doubt that it could be so.

To all of these, and infinitely more, the gratitude of boundless being is offered unconditionally from a heart whose greatest joy is the simplicity of the moment.

Evam maya e ma ho! (All hail the harmony of mind and nature!)

FOREWORD
BY BRIAN SWIMME

Among Sinologists there is a folk legend about the first westerners—a group of Jesuit scholars—to study the I Ching in the seventeenth century. The enterprise began with great energy and hope, the language was learned, the meanings deciphered and pondered over. Then tragedy struck. Several of the brilliant young men went insane. The difficulty of understanding the I Ching's wisdom within western categories of mind simply overwhelmed these dedicated men. In the end, the Society of Jesus was forced to abandon the project and even to forbid further study of this exotic Chinese scripture.

The story, even if apocryphal, throws light on Dr. José Argüelles' work, for he too has plunged wholeheartedly into what, for the western mind, is an equally baffling system of knowledge, the Tzolkin of the Maya. After a lifetime spiralling around this enigma, Dr. Argüelles has emerged with his story of what it means, and it is a wild story indeed. We are asked to consider—among other equally "outrageous" claims—the following:

First, that human history is shaped in large part by a galactic beam through which the Earth and Sun have been passing for the last 5000 years, and that a great moment of transformation possibly awaits us as we arrive at the beam's end in 2012;

Second, that the activities and world views of cultures follow the nature of the "galactic seasons", the code of which has been captured both mathematically and symbolically by the Maya;

Third, that each person has the power to connect directly—sensously, sensually, electromagnetically—with the energy/information of this beam that emanates from the galactic core, and can in this way awaken to one's true mind, higher mind, deepest mind.

Undoubtedly many will think that Dr. Argüelles has gone the way of the Jesuits who disappeared into the I Ching—mad, manic, and marooned in private delusions. Certainly Dr. Argüelles himself is aware of the shocking nature of his conclusions. He warns us honestly at the beginning: "For me the situation meant taking a leap, plunging off the edge, as it were, into mental territory that had been declared extinct or tabu by the prevailing cultural standards". And certainly his work has both the extravagance and muddiness of every fresh vision of reality, and this alone makes reading his book a challenge, even aside from the cosmic magnitude of his claims.

Having said all that, let me indicate why I think that Dr. Argüelles' vision is of profound worth. I am convinced that any vision of the universe that *doesn't* shock us is without value for us. We must bear in mind that we reasonable westerners, we rational Christian-Jewish-secular-democratic citizens are the ones who hold the Earth hostage with our nuclear weapons. We modern industrialists are the ones who carry out the ecocide that has spread over every continent.

To say a vision of the universe is "reasonable" means that it fits into this modern world view that initiated and supports this global terror. We don't need reasonable visions; we need the most outrageously wild visions of the universe we can find. Dr. Augüelles' vision qualifies.

But his vision is not just *wild*. With the unerring accuracy of all genius, Dr. Argüelles knows that western science and western society's only hope for balance is by fully assimilating the cosmology of the primal peoples, and in particular that of the Maya. Why should the primal cosmologies be singled out? Because primal peoples begin with the same conviction: the Earth, the Sun, the galaxy, the universe—everything everywhere is alive and intelligent.

What is required of us is *humility*. We who were trained in the modern world view that frames and supports our militarism, consumerism, patriarchy, and anthropocentrism need to recognize our fatal mistake—we began with the assumption that the universe is dead, devoid of feeling and intelligence and purpose. Can we find the courage to shake ourselves away from that fatal delusion? Can we find the wisdom to turn to the Maya and their science and learn the truth of the universe?

In the remainder of this introduction, I would like to comment at some length on Dr. Argüelles' three "outrageous" claims. Since my own training is in mathematical physics, my line of thought necessarily reflects the contours of contemporary science. But I need to emphasize here that I am not attempting to put the Mayan vision into modern, scientific categories. The Mayan cosmology *cannot* be put into modern, scientific categories. But there emerges in our time a post-modern science, a scientific orientation that assimilates the world view of the primal peoples with the world view of modern science. It is from the context of this holistic, pan-human, post-modern science that I speak.

First, the galactic beam, through which the Maya claim we are passing. To start, let me say that modern science has never spoken of such a beam in the way the Maya do. But physicists have recently become aware of ways in which we are influenced by beams passing through the galaxy, and this by itself is news. Current astrophysics describes these beams as density waves that sweep through the galaxy and that influence galactic evolution. For instance, our Sun's birth was the result of this wave. The density wave passed through and ignited a giant star, which exploded and evoked our own Sun's existence.

In fact, all star formation is due primarily to these beams sweeping through our galaxy. We can begin to formulate the notion of the galaxy as an organism, one involved in its own development. We speak of the "self-organizing dynamics" of the galaxy. Or, from a more organismic perspective, we speak of the galaxy as unfolding—the birth of stars are pictured as part of the galactic epigenesis. The Sun, then, is seen as activated by dynamics governed by the galactic center; just so, the eye of a frog is seen as activated by the dynamics governed by its own organismic center.

The obvious question is this: Just how far does the galactic dynamism go with respect to the development of the Sun and its evolving planets? That is, do the galaxy's dynamics have only to do with the ignition of the Sun after which the Sun and Earth are on their own? Or is the galactic beam involved with the evolution of life?

A couple of comments are needed here. First, it can be said quite simply that the galaxy is continually involved with the evolution of Earth and its life. The galactic density beams have swept through the galaxy over the entire 4.55 billion years of the Sun's existence, and whenever these pass through the Sun, they alter its dynamics and thus alter the radiant energy that bathes the Earth. I have no doubt that, as evolutionary biologists begin to reflect on this, they will articulate the ways in which the development of life on Earth has been shaped by these dynamics. We will become increasingly aware that the shape of the elm leaf has been molded not just by natural selection on Earth, but by the action of the galaxy as a whole.

Secondly, we need to recognize that it was simply impossible for modern science to notice the existence of a galactic beam such as the Maya describe. Modern science focused on material, on its change of position. All qualities—colors, smells, emotions, feelings, intuitions—were termed secondary, and dismissed. That is, we committed ourselves *from the beginning* to a mode of consciousness that was never going to recognize the Mayan galactic beam.

What needs to be appreciated at the same time is just how difficult it was to do what modern science has done. For instance, to notice empirically that the Sun has a beginning —that is an accomplishment requiring a very heightened mode of consciousness. Just think how exotic consciousness had to become to actually see the continents move! Or to actually hear the echo of the primeval fireball twenty billion years ago at the beginning of time! By recognizing modern science's particular development of consciousness, we can begin to forgive its oversights, and to appreciate other modes of consciousness, developed around different cultural projects.

The Maya were a people intoxicated with a different cultural aim which required an entirely different development of consciousness. Where the modern scientists have been able to detect experientially the physical effects of density beams sweeping through the galaxy, the Maya were able to detect experientially beams with different efficacies, beams that influenced not the birth and functioning of stars, but the birth and functioning of ideas, of visions, of convictions. Or rather, what I myself think is the case: both the modern scientists and the Maya respond to the *same beams.* The modern scientists developed a mode of consciousness enabling them to articulate the *physical* effects of these beams; the Maya developed a consciousness enabling them to articulate the *psychic* effects of these beams.

Second, the galactic seasons. The Maya, in Dr. Argüelles' presentation, taught that each era has a particular quality to it, one favoring a special type of activity, and all of this is captured in the code of the Tzolkin. By knowing the galactic code to the seasons, one can anticipate their arrival and can thus act accordingly, and with great effect. Such an orientation to the universe was common to most primal peoples, though perhaps none had the exquisite nuance of the Maya. Furthermore, early and medieval western religious tradition has a similar conception of time, where each moment or era had its special quality given to it by the heart of the divine; knowing the quality of the moment enabled one to enter deeply into divine activity.

My own way of approaching this idea of a "galactic season" is via the twenty billion years of cosmic history. When we examine our account of what has actually happened, we see that each era has its special quality, its unique moment, its particular creativity.

For instance, a half-million years into the cosmic epic, the time arrived for creating the hydrogen atoms. We need to emphasize here that this creativity is intrinsically tied to the macrophase nature of the cosmos in that moment. Until then, hydrogen atoms were not created; afterwards, hydrogen atoms were not created. But *at that time* hydrogen atoms could and *did* leap into being by the quintillion. There are dozens of such examples throughout all eras of the cosmic epic, but perhaps we can stay with the emergence of the hydrogen atoms to make the point concerning activity inherent to a cosmic season.

Prior to the emergence of hydrogen, it was in fact possible for an individual hydrogen atom to form. But to do so requried a tremendous expenditure of energy. And the atom quickly melted away in the primeval furnace. To create hydrogen atoms at other times was to work against the grain of the universe. Effortless and abundant creativity depends on both the innate urgency of hydrogen to emerge on the one hand, and the quality of the time of the universe on the other. It was only when, to quote Dr. Argüelles, "momentary need joined with universal purpose" that effective creativity happened. When the quality of the universe shifted to invite hydrogen atoms into existence, they poured forth in great abundance. The existence of these cosmic and galactic seasons is found everwhere throughout the twenty billion years of existence.

The question immediately surfaces in the western mind: "There may be seasons for the birth of atoms, or of galaxies, or of primitive cells. But what about my own thoughts? What about human culture? Are these affected by galactic times?" This brings us to our discussion of:

Third, personal interaction with the galactic mind.   Indeed, what can we say about this notion of galactic intelligence and purpose?

I saved this point for last, because here we deal with the deepest reaches of the western psyche's repression. The Maya felt they were engaged with the mind of the Sun, which manifested for them the mind and heart of the galaxy. The Maya felt that the galaxy had desires. Modern scientists heard that and relegated the Maya to the "fairy tale" bin. But our rejection of their wisdom only reveals our dangerously lopsided psychic condition.

Consider this. Our intellectual ancestors in 17th-century Europe could stand before a screaming animal convinced that the animal had no feelings. When asked how they could be so cold-hearted, they explained that these animals were just machines that had been damaged; they emitted awful sounds just as any machine does when damaged.

As their descendants, we have the same distorted sensibilities. How else can we remain apathetic as the living world howls in anguish throughout the planet today? I bring this up with the hope that once we suspect the truth—that our modern sensibility is the most deformed in all 50,000 years of *Homo sapiens'* existence—we will begin the task of awakening the full spectrum of human psychic sensitivity. Only then will we stop our assault on life. Only then will we live an ecstatic existence similar to the Maya.

Our difficulty stems from our cultural mistake of thinking of hydrogen atoms and stars and so forth as "just physical", and ourselves and our psychic life as transcendent, as utterly disconnected from the universe.

The cosmic creation story of post-modern science offers a different starting point: the universe as a single multiform energy event. And thus human consciousness and the human body and owl consciousness and the owl body are all flowerings of one numinous cosmic process. In this holistic orientation, we can begin to appreciate the way in which our thoughts and bones and intuitions (and the thoughts and bones and intuitions of the owl) are all weavings of the same fundamental sacred dynamics.

Within this perspective, "feelings" are not fabricated in the transcendent human mind. Instead, feelings are transmitted, just as photons are transmitted. This is really the most ordinary experience. A person standing in the presence of a magnificent granite cliff is suffused with all sorts of feelings; these are the feelings that the mountain has communicated to the human.

Consider, then, a Maya standing bathed in the Sun's light. What can we say is happening? This event, like every event, is simultaneously psychical and physical. We can speak of the quantum electrodynamic interaction of the Sun's photons with the human electrons; or we can speak of the feelings and intuitions that are experienced "within". The totality of the event demands that both poles be taken together. The Sun is both heating the skin and igniting the mind; the Sun is both sharing its warmth and expressing its inner feeling; the Sun is both transmitting its thermonuclear energy and projecting its ideas and demands.

It is difficult to stop reflecting on the fascinating ideas found in Dr. Argüelles' book. Jump in and see for yourself. May you return with new power for activating the health and creativity of the Earth Community!

Brian Swimme
Institute in Culture and Creation Spirituality
Holy Names College, Oakland.

INTRODUCTION:
THE MYSTERY OF THE MAYA:
SCIENCE TRANSCENDED

Ever since the triumph of rationalism and the Industrial Revolution of the eighteenth century, it has been an institutionalized truism that modern science represents the pinnacle of human achievement. This belief is the cornerstone of the doctrine of material, technological progress. The notion that there could have been a science more advanced than the prevailing one which, after all, underlies every aspect of global industrial civilization, has been virtually unthinkable. Yet the moment has come when the rationally unthinkable may be the only solution remaining in order to allow safe passage beyond the treacherous onslaught of nuclear militarism and environmental poisoning which now threatens the existence of this planet.

Entrenched and ever-vigilant in their self-support, the forces of scientific materialism have zealously guarded the portals to their domain, keeping in mind a singular goal: to maintain the myth of ever-progressing technological superiority. Thus, UFOs, varieties of paranormal experience, the discovery in 1976 of "rationally" inexplicable phenomena on Mars swiftly become classified documents, withheld from the public. Yet, on the morning of January 28, 1986, just four days after the triumphant Voyager 2 flew by Uranus with its bewildering information release, the space shuttle Challenger exploded in full televised and public view. In that awesome fiery moment, the myth of technological superiority suffered a severe blow.

It is in the window of doubt and vulnerability provided by the Challenger's fateful mission that intelligent people may question as never before the purpose of technology and the "infallibility" of modern science. Through the crack in the myth of technological superiority strange winds now blow. In the moonlight of that which transcends scientific rationalism, we may pose the questions: What if the way we are doing things is not the best or wisest? What if we are not the most intelligent civilization known to Earth? Could there have been people smarter, wiser, more advanced than us, who in our smugness we have overlooked? Could there have been a science superior to ours practiced both on this planet and elsewhere? What makes us so sure that scientific materialism is the best technique to wrench answers from a cosmos infintely more vast and mysterious than the rational mind can comprehend? In other words, what the spectre of technological crisis invokes is a paradigm shift of a genuinely radical nature. Such a shift has been in the air for a long time, thanks to pioneering research in quantum physics, but has needed an experiential jolt to get it grounded.

Throughout the twentieth century, sensitive scientific minds have been attempting to inform themselves about and alert the public to the irrational behavior of the world which rational science tries to observe. Though their message has escaped the war-lords and technocrats whose decision-making power shapes the social order, popularizers of the "new science" like Fritjof Capra, Isaac Bentov, and Gary Zukov have made admirable efforts to communicate the similarity between quantum physics and Eastern mysticism, at least to a critical thinking minority. Indeed, the conclusion to Zukov's *The Dancing Wu Li Masters* (1979) verges on the unthinkable by declaring that we are approaching the "end of science." Yet even he is incapable of surrendering the notion of the "unresting endeavor and continually progressing development of more and more comprehensive and useful physical theories."

The real "end of science," the long-anticipated, radical paradigm shift means the surrender of the notion of unceasing progress itself. Or at least the surrender of it long enough to see whether there may not be non-physicalistic or non-materialistic sciences that transcend the notion of progress—and non-progress—altogether. Of course, the myth of scientific progress and technological superiority could receive no greater blow than to discover that a more advanced science existed prior to the rise of the myth of progress, practiced by a people who, by modern estimation, were still in the Stone Age. Most specifically, I am referring to a system of thought virtually overlooked by all of the proponents of the "new science." This system of thought is the science known and practiced by the ancient people called the Maya.

The closest example to the system of Mayan science known to the champions of the new science is the Chinese legacy of the I Ching. Even the I Ching, however, has not been fully comprehended by the "new scientists," who, still immersed in the doctrine of progress, have not been able to see it for what it is: the code form of a science based on holonomic resonance rather than atomic physics.

Martin Schönberger in *The I Ching and the Genetic Code: The Hidden Key to Life* (1973), Robert Anton Wilson in *The Illuminati Papers* (1980), and my own *Earth Ascending* (1984) are some of the few efforts that approach the I Ching as an example of a system that is more comprehensive than that of present-day science. As Schönberger puts it, the I Ching represents". . .a world formula with the stature of an order of reality. . .the answer to Heisenberg's quest for those 'anonymous basic forms and polar symmetries of uniform nature'."

Like the world-order system of I Ching, the system of Mayan science is one of holonomic resonance, as much of the future as it is of the past. Indeed, from the perspective of Mayan science, the terms future and past are of little value as gauges of superiority or progress. For the Maya, if time exists at all, it is as a circuit from whose common source future and past flow equally, always meeting and being united in the present moment. Mayan science, like the I Ching, can be considered both pre- and post-scientific.

How is it, then, that at this moment of technological crisis and paradigm shift, the

Maya invite themselves into our consciousness? Who were—or are the Maya? Where did they come from? What were their achievements? Why did they do what they did? Why did they abandon their civilization at its peak? Where did they go, and why?

While Eastern forms of thought and actual practices—yoga, meditation, flower arranging, martial arts and so forth—have slowly become an increasingly prevalent phenomenon over the past half-century, relentlessly revolutionizing our culture and impacting on our scientific thinking, the Maya have remained enigmatic and remote.

Yet, to evoke the Maya of Central America is at the same time to evoke a curious resonance from the East, from India. After all, Maya is a key Hindu philosophical term meaning "origin of the world" and "world of illusion." The word Maya in Sanskrit is further related to concepts meaning "great," "measure," "mind," "magic," and "mother." Not surprisingly, we find that Maya is the name of the mother of the Buddha. And in the Vedic classic, *The Mahabharata,* we read that Maya was the name of a noted astrologer-astronomer, magician, and architect, as well as the name of a great wandering tribe of navigators.

Not only in ancient India, home of high metaphysics and spiritual adventure, do we find the name Maya, but also farther to the west. The treasurer of the renowned boy-king of Egypt, Tutankhamen, was named Maya, while in Egyptian philosophy we find the term Mayet, meaning universal world order. In Greek mythology, the seven Pleiades, daughters of Atlas and Pleione and sisters of the Hyades, number among them one called Maia, also known as the brightest star of the constellation Pleiades. And finally, we know that our month of May is derived from the name of the Roman goddess, Maia, "the great one," the goddess of spring, daughter of Faunus and wife of Vulcan.

Returning to the Maya of Central America, we find that their name is derived from the word Mayab, the term given to describe the Yucatan Peninsula, key area of the Mayan bioregional home base. So the question remains: Who were the Maya? Why is it that the name associated with this Central American civilization appears across much of the rest of the world? Is that just coincidence? Where did the Maya come from?

Current anthropological dogma has it that the Maya were part of the large group of Amerindians who crossed the Bering Strait from Asia during the last Ice Age as recently as 12,000 years ago and eventually settled in what is now Central America. To read late Mayan texts like the *Popul Vuh, The Book of Books of Chilam Balam*, and *The Annals of the Cakchiquels*, we get the distinct impression that indeed, the Maya arrived from afar, "from the other side of the sea we came to the place called Tulan, where we were begotten and given birth by our mothers and our fathers..." (Cakchiquels). Lest one think the matter is simple, we read elsewhere in the same, somewhat garbled text that there were four Tulans:

"From four (places) the people came to Tulan. In the east is one Tulan; another in Xibalbay (the underworld); another in the west where we came ourselves, from the west, and another is where God is (above, heaven). Therefore there were four Tulans."

In examining the foregoing passage, we find that the place of origins or the process

of origins described by the Maya in this late text is mandalic, celestial, and cosmic in nature. The Four Tulans represent the solar passage, east and west, as well as a superworld and an underworld. Furthermore, a reading of ancient Mayan and Mexican history and mythology in general shows that Tulan (or Tollan) is an archetypal code name as much as an actual place. What if Tulan describes not necessarily a geographic place, but a process of becoming and point of entry from one world-realm into another? In this regard, the Mayan recollection of origins resembles the Hopi, which describes passage from different worlds, of which the present is the fourth. But what are these worlds? Do they describe earlier stages of life on this planet? Or do they describe cosmic passages simultaneously occurring on this planet and/or elsewhere?

Leaving aside for the moment the question of origins, we find ourselves on firmer ground in contemplating the achievements of the Maya. Unquestionably, the Maya represent one of the great civilizational flowerings of planet Earth. Scattered across the jungles of the Yucatan and the highlands of present-day Guatemala are incredible numbers of ancient cities and temple sites. Towering stepped pyramids, finely laid-out plazas, and ceremonial centers are exquisitely adorned with sculpted stones, covered everywhere with hieroglyphic inscriptions.

Several things strike us about the magnificent Mayan ruins, chief among them being their isolation. Even in relation to the closely connected highland Mexican civlization, the Mayan artistic style is unique. Isolated in the Central American jungles, the Maya appear as aloof as they are remote. Yet in considering their pyramids towering over the jungle tree lines and their intricate hieroglyphics, we are also struck by how late in global history the Maya appear. Almost three thousand years after the peak of pyramid building in Egypt, with whose civilization they rightly beg comparison, the Maya thrust themselves onto the scene.

Even more dramatic than the relatively late rise of Mayan civilization is its sudden abandonment. By A.D. 830, after some 500 to 600 years of intense activity, the principal centers were left to time and the jungle. Of all the puzzles presented by the Maya, this seems to be the greatest one. Though efforts are made to hypothesize internal revolution, drought, or pestilence as a cause of the abandonment of the great centers, there is no convincing proof for any of these theories. The probability still remains, as stunning to our way of thinking as it may be, that the Maya consciously abandoned their civilization at its very peak. If this is the case, we must ask why?

Intimately related to the mystery of the abandonment of the key centers around A.D. 830 is the enigma not only of the meaning of the hieroglyphs but of the calendrical, mathematical, and astronomical data left behind by the Maya. If the Maya had just left behind their architecture and artwork, their civilization would still rank with the highest that humanity has achieved: the Egyptians and the Greeks, the Gupta Dynasty of India, the temples of Java, the T'ang dynasty of China, and the classic Heian dynasty of Japan. Yet, it is their scientific achievements that stand out as much as, if not more than, the harmonic heights of their artwork and continue to astonish us.

Usually, the Mayan scientific achievement is spoken of in terms of its calendrical attainments. The Maya computed the length of the Earth's revolution around the Sun to within a thousandth of a decimal point of the calculations of modern science. This, we are endlessly told, they did without our precision instruments. Not only that, but they kept calendars of the lunation and eclipse cycles; and even more, they maintained calendars recording synodical revolutions and synchronizations of the cycles of Mercury, Venus, Mars, Jupiter, and Saturn. And, on certain of their monuments, we find the recording of dates and/or events occurring as much as 400,000,000 years in the past. All of this they did with a unique and incredibly simple yet flexible numerical system that counted by twenties (instead of tens) and used only three notational symbols. Why, and to what end?

How does the Mayan calendrical knowledge relate to the mystery of their origins and to the enigma of the abandonment of their major cities by A.D. 830? And where did the Maya go following A.D. 830? Certainly there were those that remained, and yet there is such a clear break prior to the recommencement of Mayan civilization in the late tenth century that it is as if the rupture had been conscious and deliberate. Not only is the break between the so-called New Empire Maya and the pre-A.D. 830 Maya profound, but by the time the Spaniards arrived, it is as if all understanding of the past had been forgotten. And yet the calendar remained. A clue—for whom?

The archaeologists, of course, see the calendar system as just that—a way of recording time. But the question of why so much time is spent recording time remains unanswered. The suspicion dawns that the calendar is more than a calendar. Is the number system, so exquisitely proportioned, also a means for recording harmonic calibrations that relate not just to space-time positionings, but to resonant qualities of being and experience whose nature our materialistiic predisposition blinds us to ?

There is no question that in the volumes of literature written about the Maya and their bafflingly precise intellectual accomplishments, few are the writers who approach the matter with anything but the view that Mayan civilization, being a "thing of the past," was not as advanced as ours. The entrenched progressivist view, that the Maya represented one of several streams of civilization struggling against all environmental odds to attain to our level of materialism and science, is the view that informs almost everything said about the Maya. And for this reason, most everything said about the Maya may be dead wrong.

After many years of study and contemplation of the Mayan mystery, I have come to the inescapable conclusion that the Maya cannot be understood with the yardsticks that we have used to measure and judge them. Having long intuitively felt that the purpose of life according to the Maya might have been far different than our materialistic imagination can reckon, I have most recently come to the further conclusion not only that the Maya—at least the Maya whose civilization came to an abrupt halt at its peak in A.D. 830—were smarter than we are, but that their science was well in advance of ours. For this reason, it matters little that they used no metal tools or labor-saving devices such as the wheel (they also had no beasts of burden).

Because they could accomplish so much with so little, the Maya have something very important to teach us in our moment of technological crisis and paradigm shift. Indeed, the Maya may already possess not only the "new" paradigm, but also the scientific knowledge by which that paradigm may be applied. This being so, it may also be not just by chance that the Maya were the last of the ancient streams of civilization to come to flower on this planet. Nor may it be chance that the Maya represent the last overlooked ancient tradition to be examined and understood in the "light" of modern thought. In fact, it may just well be that the time is ripe for a "rediscovery" of the Maya.

In considering all of this, I have come to feel the spiritual presence of the Maya. Uncanny sages of what we call time, masters of synchronization, the Mayan presences chuckle and grin. Of course, the time is right. It has all been mapped, laid out, blueprinted. The clues have been amply left behind.

All that has been wanting is the right frame of mind to look at the clues. The breakdown of the present frame of mind allows the emergence of the possibility of reading the clues and drawing the right conclusions from them—conclusions that may have much to do with steering planetary affairs from a course of extinction to one of transformation.

In preparing the presentation of this text, I am guided by two things: the study of a phenomenon that I have come to understand as a galactic master-code, and the intuition that a dramatic break with the current scientific paradigm is absolutely necessary if we are going to not only survive but transform in the most positive and benign way possible. Having been so long overlooked, the Mayan Factor must be now examined.

The thought of doing this book came to me very suddenly. Yet, as I reflected on it, I realized I had been working with the material for over thirty years. At this stage in my life and in the life of the planet, it is necessary to present clearly, coherently, and honestly that which is true. The ways to truth are manifold. Insight, direct intuition, experience, and revelation are complemented by study, research, testing, and examining. All of these elements have been brought into play in dealing with and presenting the Mayan Factor. But more than anything else I feel it is my duty to present as simply and directly as possible the Mayan Code, the Harmonic Module.

More than a calendar, the Mayan Harmonic Module presented at this time evokes the image from the I Ching for Hexagram 49:

Revolution (Moulting):

Fire in the lake

The image of REVOLUTION

Thus the superior person sets the calendar in order

And makes the seasons clear.

It is in the interest of setting the calendar in order—the calendar as the cosmically voyaging Maya knew it—and making clear that we are involved in galactic seasons that this book is presented. Armed and reassured with such knowledge, we might set ourselves aright with the Earth and drop our childish and now very dangerous infatuation with the myth of progress and technological superiority. In this lies the import of *The Mayan Factor: Path Beyond Technology.*

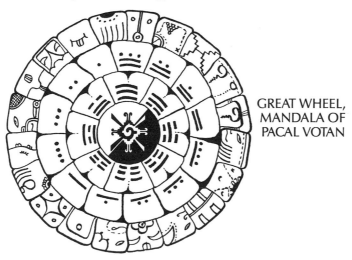

GREAT WHEEL,
MANDALA OF
PACAL VOTAN

THE MAYAN FACTOR:
PATH BEYOND TECHNOLOGY

AZTEC CALENDAR
STONE, A.D. 15TH CENTURY

1

MY 33-YEAR SEARCH FOR THE MAYA

Though I write in this book of things that may seem culturally remote or transcendentally cosmic, it would be a mistake to think of the Maya as inaccessible. As I have found through my life, the Mayan experience with its wealth of artistic and scientific lore is not so much alien or different as it is strangely, hauntingly familiar, like the numerous coincidences of the word Maya and its cognates that are scattered across the civilized world. At the same time, however, the Mayan experience, or the Mayan Factor as I have come to call it, is vast, unquestionably vast, and with implications extending far beyond the domains of our imagination.

I am 47 now, and it has taken me 33 years to fully realize that even in its vastness the Mayan Factor is friendly, approachable, communicable. In order to allow others to enter into this world, I would like to recount in a brief manner my own coming to the Mayan Factor. To begin at the beginning, I was conceived in Mexico and, though born in the States, spent my first five years in Mexico. The fact that my parents' apartment was located at 100 Calle Tula, Mexico City, struck me later as a curious synchronicity, since the name Tula is the Toltec form of Tulan or Tollan, the name of the Mayan center of origins.

It was in 1953, fateful year of the discovery of the genetic code and the Van Allen radiation belts, Earth's magnetic field, that I first encountered the Maya. That summer, my father had taken my twin brother and me to Mexico. It was the perfect opportunity for a fourteen-year-old like myself. I hadn't been to Mexico since I had left at the age of five, but Mexico City was still like my childhood reminiscence of a colonial capital. Though we didn't get any farther south than Cuernavaca, just beyond Mexico City, I received enough of an impression at the National Museum of Anthropology to stir deep and ancient feelings. But the museum, with its fantastic display of artifacts, including the great Calendar Stone of the Aztecs, was nothing compared to the experience of the great pyramid city of Teotihuacan, "Place Where the Gods Touch the Earth."

As I climbed the Pyramid of the Sun and gazed toward the mountains, cloud-dappled and shadowed beneath the still-clear-blue sky of those times, a profound sentiment arose in me, a longing to *know*. I knew it was not just a knowledge *about* things for which I thirsted, but a knowledge that comes from *within* things that I so greatly and earnestly desired. As I made my way down the steps, awestruck and filled with the wonder of the harmonic monumentality of the city of Teotihuacan, I made a vow to myself. And the vow was this: that whatever it was that had happened here I would come to know it—not just as an outsider or an archaeologist, but as a true knower, a seer.

It must have been that fall, in 1953, while working at the public library in Rochester, Minnesota that the next link occurred. I was filing books, a job I enjoyed enormously for the opportunity it gave me to encounter new and different kinds of ideas. And of all the books that tantalized me and drew my mind beyond itself, there were two in particular: P. D. Ouspensky's *Tertium Organum* and Sylvanus Griswold Morley's *The Ancient Maya*.

The former volume, with its dizzying descriptions of the possibilities of infinite numbers of parallel worlds, was enough to send my imagination into a condition of serene transcendence—or was it recollection? I really couldn't tell. For some reason or other, Morley's book on the Maya did the same thing for me. Or rather, while opening vistas on a cultural experience of exalted dimensions, Morley's book gave me a script of earthly probabilities to ground the cosmic experiences which Ouspensky described in *Tertium Organum*.

In any case, the Morley book made an indelible impression on me. The photographs of the living Maya, the curious anthropological descriptions of the Maya in relation to other members of the Mongoloid race, the diagrams of ancient temple sites and reproductions of stone sculpture of an extraordinary delicacy, harmony, and mystery, all had me completely captivated. But nothing fascinated me more than the numerical and mathematical system of the Maya. Quickly I learned the system: a dot equals one or a unit of a

● = 1 multiple of twenty; a bar, five or a multiple of five times twenty; and a shell
━━ = 5 glyph, zero or completion. It was so fantastically simple—and streamlined.
And then there were the names of the different place-values: *kin*, the ones;
◉ = 0 *vinal*, the 20s; *tun*, the 400s; *katun*, the 8,000s; and *baktun*, the 160,000s.

For long hours I marveled at the mastery which the system represented—and the mystery of what its true purpose might have been. Clearly, Morley didn't know. As great as was his appreciation of the remnants of the Maya, he, like virtually all of the archaeologists (as I was to later find out), judged the Maya by standards of material technology. Morley still viewed the Maya as being in the Stone Age. No metallurgy, no wheels. And yet, in Morley's estimation, and much to his amazement, without these material contrivances they still managed to create a science and an architecture of a proportional harmonic beauty equal to the greatest of Old World civilizations. For Morley, writing in 1947, the Maya remained an "intractable exception . . . Few if any other cultures with comparably primitive features . . . have focussed to such a degree upon intellectual attainment."

My dissatisfaction with Morley's limitations was compounded by my own lack of experience and knowledge, which were needed to formulate the actual reason for my discomfort. As much as I thrust myself into the mathematics and the astronomical and calendrical lore, such as it had been deciphered by the likes of Morely and his colleagues, there was a veil beyond which my experience could not penetrate. Here, I would retreat into reverie or fantasy. And one fantasy always would recur: that of a journey to the jungle hotlands of Mesoamerica where, through some cathartic and transfigurative experience, I would emerge, not at all as I had been, but as a bearer of knowledge, a seer. This reverie, this haunting, led me on in my pursuit of the Maya.

Through my college years, and especially in graduate school, the Maya remained an avocation. Though I studied art history at the graduate level, the University of Chicago did not offer any courses in pre-Columbian art. Nonetheless, I availed myself of every resource in the University library as well as the Art Institute of Chicago and the Field Museum. Applying the skills and discipline that I was learning in the formal study of art history, I forged ahead in my own study of the Maya and pre-Columbian art in general. For the most part, this was a satisfactory course. I was free to plunge into what was really my favorite area of art history.

And yet, as I read, studied, contemplated, and observed, it became clear that something was amiss. No one seemed to be getting the point. The archaeologists all treated Mayan civilization as if it were a happy enigmatic aberration of the Stone Age. I came to suspect that the reason archaeologists studied the Maya was precisely because their smug mind-sets would never get it, and would think instead that it was the Maya's fault that they weren't getting it!

Aside from Morley, perhaps the most prominent archaeological writer and interpreter of the Maya is a man named J.E.S. Thompson. Admirable compiler of two monumental tomes, *Maya Hieroglyphic Writing* and *A Catalog of Mayan Hieroglyphs,* as well as more general texts like *The Rise and Fall of Mayan Civilization,* Thompson, more than anyone else, wrote of the Maya as if they were idiot savants, skilled for God-knows-what-reason in abstruse astronomical mathematics to the point of devilish obsession, but to no rational end! Even more than Morley, Thompson judged the Maya by the yardstick of Renaissance European civilization and values. Thompson's discussions of Mayan art betray a condescending impatience. Because archaeologists like Thompson don't fathom what it was the Maya were about, they generally impute the worst, projecting themselves with their modern habits uncomfortably into an alien, fatalistic regime. Thus, when confronted with what is certainly the most puzzling feature of Mayan civilization—its sudden decline in the ninth century—Thompson prefers to see in it a slave revolt against despotic rulers. Yet, as Morley explains, "It is difficult to believe that so solidly established a civilization could be overturned abruptly. . . If dissatisfactions had been accumulating slowly through the centuries, they left no mark by which they can be identified."

As these unsatisfactory rumblings were going through my head in the summer of 1964, I prepared for my next journey to Mexico. Romantic fascination with place was at an all-time high. Traveling by car as I had done with my father over ten years before gave me plenty of time to contemplate the endless vistas of mountains and sky. To me, the land was mystical, living, possessing immense secrets. My openness to the mystery of place and geography was complemented by the discovery of other points of view than that of the materially obsessed archaeologists. Chief among them was that of the writer, Laurette Sejourné.

I had already been familiar with her book, *Burning Water: Thought and Religion in Ancient Mexico,* which was like fresh air in contrast to the writing of the archaeologists, for Sejourné took seriously the mental and spiritual aptitudes of the ancients. In Mexico City I came across her study, *The Universe of Quetzalcoatl.* In the introduction to that book, the eminent historian of religion, Mircea Eliade, wrote of Sejourné's approach that for her, "culture forms an organic unity. . .and thus it ought to be studied from its center and not from its peripheral aspects." This perspective resonated deeply with my own feelings. I began to perceive that the problem in coming to terms with the Maya and ancient Mexican civilization in general was actually the problem of our own civilization. Whatever it was that I had begun to feel in 1953 ran even more deeply now. Besides Teotihuacan, I now visited the ancient highland Mexican sites of Tula and Xochicalco. Armed with some knowledge, my intuition penetrated further into the mute stones. It was particularily at Xochicalco that the feelings of premonition—or recollection—gathered with disturbing intensity.

Xochicalco is high, remote in the mountain wilderness of the state of Guerrero. Its simple outlay of harmonic architectural structures is dominated by a singular presence: Quetzalcoatl, the Plumed Serpent. Dating back to the ninth and tenth century A.D., Xochicalco, "Place of the House of Flowers," represents a fusion of the Highland Mexican style of Teotihuacan, and that of the Classic Maya. Indeed, it was here in Xochicalco that

PLUMED SERPENT, QUETZALCOATL, XOCHICALCO, A.D. 10TH CENTURY

the elite of the Maya and Teotihuacan took refuge and convened following the "abrupt" decline of the Classic stage of Mayan and Mexican civilization. And it was here that the "historical" Quetzalcoatl, 1 Reed, was born in A.D. 947. For myself, the mystery intensified; and simultaneously, a new stage of unraveling had begun.

The mystery was that of Quetzalcoatl, the Plumed or Feathered Serpent, called by the Maya, Kukulkan, "Place Where the Serpent Dwells." From reading Sejourné's synthesizing work on Quetzalcoatl, it was clear that Quetzalcoatl was not just a god, but a multiple god; not just a man, but many men, not just a religion but a mythic complex, a mental structure. And it was also clear that this constellation of features, this multiple presence informed almost every aspect of ancient Mexican and even Mayan Civilization. Not just the arts, but astronomy and the calendar were affected by Quetzalcoatl, who was strongly associated with the morning and evening star, the planet Venus.

Astronomical, celestial associations, as much as his role as a religious figure of the stature of a Moses or a Christ, brought Quetzalcoatl into prophetic prominence. So it was that the tenth-century 1 Reed, Quetzalcoatl, presumed founder of the City of Tula and revitalizer of Chichen Itza in Yucatan, having prophesied his return on the day 1 Reed, in the year 1 Reed, was vindicated by the arrival of Cortés on that very day, Good Friday on the Christian calendar, A.D. 1519. This fact alone seems to have been sufficient to unstring the already nervous Montezuma II, emperor of the ill-fated Aztec empire.

Though few in our culture might have heard of Quetzalcoatl, aside from those familiar with D.H. Lawrence's novel, *The Plumed Serpent,* the prophetic facts of the matter gave me the conviction that Quetzalcoatl was not just a local affair. Rather, I saw in Quetzalcoatl an invisible and immanent force underlying and transcending the mythic fabric of mechanization. Fortified with this intuition, I returned from Mexico once again with a growing sense of my personal mission.

By the time I had completed my formal graduate studies in art history in 1965, I had arrived at a more intuitively considered position concerning the Maya and the ancient civilizations of Anahuac, "Place Between the Waters," the indigenous Nahuatl name given to Mexico and Central America. The archeologists could unearth the stones and catalog the data, giving their findings names like "god D" or "ritual object," but this said nothing about the livingness of the ancient civilizations. To me, it was obvious that one had to develop an intuitive frame of mind as well to enter into the mental states which produced the artifacts. And besides, the artifacts were but the residue. The reality was in the mental-emotional condition that went into the artifacts.

Furthermore, if it was time-transcending mystical states of mind that were aroused through whatever practices and acts of contemplation that were performed by the followers of Quetzalcoatl-Kukulkan, then what was keeping me or anyone else who applied themselves from entering those states of mind? Had not R.M. Bucke, William James, and Aldous Huxley presented convincing-enough arguments for the unity of mystical states of mind of whatever time and place? And wasn't it the purpose of mystical practices to place one in such a condition of unity? According to Sejourné, the religion of Quet-zalcoatl, as the pervading background tone of all of ancient Mexican civilization, was ulti-mately a process leading to mystical unification. From a contemplation of the most har-monious artifacts of these ancient civilizations, there was no doubt in my mind that something like this was the case.

Late in 1966, I embarked on an experiment prompted in large part by such reflections as well as by the conviction that if it had been art that provided the most creative outlet for mystical experiences, then perhaps through art one could enter into the frame of mind that had produced the ancient civilizations of the Maya and Teotihuacan. Most certain-ly, among my inspirations in the cycle of painting into which I plunged myself were the murals of Teotihuacan, the ceramic and hieroglyphic works of the Maya. The brilliance of color, the capacity to inform through condensed symbolic structures, the overall design that collected many features and forms into a single geometric yet undulating vibrant statement were aspects of ancient Mayan-Mexican art that inspired me.

The result of this experiment was a series of large free-standing panels, called by Humphry Osmond, coiner of the word "psychedelic," who saw them in 1968, the "Doors of Perception". For myself, it was the process of doing these paintings that was most mean-ingful; for indeed, they had provided me with an opportunity to enter those places where I conversed with Tlacuilo, the ancient painter, the former of archetypes. My heart opened and recollections flooded my being. I cannot say whether they were past-life recollections or not, but that they were collective recollections from the mind-stream of the ancients. I began to know from within.

The good painter is wise, god is in his heart.
He converses with his own heart.
He puts divinity into things.
—*Nahuatl saying.*

While it was the vision of the ancient Mexican and Mayan painters who guided me during the painting of these Doors of Perception, it was the study of the I Ching that gave me a perception of the primary structure of change, which was also the primary struc-ture of each of the eight panels. The panels were divided into three parts. While the top and bottom thirds were structurally mirrors of each other, the middle zone represented the zone of change or transformation. This transformative structure also possessed a com-plete bilateral symmetry. Many years later I discovered that the basic structure of these Doors of Perception was the same as the Binary Triplet Configuration, the key image embedded in the Mayan Sacred Calendar Matrix, the code key of my book *Earth Ascending.*

Having embarked on a visionary path, by the time I visited Mexico again in 1968, I was also better prepared for what I was to see. Aside from the visit to the new Museum of Anthropology, the high point of this trip was the journey to Monte Alban, the Zapotec or Cloud People citadel high in the mountains of Oaxaca. Dating back to at least 600 B.C.,

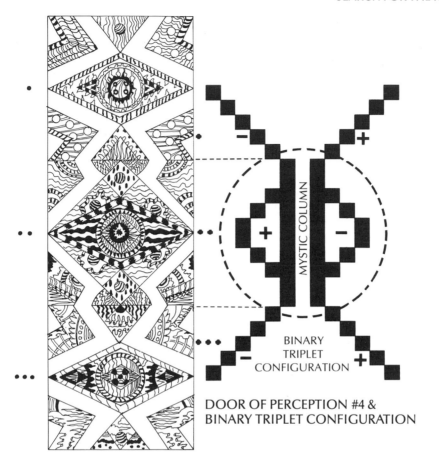

DOOR OF PERCEPTION #4 &
BINARY TRIPLET CONFIGURATION

Monte Alban represents a fusion of Mayan and Mexican influences in its own unique cultural style. Here are the sculptures of the Danzantes, the dancers—ecstatic, animal-headed shaman-priests whose body interiors are marked with hieroglyphs. Yet along side them we find the notational markings of the Mayan mathematical system, signs of the Sacred Calendar. Here also in the great plaza of the mountaintop ceremonial center is the peculiarly angled Observatory. Climbing about, pondering on the identity of the dancers and the meaning of the calendar signs, I received intimations of presences—star-beings, guardians. Who were they?

Not far from Monte Alban, in the little town of Teotitlan del Valle, ancient ceremonies are still celebrated, tapestries of exquisite geometrical and symbolic refinement are still woven. Bartering in a small shop, the proprietor, who spoke English (his brother, the weaver, spoke only Zapotec) astonished me. As his trump card, he pulled out two weavings of the same design, one in red and black, the other in blue and orange. The design of these weavings was remarkable in that it consisted of but a single line, yet the line spiraled

HUNAB KU

and projected in such a way that, in dividing the rug into two equal parts, it also created the image of an eightfold mandala. As I gazed in awe, the proprieter winked at me and said: "See, the ancient Mexicans also knew about Yin and Yang." Because of the scintillation of the complementary colors, blue and orange, I purchased that one, and drinking a ceremonial beer with the proprietor, I felt I had passed into still another intersection of time zones.

Yet it was 1968, a time of unrest and violence everywhere. As we drove out of Mexico City, we listened to the radio reports of the Tlaltelolco riots in which up to 400 students were killed. My thoughts turned more and more not only to the injustices in the world but to the distorted view that prevailed everywhere concerning the non-Western or Third World. This concern began to inform my teaching of art history, and at Davis, where I taught at the University of California, I became involved in the initial efforts at establishing a Native American college—Deganawida-Quetzalcoatl University.

It was through these efforts that I met two renegade Native Americans, Tony Shearer and Sun Bear. Tony was very involved in the prophecies of Quetzalcoatl and in the Sacred Calendar, which he very beautifully wrote about in a book called *Lord of the Dawn*. A later book of his, *Beneath the Moon and Under the Sun,* also describes the Sacred Calendar, and contains the image which I came to call the Binary Triplet Configuration, the magic 52-unit design within the 260-unit Sacred Calendar matrix. It was through Tony's inspiration that I became further involved in studies of the Sacred Calendar, or Tzolkin, as it has come to be called. It was Tony, too, who taught me about the significance of the 1987 date in relation to the prophecies concerning the return of Quetzalcoatl.

Sun Bear's efforts at founding the Bear Tribe and his clear call for a return to the land and the traditional way of life inspired me greatly at the time that I was involved in setting up the First Whole Earth Festival in Davis. That was Earth Day, 1970, the launching of the ecology movement. These activities and concerns continued while I taught at The Evergreen State College. It was there, in the winter of 1972, that I also met the traditional Hopi spokesman, Thomas Banyaca, who shared the Hopi prophecies. I shall always remember Thomas saying, "only those who are spiritually strong will survive the passing of the Fourth World and the coming of the Fifth." I understand that time to be closely related to the 1987 date which Tony had shared with me.

The studies of Mayan and ancient Mexican thought were most influential in putting together my book, *The Transformative Vision* (1975). Essentially a critique of Western civilization using the metaphor of the right and left hemispheres of the brain, I used the Mayan 5,125 year "Great Cycle," which began in 3113 B.C., and ends in A.D. 2012, along with the Hindu concept of the four ages or Yugas, and Yeats' concept of the cones and tinctures, as the framework for putting the modern "left hemisphere tyranny" in perspective. Yet, the only review of *The Transformative Vision* which appeared in an established art journal dismissed my efforts, because I had had the audacity to evaluate Renaissance and modern Western civilization from the perspective of such "alien" cosmologies as the Hindu and the Mayan.

In the summer of 1974, while teaching a class on Native American and pre-Colum-

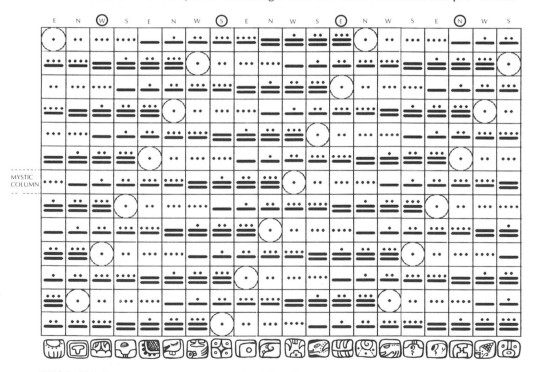

MYSTIC COLUMN

TZOLKIN, THE MAYAN SACRED CALENDAR

bian art at Naropa Institute, I completed a large version of the Sacred Calendar, using the Mayan notation system. A similar version of this calendar appears as Map 9 in *Earth Ascending*. What struck me about this version of the Sacred Calendar was the rhythmic effect of the twenty repetitions of the notations going from one to thirteen. This was the first inkling I had that the Calendar might be more than that. Was it some kind of Code?

During this time in the mid-1970s while living in Berkeley, I became involved in a short-lived educational project called the Shambhala-Tollan Foundation. While Shambhala referred to the mystic-mythic kingdom in Central Asia so fundamental to the teachings and prophetic lore of Tibetan Buddhism, Tollan (Tulan) represented the mythic city and source of the wisdom teachings of the Maya and ancient Mexicans. To my intuition, some as yet obscure connection existed between these two legendary domains, a connection not so much on the earthly plane as in the etheric body of the planet. Was there at some ancient time a congruence and synchronization of prophetic traditions between the likes of Shambhala and Tollan? Were the return of the "warriors of Shambhala" and the return of Quetzalcoatl in some way linked?

While the vision of the Shambhala-Tollan Foundation outstripped my capacity to implement anything practical with it, I found in the Tibetan Buddhist teachings a major grounding for my mind. Throwing myself intensely into the meditation practices made available to me through my teacher, Chögyam Trungpa Rinpoche, I found in the Vajrayana teachings a vast context for my continuing investigations of things Mayan. In particular, the teachings of mind-only seemed most useful for further considerations of the Mayan calendar, its origins, and especially its philosophical or scientific basis. Like the Buddhist (and Hindu) cosmologies, the Mayan describes a universe of infinite cycles of time and being. If anything, the Mayan is even more precise in its computations of these cycles. In any case, the contemplation of the far-ranging and all-encompassing cycles inevitably led to a consideration of the fact that we are not alone, that infinite other world systems exist more evolved than that of our own system. And if we are to establish greater knowledge and communication, how could it be but through the development of the mind, through the clarification and expansion of consciousness?

During the mid-1970s, two other books were published that spurred my cosmological reflections on the Maya and their calendar, *Time and Reality in the Thought of the Maya* by the Mexican philosopher Miguel León-Portilla, and *Mexico Mystique* by Frank Waters. While sympathetic to the poetry of the Mayan imagination, and extending a comparison of Mayan thought with Chinese Taoism, León-Portilla's study fails to penetrate to the actual science behind the calendar and the Mayan "obsession with time." Frank Waters' study, on the other hand, has the virtue of presenting the prophetic traditions of the Maya and ancient Mexicans in a somewhat contemporary context. In particular, he focuses on the end date of the Great Cycle, which he places at December 24, A.D. 2011, as the moment for a major shift in planetary consciousness, "The Coming Sixth Age of Consciousness."

In 1976 I travelled to Mexico yet again. This time I finally ventured on Mayan soil and visited the ancient site of Palenque. When my family and I arrived at Palenque, a tropical rainstorm burst down from the heavens. Scrambling up the nine-leveled Pyramid of the Inscriptions, we found shelter in the temple at the top. Looking out from the temple, we were greeted by a double rainbow that seemed to emanate not far from us in the Temple of the Winds.

There is no question of the magic of Palenque, double rainbow or not. Here it is that the tomb of the leader Pacal Votan was discovered in 1947—the only such Egyptian-style pyramid tomb in Mexico. There is nothing in Palenque that is not harmonious. The low-relief sculptures of the Foliated Cross and the Cross of the Sun are beyond compare, as is the sarcophagus lid of the tomb of Pacal Votan. Yet what engaged me the most were the remnants of the fresco paintings in the Temple of the Wind. Yes, I had seen them before. They had filled my mind-channel when I set about to paint the Doors of Perception some ten years earlier.

Because of the pyramid tomb of Pacal Votan, whose funerary chamber is decorated with the symbolism of the Nine Lords of Night, or Nine Lords of Time, the mystery of Palenque is especially intense. The feeling of abandonment and human silence is everywhere. At the same time, the jungle symphony washes in waves and crescendos of continuous insect ecstasy. Typical of the great classic Mayan centers that were left at their peak, Palenque begs the question: Why was Palenque abandoned? Where did the priests, the astronomers, the craftspeople go? What knowledge did they take with them, and why?

Not more than a hundred miles from Palenque but high in the Sierras of Chiapas, close to the Guatemalan border, is the town of San Cristobal. Once a major colonial center, San Cristobal now seems slightly desolate, remote. Yet, occasionally, in the streets, one sees them, the Lacandon Maya. Their long black hair hanging down past their knees, dressed in simple white tunics, the Lacandon have managed to remain their own people, leading a sedentary and simple life in the jungle lowlands, where they keep up the calendar and live a rich dream-life. Yielding few secrets, they come to San Cristobal to do a little trading, and then disappear again to their haunts.

Seeing them I was impressed. What role do the present-day Lacandons, these descendants of the ancient astronomers play in the great drama of the world? Is it as the film *Chac* suggests, to simply hold the vision, the aboriginal tone without which the world would fall apart even sooner than it now appears it might? How much occurs at the level of the native psyche that we never see or know about, that yet maintains a necessary balance with the Earth?

Taking a cab out of San Cristobal one Sunday, we visited an outlying village. In the old church, which was simply a church in appearance, the Indians conducted their service. The smell of copal incense was rich and thick. The chanting voices would periodically reach a strange harmonic and then pass back to a soft cacaphony. Outside, the *jefes*, the local leaders, passed a silver-tipped staff among each other, deciding issues raised by their constituents. Observing all of this I wondered—who speaks for these people? Or is it that they speak of and for the Earth, and that is all that counts?

The seeming gulf between the present-day Maya and the builders of the ancient cities is one that cannot be judged by our criteria of material progress. In reflecting on this matter, I am reminded of the Hopi myth concerning Palat-Kwapi, the Mysterious Red City of the South. In this story concerning the migrations to the hotlands of the South, the four-tiered temple city of Palat-Kwapi is built, but the purpose of the building is solely for that of gaining and consolidating a system of knowledge. The command is that following its construction the builders are to abandon the city, leaving it as a memorial to knowledge. Forgetful of this command, the inhabitants begin to fall into decadence, but a clan rivalry arouses them. Recalling their mission, the people finally abandon Palat-Kwapi, the Mysterious Red City of the South.

This myth fits the Maya perfectly. Their purpose was to codify and establish a system of knowledge, a science, and having codified it in stone and text, to move along. Civilization as we know it, a factory for the production of weapons of destruction and a sideline array of creature comforts, would not at all suit their purpose or knowledge system. A further factor enters the picture: since the system of knowledge and science of the Maya was so concerned with cycles of time, understanding time as a qualitative bearer of the conditions of cosmic or galactic seasons, they saw a period of gathering darkness on the horizon, and for that reason also knew it was time to call it quits and check out. Given the condition of the world today, who is to say that they weren't correct?

Such, at least, were my reasonings by the late 1970s when I entered my own hell realm of personal crisis and alcoholic breakdown. When I emerged from this dislocation of the self in 1981 and looked around, it appeared that the global crisis of the 1960s had now become endemic, so much so that it was taken for granted. My own researches had taken me to a place of synthesis, of seeing the Earth as a whole organism. Yet my inner feeling was that the thrust of modern civilization was taking things to that point where either the divine intervenes or extinction becomes our legacy. For me, the situation meant taking a leap, plunging off the edge as it were, into mental territory that had been declared extinct or tabu by the prevailing cultural standards.

For the first time in close to a decade I took to a visual form of expression as a principal outlet for what I needed to learn. Through a series of collage and sumi ink paintings on large gold or silver board—the Planet Art series—I found myself entering a phase of heightened attunement with the Earth. The time had come to take seriously the notion of planetary mind or planetary consciousness. Through my studies of art history and my own personal investigations, the conviction had arisen in me that not only was the Earth alive, but the pattern of its life actually informs, from the whole to the part, all aspects of its evolution, inclusive of the process that we call civilization. The totality of the interaction between the Earth's larger life and the individual and group responses to this greater life define "planet art." In this larger process, I dimly perceived the Maya as being the navigators

PACAL VOTAN
SARCOPHAGUS LID,
PALENQUE, A.D. 683

or charters of the waters of galactic synchronization. The Egyptians on the other hand, some three thousand years earlier, had been responsible for anchoring and setting the course of the Earth, through the Great Pyramid, in the ocean of galactic life.

Thinking, perceiving, and feeling in this expanded way led to an amazing series of explorations, meetings and coincidences. In the fall of 1981, after I had met and become involved with Lloydine Burris, a dancer and fellow visionary, I wrote a "science fiction" document entitled *The Art Planet Chronicles—The Making of the Fifth Ring.* The actual perspective of this imaginative, "planet art" tale, set sometime in the future, was from the star system Arcturus. Whatever the merits of this unpublished story, it seemed imperative to develop a consciousness that looked at our planetary affairs from afar, so that a coherence might emerge from the confusion of the daily papers and nuclear terrorism. This attitude, I was to discover, was also essential for penetrating more fully the Mayan mystery. Could the system of the Maya be a code matrix that synchronized with a galactically evolved knowledge base adopted to the idiosyncracies of this planet?

This line of thinking led inevitably to the compendium of code matrices, *Earth Ascending.* Begun initially as a text on geomancy, "earth divination," the chief point of departure in this book had been the coincidence, discovered or at least expanded into scientific or philosophical inquiry by Martin Schönberger, of the identity of the I Ching and the 64 codons, the code-words of the DNA, the genetic code. For myself, the synchronously related discovery that each of the rows, horizontally and vertically, in Ben Franklin's magic square of 8 yields the sum 260, led me to a consideration of the relation between the Mayan Sacred Calendar matrix, the 260-unit Tzolkin, and the I Ching. What followed was the unbidden flow of "maps" or matrices which constitute *Earth Ascending,* the key code figure being the "binary triplet configuration," whose base is the Mayan Sacred Calendar.

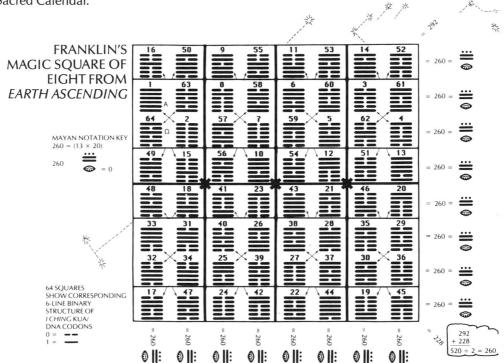

FRANKLIN'S MAGIC SQUARE OF EIGHT FROM *EARTH ASCENDING*

MAYAN NOTATION KEY
260 = (13 × 20)

260 ⊚ = 0

64 SQUARES SHOW CORRESPONDING 6-LINE BINARY STRUCTURE OF *I CHING* KUA/ DNA CODONS
0 = ▬ ▬
1 = ▬▬▬

I am acutely aware that, to many, the maps of *Earth Ascending* appear like a foreign language. That is no surprise, as even for myself the actual understanding of the maps did not come until after the publication of the book in 1984. What I slowly began to realize was that the maps, like the Mayan system itself, were from afar. Now, up to the early 1980s, I had not really considered the nature of UFOs or extraterrestrial intelligence. But with the phenomenon of "channeling" the material in *Earth Ascending*, I had been taken to a new level of possibility. Was the science fiction work that had preceded *Earth Ascending*, with its Arcturian perspective, a clue both to the origin of the information and to the Mayan mystery? If it were, then it was also clear to me that information transmission from different places in the galaxy was not dependent on space-time variables, but pointed instead to a principle of resonant diffusion.

The consideration of life and intelligence on other worlds received a major impetus in late 1983, when I met with Paul Shay of Stanford Research Institute and Richard Hoagland, a science writer formerly with NASA. Hoagland had been involved in the Viking probes to Mars that occurred in 1976. He, for one, had not been satisfied with the way NASA had handled the discovery of certain phenomena on Mars, including a large "face" that appeared to be carved into a mesa-top. On looking at the computer-enhanced photos that Hoagland was working with, I was unstrung. Something like a memory was stirred in me, but it was vaster, more profound, and infinitely more haunting than any memory I had ever known. My initital impression was that civilization—evolved life— had developed on Mars and that this civilization had met with a fateful, tragic end. In the instantaneous recognition of this fact from looking at the photos, I also perceived that the knowledge of this event was somehow still present and active in the Earth's field of consciousness.

On Christmas morning, 1983, I made a serendipitous discovery. Wanting to share with my family the "news from Mars," to my delight, I found a photo of the Martian face in a book, *The New Solar System,* which I had owned for several years but never looked at carefully. Then, because the covers looked similar, I picked up a copy of Lucy Lippard's *Overlay: The Influence of Primitive Art on Contemporary Art,* which I had purchased as a gift in Los Angeles the day before my meeting with Hoagland. Randomly opening Lippard's text to page 144, I was jolted by the photo that appeared in the upper lefthand corner: a hauntingly familiar face, a model for a sculpture by Isamu Noguchi done in 1947, 29 years before the Viking mission, entitled *The Sculpture to be Seen from Mars.*

If the NASA information had evoked the actuality of life on other worlds, the discovery of Noguchi's work, which would have been the same size as the Martian face had it been completed, evoked in me, with shocking precision, the transmission of information by the principle of resonant diffusion, a process I described then as *radiogenesis*: universal transmission of information through, or as, light or radiant energy. And of course, fresh questions arose. What is the relation between knowledge and recollection? Can the future also be our past? Can what is happening on our planet now be somehow a replay of a drama that has occurred on other worlds, and if so, how can we avoid the pitfall of extinction?

In a poetic work entitled *Earth Shaman,* written late in 1984, I attempted to deal with these questions and at the same time to describe the history of the Earth as a conscious organism, using as the mythic container the Hopi description of the passage between three earlier worlds to the present world and the imminent passage into a fifth world. The image of the Earth that is developed in *Earth Shaman,* the "crystal earth," owes much to my meeting with the Cherokee Indian lineage holder, the remarkable Dhyani Ywahoo, whom I met in the spring of 1984. It was she who, taking one look at Lloydine and myself, declared, "Your minds are very close; you should be working with crystals." We began immediately to do so and found in crystals a most precise tool for personal attunement and information gathering. Intuiting that the Earth itself is crystalline in nature, I found research both from the Soviet Union, and by mappers Elizabeth Hagens and William Becker, confirming this possibility. Somehow, the image of the Earth as a crystal seemed to go along with the notion of galactic information transmission through the principle of resonant diffusion, a key in coming to terms with the origin and nature of the Mayan matrix.

Early in 1985 I was contacted by a Maya, Humbatz Men. My name had been given to Humbatz by Toby Campion, member of an organization called the Universal Great Brotherhood whose activity is largely centered in Mexico and South America. Through a series of hilarious late-night phone calls conducted in pidgin Spanish, I learned that Humbatz was operating with 17 of the Mayan "calendars." Most archaeologists consider the possibility of only around a half-dozen such calendars. Humbatz had also written a small text entitled *Tzol 'Ek, Mayan Astrology.* Through perseverance and magic, Humbatz Men finally appeared in Boulder in March of 1985, when he gave a presentation entitled "Mayan Astrology."

The key to everything that Humbatz presented, and which he himself had received through oral transmission, was in a final aside he made during his presentation. "Our solar system," Humbatz declared, "is the seventh such system that the Maya have charted." There is no question that my meeting with Humbatz was the most crucial event in my long history of working with the Mayan material. Further discussions with Dhyani Ywahoo, as well as a meeting with Harley Swiftdeer, confirmed for me that Humbatz had left me with the most important clue yet in realizing the nature of the Mayan system of thought. Indeed, the Mayan information was transmitted from afar. But precisely how, and to what end?

It was following a gathering at the neo-shamanic think-tank, the Ojai Foundation, in April 1985, entitled the Council of Quetzalcoatl, that the presence of the phenomenon I now call the Mayan Factor finally asserted itself to me. In a simple sense, the Mayan Factor is the overlooked factor in the consideration of the meaning of human history, and in particular, in the consideration of scientific knowledge altogether. When we look at it again it can be seen that the Mayan Factor is the presence of a galactic gauge, a precise means for placing ourselves in relation to the galactic community of intelligence. Looked at even more closely, microscopically even, the Mayan Factor is the consideration that we are at a point in time 26 years short of a major galactic synchronization. Either we shift gears right now or we miss the opportunity.

My meeting with Terence McKenna, author of the intriguing *Invisible Landscape,* contributed greatly to this understanding of the Mayan Factor, for he, too, by working with the I Ching had been drawn into things Mayan. In particular, his I Ching fractal calendrics had led him to the conclusion that we are involved in a "final" cycle of time whose 67-year span takes us from Hiroshima, in 1945, to the Mayan synchronization date of A.D. 2012, the completion of the so-called Great Cycle which began in 3113 B.C. By the summer of 1985, I was certain that the code behind the Great Cycle was a key to unlocking the meaning of our own history—and current dilemma. So it was that I threw myself with renewed abandon into the Mayan Factor.

In preparation for my most recent trip to Mexico, I began working intensely with the Mayan hieroglyphs. In particular, I involved myself with the twenty Sacred Signs, the key glyphs of the Sacred Calendar. Exposure to R. A. Schwaller de Lubicz' analogical studies on ancient Egyptian symbology had given me a point of departure for my renewed studies of the Mayan glyphs. Immersing myself in the glyphs, making drawings and various arrangements of them, was profoundly revelatory. I found I was actually accessing information through the glyphs. This demonstrated to me that the Mayan Factor was nothing dead or of the past, but a living system.

In December of 1985, Lloydine and I found ourselves in the Yucatan, at the largely unexcavated and immense site of Coba. The northernmost of the Classic, pre-A.D. 830 centers of Mayan civilization and one of the largest of all the centers, with some 6,500 unexcavated structures, Coba has a presence that is the epitome of the Mayan enigma. Still overgrown with jungle, high-stepped pyramids and ceremonial plazas provide the anchors to a hub of a vast system of straight, flat roadways called *sacbeob,* marked and defined by large hieroglyphic sculptures, some containing dates—or are they harmonic numbers?— referring to events at inconceivable points in the distant past, or on some other system.

Coba provided the beginning- and end-points of a month-long pilgrimage that ended January 10, 1986. In between, we had a brief sojourn to earthquake-wracked Mexico City, Teotihuacan, and the volcanic highlands of Lake Patzcuaro and Lake Chapala. Returning to the Yucatan, we set off with our friends from the Cristaux Group, Francis Huxley, Adele Getty, Colleen Kelly, and Robert Ott, on a tour of the Yucatan that included extended visits to Uxmal and Chichen Itza, as well as the fantastic cave sites of Loltun and Balankanche, finally returning to the Caribbean Coast and Coba.

The visits to Uxmal and Chichen Itza were helpful for putting into place what I have come to call the later or second dispensation of Kukulkan-Quetzalcoatl. Arriving in the Yucatan around A.D. 987 at the age of 40, Kukulkan revitalized the centers of Uxmal and

Chichen Itza and founded the city of Mayapan before "departing" in A.D. 999. A year or so earlier I had had the opportunity to hear the Lakota medicine man, Gerald Red Elk, talk about the relation between—and indeed, identification of—Christ and Quetzalcoatl. Pondering the ancient site of Chichen Itza, the exquisitely proportioned Temple of Kukulkan, and the numerous symbolic representations associated with Kukulkan, it occurred to me that Kukulkan-Quetzalcoatl who, in A.D. 999, prophesied the arrival of Cortés and the coming of Christianity to Mexico, was himself an incarnation of the Christ.

In the light of my dawning understanding of the Maya as planetary navigators and mappers of the larger psychic field of the Earth, the solar system, and the galaxy beyond, such thoughts or intimations as that of the identity of Kukulkan and Christ seemed less and less outrageous. My discovery of the Mayan philosopher, Domingo Parédez, whose synthesizing book, *Mayan Parapsychology,* I read with avid interest, stimulated my further perception of the Maya as beings of highly evolved psychic as well as intellectual and spiritual abilities. Still, there was the question, where did they come from? Or at least, where did their information come from, and exactly how was it transmitted here?

As our tour wound its way down the Caribbean, further intuitions concerning the Mayan Factor formulated themselves. It was at Coba again, while standing atop the great pyramid, the Nohoch Mul, that the significance of the "solar cult" of the Maya (as well as the Egyptians and the Incas) began to make more sense to me. Indeed, the Sun is not only literally the source and sustainer of life, but it is also the mediator of information beamed to and through it from other star systems.

So-called sun worship such as is imputed to the ancient Maya is in actuality the recognition and acknowledgement that higher knowledge and wisdom is literally being transmitted throught the Sun, or more precisely, through the cycles of the binary sunspot movements. The Tzolkin, or Sacred Calendar, is a means of tracking the information through knowledge of the sunspot cycles. The Tzolkin is also the information matrix that is communicated by at least two star systems, creating a binary communication field through the sunspots. As for the sources of information, it seems clear that the Pleiades is one source; Arcturus is most likely the other.

The last evening in the Yucatan was spent in a simple thatched-roof-and-hammock-style hostel called Chac Mool. The waves of the Caribbean break and beckon ceaselessly on the timeless beach. At night, the stars spread their canopy of infinite recollection across the blackened sky. Gazing long at the endless interpenetrating geometries of star patterns, I felt incredible satisfaction welling through my being. In the sound of the wind, in the sound of the surf, in the sight of the dazzling magnificence of the stars, a deep and wondrous knowledge spread touching every cell in my body. The Maya were returning, but not as we might think of them. Ultimately their being, like ours, transcends bodily form. And precisely for that reason, their return can occur within us, through us, now.

We woke up to greet the dawn at Chac Mool. Swimming naked in the joyous surf, I gazed upward. The sky, ablaze with pink and orange clouds, heralded the coming day. Saying good-bye to friends and acquaintances, we headed up the coast for Cancun, the airport, and the Late Industrial world. This time I returned more as myself than ever, and at the same time as another. The Mayan Factor had been retrieved. Perhaps the world cycle would yet make its appointment with galactic destiny.

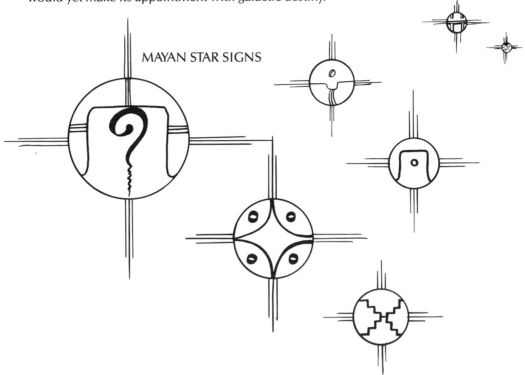

MAYAN STAR SIGNS

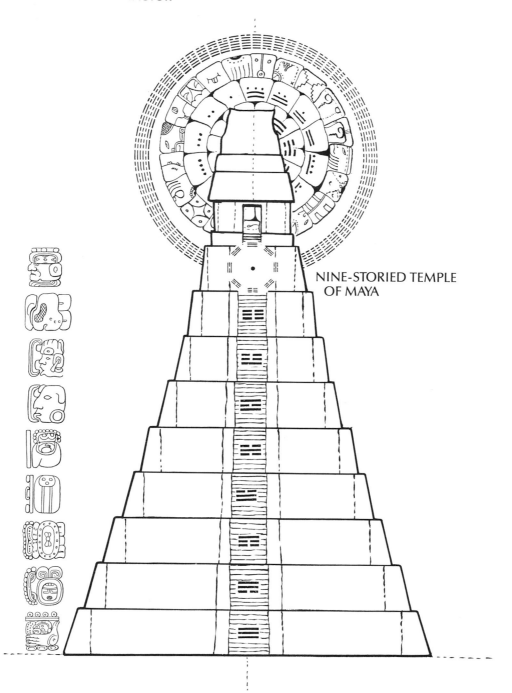

NINE-STORIED TEMPLE
OF MAYA

2

THE MAYA: DIVINERS OF HARMONY

Most happily, my personal route to the Mayan Factor blossomed through interests that were seeded by art historical studies, leading eventually to wondrous contemplations and mind-boggling insights of a galactic nature. Indeed, that the Maya are known about at all owes to their having secured an anchor in our imagination through art exhibits and archaeological text books. While the National Geographic Society has most recently brought the Maya to popular attention through full-page color glossies of their mysterious ruins and stoneworks in the Central American jungles, it should be borne in mind that modern knowledge of the Maya dates back scarcely more than 140 years.

When the artistic/archaeological team of John Stephens and Frederick Catherwood published their various exquisitely illustrated books documenting their travels through the Yucatan and Central America in the 1840s, the result was nothing less than sensational. It amounted to the virtual discovery of a "lost" civilization, with all the attendant romance and fantasy such an image conjures up. Nineteenth-century writer-explorers like Charles Brasseur de Beaubourg, Lord Kingsborough, and Auguste Le Plongeon, while bringing to light some matters of archaeological interest, were also quick to relate the Maya to ancient Egypt and Atlantis. Other writers like James Churchward and Lewis Spence made the most of the Atlantean-Lemurian aura which they attributed to the Mayan ruins and hieroglyphic writings.

At the same time, by the end of the nineteenth century, more purely "scientific" archaeologists and thinkers like Alfred P. Maudslay, Ernest Willem Förstemann, and Herbert J. Spinden had seized upon the Mayan mathematical and astronomical system, which clearly, to the scientific mind, was the most fascinating aspect of the Maya. By 1927, what is cumbersomely known as the Goodman-Martinez Hernandez-Thompson correlation of Mayan and Christian chronology was completed. This meant that the "beginning" of the Mayan "Great Cycle" had been variously located between August 6 and August 13, 3113 B.C. on the Christian calendar. In Mayan chronology, this date is written: 13.0.0.0.0. This same date, 13.0.0.0.0, will occur again, December 21, A.D. 2012.

What this means is that between the first 13.0.0.0.0 date and the second one, thirteen cycles of slightly less than 400 years each have elapsed. These large 394 + year cycles are called *baktuns* by the Maya. Since the coefficient 13 in the date 13.0.0.0.0 refers to the completion of a Great Cycle of thirteen baktuns, the first baktun of the new cycle is actually Baktun 0, the second cycle, Baktun 1, and so forth. Thus, the date corresponding to 2993 B.C. would be written: 0.1.0.0.0. What is called *Classic* Mayan civilization occurs largely in the tenth cycle, Baktun 9, A.D. 435-830, and so most of the deciphered dates look something like this when written in our notation system: 9.13.10.0 (A.D. 702). But of this, more will be said later.

It was in 1935, that Sylvanus Griswold Morley, perhaps the most sensitive of the scientific archaeologists, in his otherwise somewhat arid study, *Guidebook to the Ruins of Quirigua,* summed up what is still the most enlightened prevailing view of the Maya:

> When the material achievements of the ancient Maya in architecture, sculpture, ceramics, the lapidary arts, feather-work, cotton-weaving and dyeing are added to their abstract intellectual achievements—invention of positional mathematics with its concomitant development of zero, construction of an elaborate chronology with a fixed starting point, use of a time-count as accurate as our own Gregorian Calendar, knowledge of astronomy superior to that of the ancient Egyptians and Babylonians—and the whole judged in the light of their known cultural limitations, which were on a par with those of the early Neolithic Age in the Old World, we may acclaim them, without fear of successful contradiction, the most brilliant aboriginal people on this planet.

As high as this estimation may be, the conjecture remains that despite their brilliance, the Maya were nonetheless *Neolithic* and *aboriginal*. What does the use of these terms actually imply? Neolithic—later Stone Age—and aboriginal—from the beginning of time, before civilization—are measurements on the yardstick of progress. Their use dooms the mind to the view that whatever brilliance might have been achieved by these people it is nonetheless hopelessly of the past, an anomaly, and hence of little use in the present.

Yet, the question is often asked, if the Maya were aboriginal, Neolithic, virtually without metallurgy or the use of the wheel, what were they doing with a mathematical system of such exquisite refinement? Why were they so intellectually bent? And, when one considers the matter, the Classic Maya, flourishing at their peak between A.D. 435 and 830, the time of the European "Dark Ages," were really not so distant, at least in time. By general standards, the later Stone Ages occurred elsewhere in the world some 12,000-6,000 years ago. Something is amiss—is it the Maya, or the yardstick by which they are being measured?

Since Morley wrote his quintessential archaeological assessment in 1935, there have been a few spectacular finds in Mayan archaeology, such as the murals at Bonampak, discovered in 1946, and the pyramid tomb at Palenque, excavated in 1952. Overall, a gradual refinement of Mayan archaeology has occurred, inclusive of the rise of the new

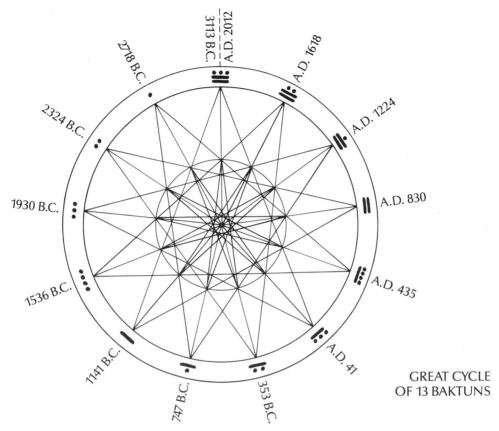

3113 B.C.
A.D. 2012
2718 B.C.
A.D. 1618
2324 B.C.
A.D. 1224
1930 B.C.
A.D. 830
1536 B.C.
A.D. 435
1141 B.C.
A.D. 41
747 B.C.
353 B.C.

GREAT CYCLE
OF 13 BAKTUNS

discipline of archaeoastronomy. In addition, use of the computer has made inroads in the decipherment of the hieroglyphs, but for the most part, only in the identifications of names of what are considered "dynastic" leaders, such as Pacal Votan of Palenque.

Yet, despite these "advances" in archaeology, the true story of the Maya remains a closed book. At sites like Quirigua and Copan, the hieroglyphs incised in stone with astonishing precision and elegance tease the mind with their awesome quantity and baffling sense of order. Are they really so impenetrable? In our reflections, several other facts about the Classic Maya present themselves. Though there are depictions of what appear to be captives in the late Classic stage, in all of their sculpture there are virtually no scenes of warfare. And, when the Maya began building their astronomical-ceremonial centers in stone late in the eighth baktun (A.D. 200-400), the system of hieroglyphs and mathematics is fully formed, perfect in every detail. There is little evidence of formative stages, of trials and errors; it is a complete system of notations, mathematics, and astronomical calculations with an accompanying highly developed hieroglyphic code.

Add to this the abrupt cessation of building and particularly of recording dates around

A.D. 830 and you have the Mayan mystery complete. Let us sum up, then, what is generally known about the Maya.

Sometime over two thousand years ago in Central America, the people called Maya began to leave clues or indications of their presence. In the general area, called by archaeologists Mesoamerica—Mexico and Central America—the Maya had been preceded by a mysterious group called the Olmecs, whose origins along the Gulf of Mexico coastline date back at least 4,000 years, and by the Zapotecs of highland Oaxaca, in southern Mexico, whose great center, Monte Alban, was founded as early as 600 B.C.

Coincident with the rise of the Maya in Central America was the flourishing of the great pyramid metropolis, Teotihuacan, in central Mexico just northeast of present-day Mexico City. Yet, though possessing in common with their highland Mexican neighbors an agricultural base with collectively shared cultural traits, such as the 260-day Sacred Calendar and the ritual ball game, the Maya, in their jungle domain, remained artistically and intellectually distinct.

Beginning around A.D. 300 at a site called Uaxactun in the heart of the jungle region known as the Peten, and thence spreading to Tikal, Palenque, Copan, and Quirigua, by A.D. 500 the great push of Mayan civilization was on. For the next 300 years or so, the duration of Baktun 9, the Maya built their harmoniously proportioned stepped-pyramid temples, and left behind great numbers of large stone markers, called stele, on which were recorded dates—and other related information—every five, ten, or twenty years. Then, with the transition from Baktun 9 to Baktun 10, A.D. 830 A.D., came the abrupt decline or disappearance of the Classic Maya.

At the end of the tenth century A.D., when the curtain goes up again on the Maya, or rather on the descendents of the Maya, it is an altogether different scene. Northern Yucatan is the home base. A mingling has occurred between the Maya and their Mexican neighbors, the Toltecs. The religious dispensation of Quetzalcoatl/Kukulkan 1 Reed— A.D. 947 to 999—is the cultural binding factor. Though great architectural achievements occur, such as we find at Uxmal and Chichen Itza, no longer are great monuments carved in stone recording endless dates and astronomical data. Rather, a shorthand version of the chronological system has been developed, and much of the writing is done in hieroglyphic manuscripts called codices, of which only three survive. Warfare and human sacrifice are on the rise, and an unprecedented political alliance, the League of Mayapan, has replaced the virtually autonomous, apolitical era of the Classic Maya.

With the fall of Mayapan through internal warfare in A.D. 1441, the later Maya phase comes to an end. When the Spaniards finally arrive in full force in the Yucatan in 1527, as predicted by the twelfth-century Mayan prophet, Ah Xupan, the Mayan descendents are in a condition of disunity. By 1697 the intolerant cruelties of the new Christian order, along with smallpox and other diseases, have all but put an end to the Maya as a cultural or political entity. Despite the terrible hazards of fortune, the Maya have persisted, culturally at least, to remain distinct to the present time. And, here and there, wizards, keepers of the most ancient traditions have managed to keep alive the knowledge, the code, the lines of truth that lead directly to the stars.

When we look at the history and review what was left behind by the Maya, one fact becomes very clear: not only did the Spaniards have no idea that a separation in time had occurred between the Classic ninth-baktun Maya and the later Maya of the League of Mayapan, but the texts and manuscripts of the later Maya themselves—*Popul Vuh, The Books of Chilam Balam,* and *The Annals of the Cakchiquels*—give us virtually no information about their predecessors, the Classic Maya. Not only did the Christians garble or misinterpret what was told them by the Maya, but the later Maya themselves seem to have intentionally confused their texts. Why?

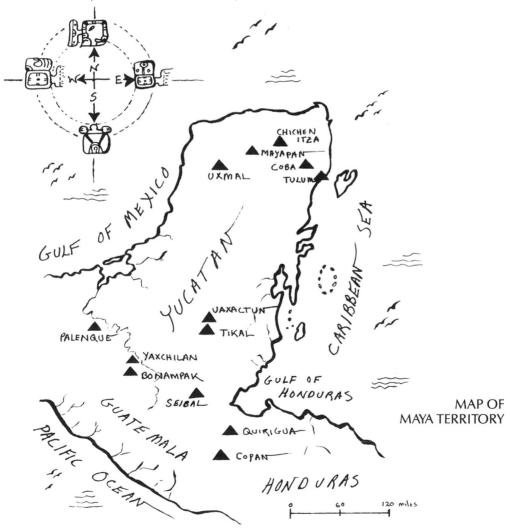

MAP OF
MAYA TERRITORY

When Stephens and Catherwood stumbled 150 years ago upon the jungle centers of the classic Maya, they had indeed stumbled upon a "lost civilization," but one lost only to our mind. When everything is said and done, all that archaeology has described of the Classic Maya are the visible contours of the scientifically materialistic mind. What actually lies in the jungle lowlands of the Peten is very different than what is described by archaeology. Like a stellar constellation imprinted upon the Central American jungles, the pattern connecting the various classic era centers peeks through the labyrinth of time. Pyramid temples and plazas strewn with large stone monuments, intricately incised with elaborate hieroglyphs and astronomical data, represent as precise a scientific record-keeping operation as any known to humankind.

Indeed, taken as a whole, the Baktun 9 Classic Maya centers appear as a veritable cosmic calling card. "Oh, you of the Earth," the monuments seem to sing out to us, "those who built us have been here, appearing as humans, like you, oh Earthlings. Can you not see, can you not understand what it is that we have left for you? Could you but open your eyes without attachment, you would see and know the gift that awaits you."

Clearly, more important for the Classic Maya than territoriality and making war was the need to track the cycles of planet Earth by means of a unique mathematical system. The purpose of this elaborate record-keeping seems to have been the correlation of terrestrial and other planetary cycles within our solar system with the harmonic matrix of a master program. This matrix, encompassing the cyclical harmonics of the planets within our solar system, was *galactic*, as it represented a larger, more encompassing view than could be obtained from within our solar system. Unique by any known standard, this perspective implies that the Classic Maya were possessed with a distinct mission. Anyone with a mission also has a message—a fact which seems quite obvious, but all too often escapes the mind of materialistic archaeologists.

That Classic Maya was a civilization unparalleled in its accomplishment and unique in the self-termination of its achievement is owing completely to the mission which it was its duty to fulfill. This mission, it seems, was to place the Earth and its solar system in synchronization with a larger galactic community. That is the meaning of the dates and their accompanying hieroglyphs. Once the purpose had been achieved, for this is the cause and meaning of the intense acitivity of Baktun 9, the Maya departed—but not all of them.

Some remained behind as caretakers, overseers, speaking the language of the *Zuvuya*, the cryptic code-language of the significances of the different cycles of time. The key and the code left behind by the Classic—or shall we say the galactic—Maya describing their purpose and their science is embedded in the deceptively simple system of thirteen numbers and twenty symbols called the Tzolkin. In fact, in the Tzolkin, the harmonic matrix, lies all we need to know about the Mayan Factor. But how was all this done? How did the Maya get here? What is the meaning of galactic synchronization, and what bearing does all of this have on us now?

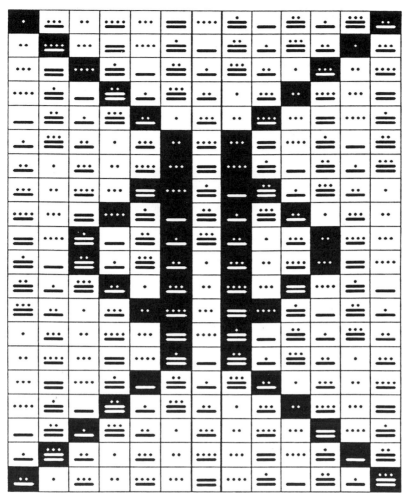

TZOLKIN
AS THE
HARMONIC
MODULE

In answer to these questions, this much we may say: what distinguishes Mayan science from present-day science is that it is a system operating within a galactic frame. A science operating within a genuinely galactic frame of reference cannot be separated from what we call myth, art, or religion. For, as a comprehensive world-view, the Mayan galactic frame of reference synthesizes rather than separates. In this regard, not only do the Maya challenge our science, but they play with our myths, and, as we shall see, they reinvest our history with a meaning and a scope that places our destiny within the unseen purposes of the starry firmament—but in a way undreamed of by the tinker-toy builders of our modern space programs.

Having considered the Maya from the perspective of archaeology and materialistic modern science, let us now consider them from the comprehensive galactic view provided by the Mayan Factor. Two Mayan terms, *Hunab Ku* and *Kuxan Suum*, are essential in providing us a galactic view which synthesizes science and myth.

Hunab Ku is usually translated as "One Giver of Movement and Measure"; it is the principle of life beyond the Sun. In this regard, Hunab Ku is the name of the galactic core, not just as name but as a description of purpose and activity as well. Movement corresponds to energy, the principle of life and all-pervading consciousness imminent in all phenomena. Measure refers to the principle of rhythm, periodicity, and form accounting for the different limiting qualities which energy assumes through its different transformations.

Kuxan Suum, literally "the Road to the Sky Leading to the Umbilical Cord of the Universe," defines the invisible galactic life threads or fibers which connect both the individual and the planet, through the Sun, to the galactic core, Hunab Ku. These threads or fibers are the same as the luminous threads extending from the solar plexus described by the seer, Don Juan, in Carlos Castaneda's series of Yaqui wisdom books. According to the extant Mayan texts, *Popul Vuh* and *The Annals of the Cakchiquels,* the Yaquis were the first of the Mayan tribes to separate from the rest of the clans following entry into this world. The purpose of the Yaquis in so doing was to keep at least some of the original teachings of the Maya relatively pure and in a remote place.

In any case, the fibers, or Kuxan Suum, define a resonant pathway, like a walkie-talkie, providing a continuing channel of communication, a cosmic lifeline. Through Kuxan Suum, each of us has a connection that extends from the solar plexus through the reflective membrane of the planetary field on to the Sun and, ultimately, to the galactic core. Could this lifeline have something to do with the origination of the Maya on this planet? And if so, how?

HUNAB KU:
ONE GIVER OF
MOVEMENT & MEASURE

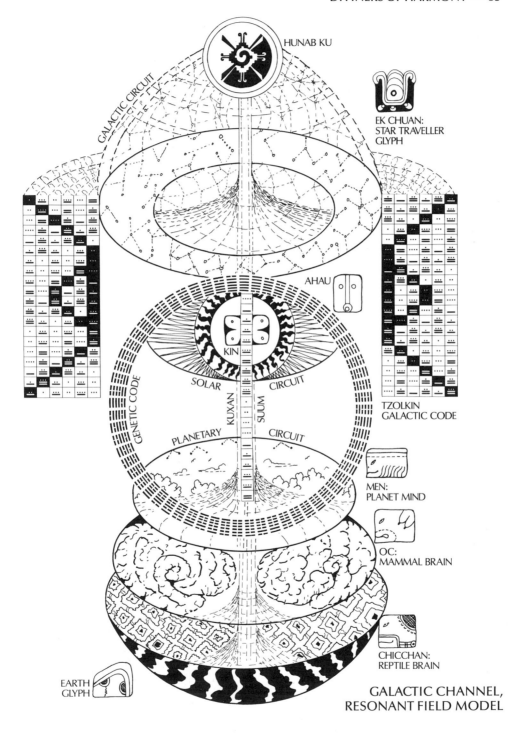

HUNAB KU

EK CHUAN:
STAR TRAVELLER
GLYPH

GALACTIC CIRCUIT

AHAU

KIN

SOLAR   CIRCUIT

GENETIC CODE

KUXAN   SUUM

PLANETARY   CIRCUIT

TZOLKIN
GALACTIC CODE

MEN:
PLANET MIND

OC:
MAMMAL BRAIN

CHICCHAN:
REPTILE BRAIN

EARTH
GLYPH

GALACTIC CHANNEL,
RESONANT FIELD MODEL

As much like a telescope as a walkie-talkie, the resonant pathway described by the Kuxan Suum can be understood as a series of vibratory or resonant lenses. On one end is the lens of Hunab Ku, the center of the galaxy, the galactic core. On the other end is the lens of the individual human being. Indeed, as a cosmic resonator, the individual human actually contains three lenses. One corresponds to the reptilian brain or autonomic system; the second corresponds to the mammalian brain, or neo-cortex; and the third corresponds to the higher mind, connecting the individual to the larger planet body. It is this last lens that actually extends from the solar plexus.

Through aligning these three lenses, a fourth lens comes into focus corresponding to the solar mind, the consciousness of the Sun and the solar system. A fifth lens is provided by the Sun itself. Finally, there are two lenses intermediate between the Sun and the galactic core, Hunab Ku. One is a lens for focussing galactic information from one star system to another; the other lens, closest to Hunab Ku, is imprinted with the common galactic information core, the harmonic matrix. In this way, information passing through the Kuxan Suum, the galactic life-fibers, is articulated, and, depending upon which of the eight lenses is brought into focus, different levels or stages of being and knowledge may be emphasized.

Looking through this galactic telescope of vibratory lenses, rather than an atomistic world of space and time, distance and separateness, the Mayan Factor brings into focus a world of coherence and unity, a resonant matrix within which information transmission is virtually "instantaneous." If we were to give a modern name to this process of galactic focussing and transmission of information it would be the *principle of harmonic resonance.*

But resonance—what is it? Everybody talks about it—electricians, physicists, musicians, and healers. But what is resonance, really? *Resonance* means the quality of *sounding again.* To resonate is to reverberate. Reverberation implies give and take, the definition of communication which is always simultaneous and between at least two agents. Any communication implies an exchange of information. People talk about the "information age," but what is information? From the perspective of resonant harmonics, information is the form-vehicle of qualities of energy passing between two agents or parties. As a sounding again, resonance *is* information.

The essense of information, then, is not its content but its resonance. This is why feeling or sensing things is so important. To sense the resonance of incoming information co-creates a resonant field. If we try to conceptualize experience before we have actually resonated with the experience, the field is off or even broken. If the field is broken it means the Kuxan Suum is obscured at the solar plexus—in a word, we've stopped feeling things and our resonance has been damped!

When people speak of resonance, they also speak of frequencies and tones. Frequency refers to rate of vibration. As everybody knows, there are higher and lower rates of vibration, while all vibration is pulsation of waves. A frequency held for but a single wave-cycle, otherwise known as a beat, becomes a tone. A tone, then, is any sustained frequency, whose level determines which of our sense organs may be affected. In other words, touch has its tones; perfume is a tone of the sense field "smell"; even "mind" experiences its high-frequency sensory tones.

Inclusive of all the sense-fields, harmony is the synchronization of two or more tones. The skill in synchronizing tones and synthesizing sense-fields is an art as much as it is a science. The practice of this science yields opportunities unthought of from a materialistic perspective, which, for instance, leads one to think that flying is the air-borne passsage of a physical body between two points. But what is flying to the sense-fields of the passenger in the airplane? The coarse, vibratory shudder of jet engines, the odor of jet fuel, and a microwave meal. What if flying is, instead, a capacity to identify consciousness with resonance and ride the frequencies of different levels of reality?

Indeed, harmony *is* a science. Those who practice this science are the real artists, the diviners of harmony, for it is they who transmit—not as any doctrine but as reality itself— the principle of harmonic resonance. Applied galactically, this principle describes the totality of the universe as a field operated by resonant lenses or plates. Through proper attunement or "striking" of these lenses, overtones may be sounded which penetrate to higher or lower levels of tonal activity. Through such a sounding of tones and overtones, like plucking the strings of a harp and observing the effect of the vibrations rippling across a bowl of water, information from different levels or octaves is transmitted to other levels or octaves.

If this world-view sounds Pythagorean—music of the spheres—it is! Yet the difference between the Pythagoreans and the Maya is this: the Maya demonstrated to no uncertain degree that this is not merely a philosophy but the basis of an entire civilization. Such a civilization based on the principle of harmonic resonance is obviously different in nature and purpose than a civilization such as ours, which is based on the acquisition of material goods and the defense of territory.

To understand the Maya and their scientific base as an alternative to our present disorder, we must pursue the description of such a civilization even further. For instance, what would a civilization founded on the principle of harmonic resonance have as its goals or purpose? Could it be anything else but to place the system Earth in resonance with the Sun as an evolving member of a larger galactic family? How does this compare with the goals of our present civilization? Who can say what the goals of our civilization are? Do these goals even have a relation to the planet, much less to the solar system?

Precisely, because it is based on the principle of harmonic resonance, a civilization such as the Mayan can be described as *galactically informed*. That is, by the principle of harmonic resonance, there is a two-way information wave that ripples to and from the individual being to the collective or planetary mind, and from the planetary mind through the Sun to the galactic core.

If the Maya are "galactic agents," does being galactically informed describe a process of information dissemination only, or does it also describe a process of what we today would call "space travel"? Or, rather, might it not be that from the perspective of harmonic resonance and the two-way galactic information flow, there is no difference between information dissemination and space travel?

I think at this point that there is an important distinction to be considered. Unlike Western science, which bases itself on an investigation of matter—hence scientific materialism—Mayan science bases itself on mind as the foundation of the universe. Universe *is* mind, and the different qualities of mind can be described by simple, whole-number relations. For Mayan science, what we call *matter* represents different tones holding together as a harmonic frequency-spectrum perceptible to the sense of touch. Like all other resonant experiences, matter can be represented by whole-number relations. As any mathematician knows, number itself is a purely mental structure.

A further corollary of the Mayan perspective is the universality of consciousness. Since the universe is mental rather than material in nature, or rather, since the notion of the material is derived from the mental, in actuality there is only consciousness—intelligent energy—be it a piece of quartz, an ant, a human, or something beyond. Everything is alive. There is nothing without feeling. The field of reality is saturated with purpose.

In this view, the form of things is the shape of consciousness at a particular *resonant frequency juncture*. A resonant frequency juncture can be defined as the synchronization of two or more tonal spectrums which join momentary need with universal purpose. The environment may need "ant" to perform a task, to aerate the Earth; ant then is the tonal spectrum joining momentary need with the universal purpose of aerating the Earth. In a similar way, at one point in its evolution, the Earth may need synchronized intelligence to place it in more conscious relation to the Sun and to the galaxy as a whole. Or rather, at the same time, the Sun may need a planetary body to consciously ground galactic information it is receiving from the galactic core and/or from more evolved star systems. It is to precisely this situation that the Mayan Factor corresponds: the synchronization of galactic information with the mutual needs of the Earth and the Sun. Like galactic ants, the Maya and their civilization would be the synchronizers of momentary need—represented by planetary or solar intelligence—with universal purpose, full conscious entry into the galactic community.

Let us, for a moment, consider a scenario. Let us assume the galaxy to be an immense organism possessing order and consciousness of a magnitude transcending the threshold of the human imagination. Like a giant body, it consists of a complex of member star systems each coordinated by the galactic core, Hunab Ku. Cycling energy/information in clockwise and counter-clockwise directions simultaneously, the dense pulsing galactic heart emits a continuous series of signals, called by ourselves radio emissions. In actuality these radio emissions correspond to a matrix of resonance—a vast galactic field of intelligent energy whose primary on-off pulsation provides the basis for four universal wave function: a *transmitting* or informational function; a *radiative*, or electromagnetic function; an *attractive* or gravitational function; and a *receptive* or psychoactive function.

The sole purpose of the continuous emission of intelligent wave-information from Hunab Ku, the galactic core and cosmic radio station, is the superior coordination of the member organisms, the star systems. By superior coordination is meant, first of all, the ability of local intelligence, through a focussing of the lenses of the Kuxan Suum, to arrive at the threshold of perceiving the whole and aligning itself accordingly. By local intelligence is meant the planetary mind or field of consciousness constituting the self-reflective field of a planet (or planets) within a given star system. Then, once alignment with the whole has been perceived and realized by a local system, the purpose is to extend the process to member systems in which the threshold of perceiving the whole has not yet been attained. In this way, the community of galactic intelligence is slowly evolved.

Realization of the whole implies direct conscious communication via the local star, with the galactic core. This also implies a continuous activation of the galactic walkie-talkie lifeline, Kuxan Suum. The capacity to maintain direct communication and to continue to establish and extend realization of the whole is the conscious attainment of harmony. The end of the process may be nothing more than a transcendent passing of the entire galaxy into an inconceivable stage of harmonic synchronization.

In the process we are describing, some local systems attain alignment with the whole earlier than other systems. Let us say that the intelligence that reaches this stage is called Maya—diviners of harmony. To divine is to know directly by mind. To be a diviner of harmony, a Maya, would then be to know directly the harmonic frequencies of a level or stage of being, and, in a manner of speaking, to be able to tune into and even take on the qualities of that level or stage of being.

Because of the attainment of such knowledge, one of the powers of Maya would be that of *resonant transduction*. Through direct knowledge of wave harmonics and frequency changes, resonant transduction is the ability to apply this knowledge and pass directly from one condition of being to another—and, consequently, from one star system to another. Of course, the imperative of attaining alignment with the whole and becoming Maya, diviners of harmony, is to extend such realization to other local star systems. In this manner, the galactic matrix begins to be woven into a web of self-reflective intelligence.

Furthermore, in order that all systems may attain the same level of harmonic coordination, knowledge or information would have to be systemized into the simplest code possible so that it might be used in common. To systematize and transmit this code is also the responsibility of Maya. The code, as we shall see, is referred to as the *harmonic module*, or Tzolkin, the simplest possible mathematical matrix to accommodate the largest possible number of harmonic transformations, transmissions, and transductions—a veritable periodic table of galactic frequencies.

Intrepid voyagers of the Kuxan Suum, galactic travellers scouting for star systems in which the potential for realization of and alignment with the whole is just ripening, the Maya, diviners of harmony, are tirelessly on the roam. Once a system has been surveyed, monitored and found to have the evolutionary potential for harmonic attainment, the

Maya make ready for final adjustments. Of course, as the local systems that attain harmonic synchronization increase in number, the level of cooperative coordination for less evolved systems also increases. And as much as the Maya operate with a uniform galactic information code, the harmonic module, in fulfilling the imperative of extending the harmony, they would also operate with a galactic code of honor. Why?

As anyone knows, there is no intelligence in coercion or forcing another into action or realization. And if the name of the galactic game is superior, intelligent harmonization, it must be played so that the local intelligence is taught or shown how it works in such manner that it comes to its own conclusions. In other words, the galactic code of honor is to manifest and demonstrate harmony by whatever means possible. Always playing by the rules of harmony, but at the same time respecting the local intelligence, the code's chief command would be to do nothing to further any notion of duality or separateness. A key Mayan phrase in this regard is: *"In lake'ch:" I am another yourself.*

Skilled in resonant transduction—the wave-harmonic means of transmission, communication, and passing from one condition of being to another—through skilled use of the Kuxan Suum, the Maya would act as mediators between Hunab Ku, the galactic core, and the evolving intelligence of a local star system. But while it may be easy enough to imagine information being transmitted through the Kuxan Suum, like waves propagated through a tin-can walkie-talkie, what about space travel? According to the Mayan Factor, space travel *is* information—information transmitted through the principle of harmonic resonance. We are information. The universe is information. Information, like number, is ultimately a resonant property of mind.

Information is energy structured according to the receiver for which it is intended. The limiting or form-bearing aspect of information does not conceal the fact that the container is in-formed by a quality of energy. We hear music, "sound-waves propagated through space," and someplace within we experience an emotional charge. A transduction has occurred—a transformation of sound, one kind of information, into emotional energy, another kind of information.

All energy possesses transductive wave properties. All wave property is susceptible of being transmitted resonantly as frequency overtones. A coherent cycle of frequencies is an octave, and in all octaves any tone can be sounded to produce its overtones in other octaves. Add to this the fact that any wave property can be transduced from one form to another through a particular medium, such as quartz crystal, and you have the basic principles underlying harmonic resonance.

As we are only now beginning to discover, DNA, the genetic code,—the code of life—possesses a wave character infrastructure. This implies that between the cells of the body there is a universal system of communication operating at speeds ranging between those of sound and light. As we also know, the DNA code corresponds to a whole number formula which represents a binary progression to the 6th power—2, 4, 8, 16, 32, 64—producing 64 six-part code words or codons.

A science based on the principle of resonant harmonics could translate the whole-number mathematics of these codons into wave structures of different frequencies and transmit the information through the Kuxan Suum as resonant transduction. Like maximum velocity Star Trekkers beaming through the galactic ether, the Maya could transmit themselves as DNA code information from one star system to another.

Yet, to respect the perspective of the whole system, transmission of genetic or other kinds of information from a more evolved system to a lesser one must go through a proper hierarchy of command. The basic chain of command goes from Hunab Ku—galactic core, to star, and from star to reflective intelligence—planetary mind or consciousness. Once a particular planetary consciousness has placed itself in alignment with the whole—that is, through its parent star to the galactic core—then, through playing changes on the universal code—the harmonic module—communication could be established with another star system.

It is important to bear in mind that the information communicated from one system to another must pass through the star of the receiving system. It is the star, of which our Sun is an example, that mediates the Kuxan Suum between Hunab Ku, the galactic core, and the planet evolving into conscious reflective intelligence. How would this information tranmission occur using the Sun as the chief mediator?

Assuming a surveillance had occurred and a monitoring of the local system had verified that the system was evolved enough to be on the threshold of whole alignment, then the proper code information would be readied. An intelligence probe transmitted as a synchronization code would be beamed through the local star, say, our Sun, called by the Maya, *Kin*. Since Kin, our Sun, has a cycle of just under 23 years divided into two pulsations averaging 11.3 years each, the intelligence probe would first synchronize itself with this solar cycle. Incidentally, the 11.3-year cycle pulsation produces a phenomenon known as the *heliopause*: a fluctuation in the virtually imperceptible bubble that forms the *heliocosm*—the totality of the sun's gravitational and electromagnetic field, encompassing the orbits of the planets of the entire solar system.

Once the information field of the Sun had been synchronized with the information flow of the more evolved systems, the critical information transduction could occur: the genetic impregnation of the selected planetary field. Like a subtle beam keyed to the solar cycle, the genetic information wave coded to the particular frequencies and qualities of the select planet would instantaneously burst into manifestation. The Maya, galactic navigators and diviners of harmony, would have penetrated to another system. What would this be like? How would this actually occur?

The beginning of the most coherent of the extant Mayan texts, *Popul Vuh: The Book of the Community or of the Common Things,* though written after the Spanish conquest, contains some interesting clues.

Here we shall set forth the revelation, the declaration, and the narration of all that was hidden, the revelation . . . and at the same time the declaration, the combined narration of the Grandmother and the Grandfather. . .we shall bring to light because now the Popul Vuh . . .cannot be seen anymore, in which was clearly seen coming from the other side of the sea . . .The original book, written long ago, existed, but its sight is hidden to the searcher and to the thinker.

Great were the descriptions and the account of how all the sky and Earth were formed, how it was formed and divided into four parts; how it was partitioned, and how the sky was divided; and the measuring cord was brought, and it was stretched in the sky and over the Earth, on the four angles, on the four corners, as was told by the Creator and the Maker, the Mother and the Father of Life; of all created things, he who gives breath and thought, she who gives birth to children, he who watches over the happiness of the people, the happiness of the human race, the wise man, he who meditates on the goodness of all that exists in the sky, on the Earth, in the lakes and in the sea.

Similarily, in another text, *The Annals of Cakchiquels,* it is written:

. . . from the other side of the sea we came to the place called Tulan . . . From four places the people came to Tulan. In the east is one Tulan; another in Xibalbay; another in the west from where we came ourselves, and another is where God is; therefore there were four Tulans . . . And setting out we arrived at the gates of Tulan. Only a bat guarded the gates of Tulan . . .then we were commanded by our mothers and fathers to come, we the thirteen clans of the seven tribes, the thirteen clans of warriors . . .

From these cryptic descriptions, several things immediately attract our attention. First of all, these are descriptions of a coming into being, a passage from an elsewhere that is described as "the other side of the sea." Is this "other side of the sea" an actual ocean, or is it a metaphor for the galactic sea? Secondly, there is the mandalic description, whether of the four Tulans or the four-part division of the sky and the Earth. What does this actually describe? Is the measuring cord by which the center determines the relation of the four corners or four directions also a reference to the Kuxan Suum?

Then there is the reference to the thirteen clans of warriors and the seven tribes. These are the key numbers of the Mayan matrix. Thirteen, representing the movement present in all things, repeated twenty times, yields 260, the harmonic number of the Tzolkin or galactic matrix. Seven is the number of the mystical center. Six subtracted from seven is one, the number of unity. Six added to seven is thirteen, the heavenly harmonic of movement and totality. Seven added to thirteen is twenty, the factor combined with thirteen which creates the harmonic module. The numbers located at the four corners of the Tzolkin, or harmonic matrix, are one at the beginning, thirteen at the end, and seven at the two intermediate corners.

In these descriptions of origins, are we actually dealing with the code-language of the Zuvuya, describing passage via the Kuxan Suum to the Earth? Is the four-part mandala or fourfold Tulan a description of a primary harmonic pattern through which genetic and other information could be transmitted intact? Do the thirteen clans and seven tribes

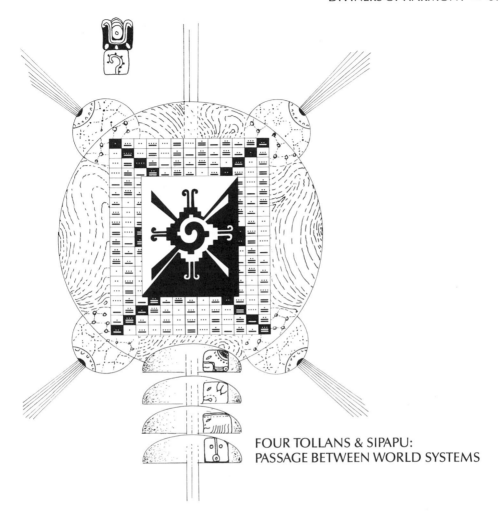

FOUR TOLLANS & SIPAPU:
PASSAGE BETWEEN WORLD SYSTEMS

represent code language for the recollection of the galactic matrix? Do the Grandmother and Grandfather, in other Mayan and Mexican texts described as dwelling in the thirteenth or highest heaven, represent the benevolent commanding intelligence in the system from which the Maya, or at least the Mayan information stream, originated?

If the Kuxan Suum, like a resonant, galactic walkie-talkie, could be the transmitting agent of the information necessary to transport the Maya as high-frequency synchronization scouts from a system outside of ours to our planet, Earth, it also bears resemblance to the Hopi *sipapu*. Described as the tunnel or passage leading to and from the different worlds, the sipapu is the thread or lifeline not only linking galactic core, star systems, and different planets, but linking different world eras as well. Thus, when one world era closes and another is about to begin, the sipapu is the passage showing the way.

Following this hypothetical route of resonant transmission between galactic star systems, we would find the Mayan information stream implanting on this planet perhaps as early as 3,000 years ago, if not earlier. Setting about their purpose of gathering information about Earth in relation to the Sun, Moon, and the rest of the solar system, the Maya observed, adopted, interacted, and assimilated. Always maintaining communication with central headquarters, when the time ripened to leave their calling card—the brilliant heights of classic Mayan civilization—they went about it with precision, artistry, and total aplomb. Since they were still in communication through Kuxan Suum with the galactic core, Hunab Ku, the mathematical system "arrived" already fully developed. Following observation and adaptation to the new planetary system, the twenty key hieroglyphs would have then been modified accordingly. And following the completion of their mission, the correlation of the planetary cycles of our solar system within the galactic frame of the harmonic matrix, the key agents would have then returned whence they had come via the mediating lens system of the Kuxan Suum. In this way, the "mystery" of the Maya may be accounted for.

PACAL VOTAN,
NAVIGATOR

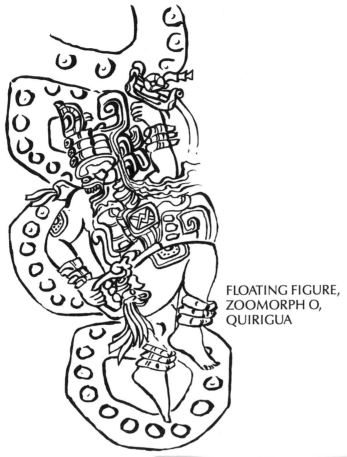

FLOATING FIGURE,
ZOOMORPH O,
QUIRIGUA

Given this scenario, there is a genre of sculpture that the Maya left behind at Quirigua and also at Palenque which depicts humans or human-like figures in positions that show the feet slightly akimbo, as if soaring or floating, ascending or descending, coming into being or going out of it. The most famous of these is the figure on the tomb-lid of Pacal Votan at Palenque, in which it appears that the tree of life emerges from the main figure's abdomen or solar plexus. Is this tree of life actually the Kuxan Suum? Far more intriguing are the two figures from Quirigua, which, without a doubt, was the most brilliant intellectual center of the Maya. Interesting also is the fact that, as the most brilliant of the Mayan centers, Quirigua reached its pinnacle of artistic and intellectual achievement in the final stages of Baktun 9—A.D. 790 to 830.

One figure on the massive stone altar of "Zoomorph O," Quirigua, possesses a fantastically grotesque head, a phenomenal headdress and an otherwise human form. In its right hand it holds a handle of some kind. Behind the body is a large organic enclosure consisting of three oval or circular discs, in which are incised smaller circular forms. The position of the legs, arm, and head turned sideways, in particular, give this figure the appearance of soaring or floating.

In another related sculpture at Quirigua on the equally monumental stone altar of "Zoomorph P," only the feet and lower legs appear humanly recognizable. The rest of the body, which appears as if it might almost be seated, disappears into a maze of strange but organic structures. Facing the altar of "Zoomorph P" is the sculpture of a contemplative seated figure, holding a sceptre. All of the Quirigua figures are accompanied by a wealth of hieroglyphs. The Palenque figure is adorned in the tomb by depictions of the Nine Lords of Time or the Underworld. What is happening? Are these depictions of form either coming into manifestation or subsiding back into the vibratory field of the Kuxan Suum?

While, by current standards, all of this may seem to be speculation—wild hypothesis—we are on firm ground in dealing with the harmonic matrix, the 13×20 harmonic module, commonly called Tzolkin. By turning our attention to this one intriguing and coherently unique piece of evidence, we shall penetrate farther into the galactic mystery of the Maya, diviners of harmony. At the same time, through our understanding of the Tzolkin, we ourselves may come to divine the purpose of the Maya in coming to this planet.

SEATED FIGURE,
ZOOMORPH P, QUIRIGUA

THE GALACTIC MASTERS & THE NUMBERS OF DESTINY

3

When we first confront the Maya we sense their richness, yet we miss their gods, their myths, their beliefs. While the myths and stories are there, hidden in the texts, peeping out from the jungle creepers, winking at us from among the brilliant flowers growing out of hewn stone, what forces itself upon our attention are the numbers. As we have seen, the insistence of the numbers occurs in the telling of the times of "origins." The numbers also speak when we read the garbled texts of the prophets of Chilam Balam, who, going into trance, speak everything in numbers: the **1**, the **13**, the **7**, the **9**, the **4.** Are the numbers living? Are they entities, etheric and intangible, occupying dimensions of mind, the existence of which is unsuspected by our materialistic head-sets?

Rubbing our eyes and clearing our heads, it is hard to believe that the whole of the story can be told with numbers. Thirteen numbers and twenty symbols, to be precise. And the twenty symbols themselves—are they but more numbers, masked in cryptic forms called hieroglyphs? Even further, how could the whole of the story—science, myth, galactic measure, and divine strategy—be contained in a matrix measuring 13×20 units?

Called by archaeologists the Tzolkin—literally, the count of days or actually the count of *kin* (Sun, day, primary harmonic unit)—the original name of the 13×20 matrix is not known to us. Also referred to as the Sacred Calendar, the Tzolkin appears as one of those bizarre, numerological anomalies. But then, did the I Ching seem any different to Leibnitz, Hegel, or Jung when they first encountered it? We do know that the Tzolkin, what I call the Harmonic Module, is also the same as the permutation table called the Buk Xok. Yet when we examine the permutation table, as playful as it is, its profundity eludes us. Come now, we say, what is meant by the Mayan numbers? How can this arrangement of thirteen numbers in twenty sets speak of universal resonance?

Of course, the Tzolkin is just a code. So is the alphabet with which we write. Yet, as we know, the alphabet encodes a language, and the person who knows to write that language with the alphabet—26 letters—can command tremendous power and communicate at least a suggestion of the knowledge and wisdom of the universe. In the same way, knowing the code language of the Tzolkin, the Mayan harmonic module, can open up channels of understanding and communication with equal if not greater power than is available to us through the alphabet. For number, no different than symbol, is a condensation of overtones and levels of meaning. And each individual number is a resonant field unto itself. It is for this reason that only thirteen numbers are necessary to describe the entire complex we call galactic being—thirteen numbers each occupying a possibility of twenty positional places, for a total of 260 permutations.

In order to explain and appreciate the workings of the 13×20 Mayan matrix and the richness of its actual and symbolic applications, it may be well to get an even deeper feeling for the magical potency which "numbers" have for the Maya. These numbers, the **13**, the **7**, the **4** and the **9**, in particular, as well as the **20**, so pervade the thought of the Maya that it is important to understand that each of the numbers represents a multitude of qualities, and the sum of the qualities, like the sum of the numbers, represents what we call "the world," or rather "the universe."

Today we generally think that numbers represent *quantities* such as 7 apples or 13 oranges. But quantification is only one function of number. To think of number as harmonic qualities the analogy of music is helpful. Each musical tone may be said to represent a number or vice versa. *C* could be represented by *1*, *D* by *2*, and so forth. Within an octave range there may be a set number of tones—*7*, to be exact—do, re, mi, fa , sol, la, and ti—the eighth tone being high C or do.

Each tone of a given octave has its overtones in both higher and lower octaves. The possibilities of the sequences of tones, the sharpening or flattening of tones, the richness and timbre of tones, the play of octave ranges and harmonic synchronizations of two or more tones are virtually endless. And yet to begin with we had only a small set of tones. This analogy demonstrates that number, representing sensory as well as symbolic mental qualities, is vital, possesses multiple overtones of depth and meaning, and is capable of expressing the whole range of universal possibilities. The analogy also shows that a very limited range of numbers can accomplish all of these ends.

For the Mayan Factor, the qualitative, harmonic function of number is paramount. Thus, while for us the measurement of time is the counting of a sequence of quantitative units, be they days or minutes, years or hours, for the Maya what we call time is a function of the principle of harmonic resonance. Thus, days are actually tones, called *kin*, represented by corresponding numbers; sequences of days (kin) create harmonic cycles, called vinal, tun, katuns, baktuns, and so forth; and sequences of harmonic cycles taken as larger aggregates describe the harmonic frequencies or calibrations of a larger organic order, say, the harmonic pattern of planet Earth in relation to the Sun and the galaxy beyond.

Yet, to follow the musical analogy, while any day represents a particular tone or number, it also has its overtones. Properly tuned into, then, the quality of a day can lead to experiences in other octaves, in other dimensions of being. Though this view bears some analogy to astrology, the meaning is somewhat different, because the numbers are cued to galactic harmonics rather than, or as well as, to planetary cycles. As a result of this

1	8	2	9	3	10	4	11	5	12	6	13	7
2	9	3	10	4	11	5	12	6	13	7	1	8
3	10	4	11	5	12	6	13	7	1	8	2	9
4	11	5	12	6	13	7	1	8	2	9	3	10
5	12	6	13	7	1	8	2	9	3	10	4	11
6	13	7	1	8	2	9	3	10	4	11	5	12
7	1	8	2	9	3	10	4	11	5	12	6	13
8	2	9	3	10	4	11	5	12	6	13	7	1
9	3	10	4	11	5	12	6	13	7	1	8	2
10	4	11	5	12	6	13	7	1	8	2	9	3
11	5	12	6	13	7	1	8	2	9	3	10	4
12	6	13	7	1	8	2	9	3	10	4	11	5
13	7	1	8	2	9	3	10	4	11	5	12	6
1	8	2	9	3	10	4	11	5	12	6	13	7
2	9	3	10	4	11	5	12	6	13	7	1	8
3	10	4	11	5	12	6	13	7	1	8	2	9
4	11	5	12	6	13	7	1	8	2	9	3	10
5	12	6	13	7	1	8	2	9	3	10	4	11
6	13	7	1	8	2	9	3	10	4	11	5	12
7	1	8	2	9	3	10	4	11	5	12	6	13

TZOLKIN & BUK XOK PERMUTATION TABLE

perspective, what scholars have taken to be the Mayan obsession with time is not that at all. Rather, the number sequences that so intricately adorn the Classic Mayan monuments are primarily intended to describe calibrations of a galactic harmonic as it corresponds to solar and earthly cycles of time. We shall return to the implications of this statement shortly.

For the Maya, then, the meaning of number does not necessarily come from sequential relationship, i.e., ten is greater than nine, nor the quantities that any sum of numbers might necessarily represent, but from the qualities derived from juxtapositions, permutations, and overtones of a given set of numbers. In other words, the meaning of number as representative of harmonic orders is not linear or progressively quantitative but *radially reciprocal*. But what do we mean when we say that the meaning of number is radially reciprocal ?

Radial describes a dynamic field of radiance, of radiant qualities like a starburst firework on the Fourth of July. The idea is that each of the thirteen numbers is radial, expressing its qualities in all directions simultaneously, each contained in and penetrating all the other numbers. Reciprocal means that each number feeds back to and is referenced by all the other numbers within a self-contained circuit. A circuit describes a stream of energy whose origin and end are one.

As a giant circuit, the galaxy may be represented by a set of streams of energy, each of whose radial pulses may be described by one of a set of primary numbers. Like any circuit, each of the pulsing energy streams have a common end and point of origin: the galactic core, *Hunab Ku*. The circuit itself as described here is called by the Maya, *Zuvuya*, the current by which everything issues from and returns, simultaneously forwards and backwards, to the source.

Let us return then to Hunab Ku, the unspeakably brilliant galactic core. Like the heart of a hurricane, Hunab Ku may be described as possessing a simultaneous spin and counter-spin motion radiating outward from a center-point of indescribable energy that pulses at a particular rate. Let us say that the counterpoint currents of energy may be described by a series of numbers going in opposite directions to each other. Let us further say that one current pulses at frequencies represented by the series *1* to *13* and the other pulses by the series represented by *13* to *1*. That is, the former goes from a simple to a more complex pulsation, the latter from a more complex to a simple pulsation. If we match the pulsations in the spin and counter-spin currents, this is the sequence that we get:

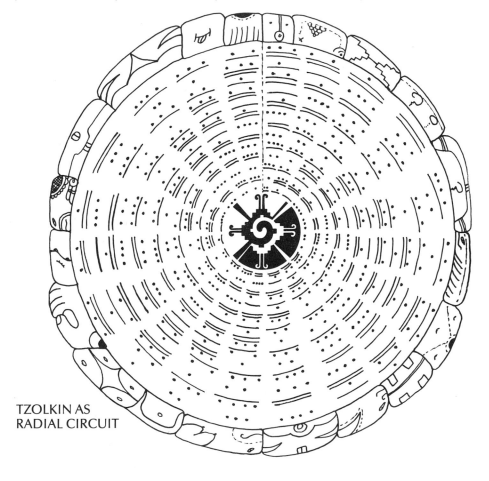

**TZOLKIN AS
RADIAL CIRCUIT**

Spin	**1**	**2**	**3**	**4**	**5**	**6**	**7**	**8**	**9**	**10**	**11**	**12**	**13** (=91)
Counter-Spin	**13**	**12**	**11**	**10**	**9**	**8**	**7**	**6**	**5**	**4**	**3**	**2**	**1** (=91)
Paired Sums	**14**	**14**	**14**	**14**	**14**	**14**	**14**	**14**	**14**	**14**	**14**	**14**	**14**

The entire cycle of spin/counter-spin can also be described by the numbers representing the differences between each of the adjacent numbers of the two cycles, i.e, the *difference* between *1* and *13*, *2* and *12*, *3* and *11*, etc. The sequence of the *differences* between the two series is described by the following set of numbers:

Differences **12 10 8 6 4 2 0 2 4 6 8 10 12** (=84)

We also see that the sum of the numbers *1+2+3+4+5+6+7+8*. . . *+13* equals *91*, which is also *13×7*, while the numbers in the series represented by the differences of the two cycles equals *84*, or *7×12*, the difference between *84* and *91* again being *7*. As an even number *12* can also be factored by *3* (*3×4*), and *84* is also *3×28*, while *28* is represented by *4×7*.

In this example, it is interesting that *7*, the middle number in each series, represents a difference of zero. Being at the center of a set of *13* numbers, *7* represents mystic fullness or potentiality. By adding the two sets of thirteen numbers as they are matched with each other— *1+13*, *2+12*, *3+11*, etc.—in every case the sum is *14*, or *7×2*. The total number of numbers in the spin/counter-spin series is *13×2* or *26*.

In this simple example, we see that from the galactic core numbers can radiate in at least two directions simultaneously. We also see that the relation between the cycle of numbers in each energy arm creates a simple set of reciprocal relations. It is also apparent that *7* has a peculiar relation to *zero*, to the sums of the whole series (*91*), to the sums of the paired numbers of the series (*14*), and to the sum of the differences between the series (*84*). If there were any two key numbers to emerge from this exercise they would be *13* and *7*.

This example demonstrates what we mean by number being radially reciprocal. What appeared to be just two lines of numbers matched with each other actually yields a magical range of permutations and possibilities. Keeping in mind that the numbers represent different resonant tones, wave pulsations, or qualities of radiant energy corresponding to different sensory and mental ranges, we can begin to appreciate the Mayan "meaning" of number. As the active agents of the different levels of resonance, numbers are indeed magical entities, harmonic beings that jump octaves, transform identity, switch dimensions, and travel relentlessly backward with the same ease that they display in marching progressively forward. (For greater detail on the radially reciprocal Mayan number code, see *Appendix A. Radial & Directional Numbers*.)

That the Maya accorded a directional significance to each of the numbers, following an East-North-West-South pattern repeated five times, contributes to the richness of meaning and symbolism of each of the *13* numbers. The factored result of the *20* directional positions and *13* numbers, of course, is the *260*-unit Tzolkin.

If we continue to assume that this *260*-unit permutational matrix is the primary matrix spun out by and counter-spun back into the galactic core, Hunab Ku, then we may also assume that in one way or another this pulsing matrix—the galactic constant—will penetrate into and underlie all aspects of galactic functioning throughout all the far-flung star systems of the galaxy. The numbers and the directional positions, remember, describe the total range of tonal harmonic relations, with all of their resonant overtones and transformative possibilities. In short, the Tzolkin is a keyboard or table of universally applicable periodic frequencies.

And just as the primary galactic matrix—Tzolkin—is radial and simultaneous at its core, then, as dissipated and distant from the core as it may sometimes seem, the functioning of the matrix nonetheless maintains its radial and simultaneous integrity throughout. Thus, as the sweeping galactic arms are described by numbers moving backward and forward in relation to each other, so what we call time, for instance, is actually the simultaneous movement out from and back to the galactic core. Indeed, as long as we are attuned to the movement of "time" going in only one direction, what we perceive of the galaxy and of the universe is only half of the picture.

To complete this general consideration of the qualitative nature of number in the Mayan scheme, we should not lose sight of the *overtone* function of number. This function, which is referred to mathematically as the *fractal principle*, describes the capacity of a number to remain proportionally constant. Thus *2* is to *10* what *20* is to *100* and *200* is to *1,000*. Though the quantity of the number changes, the proportion in this series is constant. It is from the proportion, furthermore, that the whole may be reconstructed. In the Mayan code, one is struck by the continuous appearance of certain numbers which refer to specific holographic proportions or fractals, including *26, 260,* etc. and *52, 520,* etc. Indeed, it is through fractal properties that the numbers resonate at different octaves, bringing to the senses and mental spheres higher informational ranges to be decoded through cellular attunement. (For more information on fractals in the Mayan system, see *Appendix B. Mayan Factors & Fractals*.)

So we see that the purpose of the Mayan mathematic was for understanding and recording of the galactic constant—Tzolkin—spinning through its endless fractal harmonics and overtone permuations. Only secondarily did the Classic Mayan recording of numbers have to do with calendars. Indeed, what we find recorded on the great stone monuments and certain of the extant *codices*, or painted manuscripts, is actually the skill the Maya demonstrated in showing the relation between the galactic harmonic and the annual cycles of the Earth, Moon, and other planets of the solar system.

It is for this reason that at places like Copan, Quirigua, and Tikal the Maya erected "time markers" every five, ten, and twenty years. It was not years that were being commemorated so much as harmonic numbers occurring at *factoral equivalants* of five, ten, or twenty years. Thus five "years" is actually a calibration of 1,800 *kin*. 1,800 kin, a *holtun,* is actually 25 days short of five solar years, 1,825 (5×365) days. Likewise, ten "years" is 3,600 kin, and twenty "years," 7,200 kin. As a point of interest, each of these numbers—*1,800, 3,600, 7,200*—possesses 9 as its base factor (*18=9×2; 36=9×4; 72=9×8*). As we shall see,

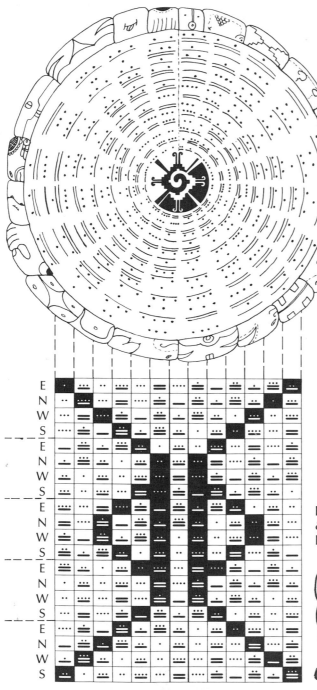

RADIAL MATRIX & TZOLKIN WITH DIRECTIONAL GUIDE

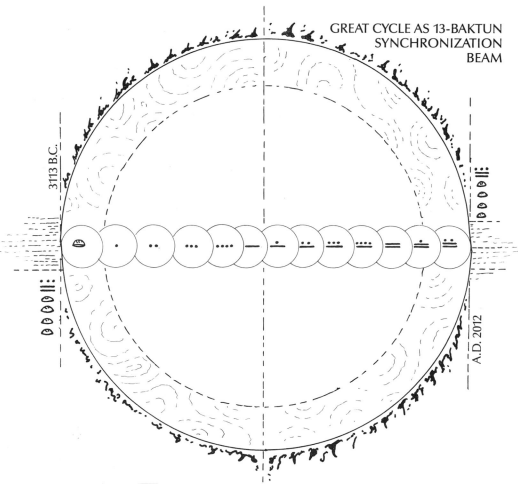

GREAT CYCLE AS 13-BAKTUN
SYNCHRONIZATION
BEAM

3113 B.C.

A.D. 2012

9 is the key number related to computations that correlate to what we call time.

These harmonic calibrations—*1,800 kin, 3,600 kin, 7,200 kin*, etc.—correspond to measurements of a galactic pattern or synchronization beam. To think about this, let us imagine a beam emanating from the galactic core. Like a beam from a lighthouse, the greater the distance, the wider the beam. Suppose a small boat, far out at sea, passes through the beam. Even though both boat and beam are moving, there will be an interval of time during which the boat is actually bathed in the beam. So it is with the spaceship Earth passing like a boat through the galactic synchronization beam. From the perspective of Mayan harmonics, this beam is 5200 *tun* in diameter. That comes out to approximately 5125 Earth years in diameter. How is this so?

The commencement of our point of passage through this beam corresponds to the Mayan "beginning" date, August 13, 3113, B.C. Being 5,200 tun in duration, the galactic harmonic pattern belongs to the fractal series based on 52, while 52 itself is based on 26 (×2), and 13×4. Since 26 is the base fractal of 260, the number of the Tzolkin, the beam is imprinted and saturated with the galactic constant throughout. Because the beam is calibrated by 5,200 tun, and because a tun of 360 kin, or the equivalent of 360 days, is some five days short of a vague solar year of 365 days, the entire pattern of 5,200 tun is actually the equivalent of some 5,125 years duration. Again, we are assuming it was not the Classic Mayas' primary intention to record time, but to record the harmonic calibrations of the 5,200-tun harmonic synchronization beam.

Naturally, most Mayan scholars are puzzled by what appears to be the use of 260- and 360-unit "calendar" cycles that do not correspond in any precise way to perceivable astronomical or organic planetary cycles. The reason for the bewilderment lies in the fact that the 260- and 360-unit cycles are not originally calendrical or time-marking cycles but fractal indices of the galactic harmonic. As a fractal, *260* is actually an overtone of *26* or *2×13*, and *360* is an overtone of *36* or *2×18, 4×9*. So we see, in the numbers 260 and 360, the key Mayan factors, *4, 9,* and *13*.

The 260-unit "calendar" is the *galactic constant*. The 360-unit "calendar" is the *harmonic calibrator*. 260 is constant because it represents the ceaseless round of permutations generated by the 13 numbers and the 20 directional positions that define the least possible set of changes accommodating the greatest number of galactic possibilities, from wave frequencies to archetypes. Both 260 and 360 are counts that are based on the smallest unit, a kin. 360 kin, or one tun, is the harmonic calibrator by virtue of its being a multiple of 9, its representation of the number of degrees in a circle, and its approximation of the 365 days in a solar year. (For more detailed information on the harmonic progressions of the 260- and 360-unit "calendars," see *Appendix C, Calendar Harmonics*.)

Equipped with a disarmingly simple though highly flexible number system, the purpose of the Maya in coming to our planet was to make sure that the galactic harmonic pattern, not perceivable as yet to our evolutionary position in the galaxy, had been presented and recorded. Of course, the Maya may not have been the first of the galactic masters to communicate information from outside the solar system to our planet. The facts point to various others having at least seeded the planet sometime around entry into the current harmonic beam, 3113 B.C. But by their place in the history of global civilization, the Maya's greatest and most unique signficance lay in their being the most recent wave of galactic masters and in their bringing the galactic information matrix in its entirety to us.

The Classic Maya showed with great dexterity and ease how our annual cycles correlate with the galactic harmonic pattern. This is easy enough to understand if we do not consider ourselves to be superior to the Maya. But if we think of them as having been Stone Age or as representing an earlier, less advanced stage of our own civilization, struggling to create a solar agricultural calendar, then this point will be harder for us to understand.

In order to obtain a better grasp of the matter let us flesh out a little more the scenario we began to develop in the preceding chapter.

At Monte Alban in the Oaxaca highlands of southern Mexico, we find a curious phenomenon. There among the earliest ruins, which archaeologists date to a period between 500 and 600 B.C., are an amazing set of sculpted figures. Animal-headed and with glyphic representations vertically aligned through the centers of their bodies, these otherwise human-like figures are accompanied by what is considered to be the earliest example of the bar and dot notation system associated with the mathematical "texts" of much later Mayan civilization. In this notational system, a dot equals one unit, a bar, five units, and a stylized shell, zero. With these three notational symbols, the Maya achieved mathematical miracles.

In considering the current Great Cycle running from 3113 B.C. to A.D. 2012, we find that its exact midpoint, 6.10.0.0.0, in the seventh, or middle, of the thirteen-baktun cycles comprising the Great Cycle, corresponds to the date 550 B.C. This represents the approximate time of the Danzante sculptures of Monte Alban. In transposing Mayan calibrations from the initial point, August 13, 3113 B.C., the so-called long count, a five positional figure is used, e.g., 6.10.0.0.0. The first number, 6, records the number of baktuns passed since the initial date; the second position records the current katun period, the third position the tun, the fourth the vinal, and the fifth, the kin.

In terms of the number of kin or days passed since the initiation of the Great Cycle, the date 6.10.0.0.0 equals 936,000 kin. Like all key Mayan dates, the key factor in the number 936,000—*harmonic 936*—is 9. The number symbolizing periodicity and completeness, 9 is also the number of the mythic Lords of Time, the number representing the original Mayan galactic masters themselves. The midpoint date, 6.10.0.0.0, at which moment the sculptures at Monte Alban were executed, refers to the "coming of the Nine Lords of Time" and the bringing of galactic measure to the planet.

Whether this first galactic wave, represented by "the Nine Lords of Time," arrived at or about 550 B.C., or whether the date precisely midpoint in the Great Cycle was chosen to commemorate their earlier arrival, is an open question. Suffice it to say that the Monte Alban sculptures commemorate the first wave of galactic Maya in Mesoamerica.

If we look at the Mesoamerican cultural scene around 550 B.C., what we find is the climax of what is considered the first advanced stage of high civilization in this part of the world, the *Olmec*. The name Olmec literally means "rubber people," for it is the Olmec who supposedly invented the ritual ball game and the use of the rubber ball. Having begun their rise to civilization around 1500 B.C., the Olmec are characterized by powerful stone and jade sculptures depicting helmeted jaguar or feline-faced creatures. It is assumed that the religious basis of the Olmec grew out of a late Neolithic shamanic culture centered around the *nagual* or spirit of the jaguar. The Olmec also included among their rites the ingestion of the hallucinogenic mushroom, psilocybin, called by natives, *teonanacatl*, flesh of the gods.

Let us assume that following their materialization into Mesoamerica, commemorated

by the recollections of fourfold Tulan, certain of the Maya became friendly with and infil-
trated the advanced jaguar priest orders of the Olmec. The name for high priest accorded
the Maya in later times was *Balam*, which means jaguar or jaguar priest. Through such
infiltrations, the Maya were able to introduce the bar-and-dot notation system as well as
the "Sacred Calendar": the ceaseless permutations of the thirteen numbers and the twenty
directional positions, adopted for use on this planet as the sacred hieroglyphic signs.

While key galactic Mayan emissaries became assimilated into the high culture of the
Olmec, being remembered as the Nine Lords of Time, others settled their thirteen warrior clans and seven tribes in the highlands of Guatemala and the jungle lowlands of the
Peten, located in present-day Honduras and Guatemala. In the meantime, following the
seeding of the galactic harmonic represented by the 260-day Sacred Calendar, and commemorated by the founding of Monte Alban, a great center arose in central Mexico,
Teotihuacan.

DANZANTES OF MONTE ALBAN,
6.10.0.0.0 OR 550 B.C.

Emerging by the third century B.C. as a major ritual and civil center, Teotihuacan was to become the largest and most extensive ceremonial center in all of Mesoamerica. In actuality, Teotihuacan—"Place Where the Gods Touch the Earth"—like all other major centers in Mesoamerica, was built as a recollection of the primal Tollan or Tulan, the place of origin, as well as the place of entry to this world. Dominated by the Pyramid of the Sun, whose base is almost exactly the same measurement as that of the Great Pyramid of Giza, Egypt, Teotihuacan grew to unparalleled splendor as a city of abundance and artistic glory. The intensely spiritualized artistic vision of Teotihuacan came to be commemorated by the name *Toltec*, meaning master builders, artists, and seers.

Teotihuacan also became the first great center of the religion of Quetzalcoatl, the plumed serpent. As the primal-culture hero, Quetzalcoatl is associated with the sky, the stars, the sea, water, abundance, and the cultivation of all of the arts and sciences of civilization. Representing the union of Heaven and Earth, the imagery of the plumed serpent, as well as that of the plumed jaguar, abounds everywhere in Teotihuacan—on ceramic ware, murals, and the great sculpted figures of the citadel of Quezalcoatl. And here in the citadel of Quetzalcoatl we find the symbolism of the *13* once again: twelve low platform temples, surrounding a thirteenth, which represents the Quetzalcoatl itself.

By the third to fourth century A.D., toward the end of the eighth baktun, the influence of Teotihuacan had begun to extend throughout Mesoamerica. The presence of the Toltec seers and the imagery of Quetzalcoatl became synonymous. And in the jungles of the Peten, the Toltec seers of Quetzalcoatl encountered the tribes of Maya. It was at Tikal that the marriage of Teotihuacan and the Mayan presence occurred. Infused with the spiritual luster of Quetzalcoatl, called by the Maya *Kukulkan*, the Maya began their civilizational rise.

Even more energetically than at Teotihuacan, the priests of Tikal began to construct pyramid temples. But while the pyramids of Teotihuacan were of five levels, those of Tikal tended to be nine—to commemorate the original galactic masters, the Nine Lords of Time. And then occurred the closing of the eighth baktun and the beginning of the ninth. Commencing at A.D. 435, the date 9.0.0.0.0, represented the *harmonic 1296* (1,296,000 kin or days elapsed from 3113 B.C.). Throughout the Mayan centers, it was known: now was the time to prepare for the second galactic wave. Baktun 9, the tenth cycle, was a phase for maximum synchronization. It was the critically important period in which to record the harmonic correlations of the galactic beam with the annual cycle of the Earth, the Sun, the Moon, and the other planets of the solar system.

So it was that the Maya, spiritually renewed by the infusion of the Kukulkan religion and remembering their galactic mission, began to construct and record with an unheard-of fervor. Not only at Tikal, but at Copan, Quirigua, and Palenque, as well as numerous other centers, the activity occurred. Everything had to be made ready. For at exactly the right moment—that is, at exactly the right harmonic calibration—the second galactic wave would be initiated.

Of course, the moment was no mystery. In the sequence of fractal harmonics, the great

Mayan number of synthesis as recorded in the Dresden Codex and re-discovered by Ernst Förstemann is *13 66 560*, a phenomenal number, divisible or capable of being factored by all the key numbers corresponding to all of the harmonic cycles. (See Appendix D. *13 66 56* and the Mayan Harmonic Numbers.)

As the number of kin elapsed since 3113 B.C, *13 66 560* corresponds to a date in the year A.D. 631. While 1,366,560 kin, A.D. 631, is also the equivalent of *3,796* tun or 360 day cycles completed since the initiation date, A.D. 683 corresponds to *3,796* solar years elapsed from the same beginning date. It is interesting that both of these dates—A.D. 631 and A.D. 683—have corresponding number harmónics of *3,796*, the former as tun, the latter as solar years. It is also most significant that the 52-year span between these dates corresponds to the span of the earthly life of Pacal Votan.

If there were to be a significant galactic phase according to the Mayan harmonics, it would occur in the 52-year calendar-round period between A.D. 631 and 683, or between harmonics 13 66 560 and 13 85 540. Indeed, these are the precise dates of the avataric incarnation known as Pacal Votal of Palenque. His "tomb," the only one like it in all of Mesoamarica and the only one comparable to the tomb in the Great Pyramid of Giza, is dated A.D. 683. It lies within the nine-storied Temple of the Inscriptions at Palenque. In the Chamber in which the tomb is found are sculpted representations of the Nine Lords of Time.

Only discovered in 1952, the tomb of Pacal Votan has recently become one of the most celebrated and sensational wonders of the mysterious Maya. The sculpture on the tomb lid, which we mentioned at the end of the last chapter, has been variously interpreted as an astronaut in a space capsule or the representation of a dynastic king being "lowered" at his death into the jaws of the Earth monster.

Here, however, is the legend of Pacal Votan, galactic master, who declared himself to be a serpent, an initiate, a possessor of knowledge. By decree of those above him, Pacal Votan was ordered to leave his "homeland," the mysterious Valum Chivim, and to proceed to the Yucatan, the land of the Maya on Earth. Departing from Valum Chivim and going by means of the "Dwelling of the Thirteen Serpents," Pacal Votan arrived at Valum Votan, on the Usuamacinta River not far from Palenque, which Pacal Votan supposedly then founded. Through making several visits back to his "homeland," Pacal Votan discovered a tower, which came to be destroyed because of a confusion of tongues among its builders. By means of a subterranean passage from the tower, however, Votan was allowed to reach the "Rock of Heaven."

What are we to make of this story? Valum Chivim is a reference to one of the Mayan star-bases, perhaps in the Pleiades, perhaps in Arcturus. These bases, of course, had been monitoring the Mayan mission since the first wave of galactic masters, the Nine Lords of Time among them, had originally seeded planet Earth. Galactic master, Pacal Votan, assigned by his superiors to oversee the initiation of the final phase of the Mayan terrestrial project, would also be known as *Galactic Agent 13 66 56*, corresponding to the harmonic

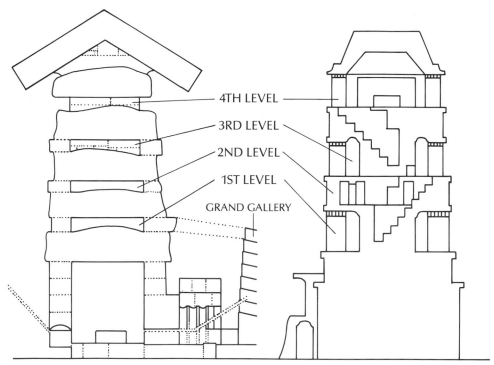

CROSS-SECTION OF KING'S CHAMBER, GIZA, &
TOWER OF THE WINDS, PALENQUE

equivalent date, A.D. 631, of his incarnation/manifestation on this planet. Numerologically, 13 66 56, like all factors of 9, also adds up to 9 (1+3+6+6+5+6=27=2+7=9).

Pacal Votan's travel by means of the "Dwelling of the Thirteen Serpents" refers to intergalactic passage by means of the Kuxan Suum. As the galactic life-fiber, it would be natural
to represent the Kuxan Suum by a serpent or serpent forms. *13*, number of movement, is
also the number of the highest, most exalted of the heavens or levels of being beyond our
solar system, the one closest to central information—the galactic hub, Hunab Ku.
Sculpted serpent beings in transformation, similar to those at Quirigua, adorn the Temple of the Inscriptions at Palenque, a plastic record of the Kuxan Suum transport of Pacal
Votan, Galactic Agent 13 66 56.

Arrival at Valum Votan near present-day Palenque would signify the place of arrival
and/or birth of Pacal Votan in A.D. 631, Harmonic 13 66 56 0. The timing of his arrival
would also coincide with the expectation of the next Kukulkan avatar, whose role Pacal
Votan would assume. In this role, it would only be natural to found a city—corresponding
to the mythic Tollan—to be called *Xibalanque*, or in modern form, Palenque. In the Popul
Vuh, Xibalanque would correspond to the mythic *Xibalba,* the place of the underworld,
or the world of manifestation and the heroic testing of mortality. This would refer to the

taking of a "mortal" human form by Galactic Agent 13 66 56, to be marked and commemorated by the underworld "tomb" within the nine-storied Temple of the Inscriptions.

Maintaining his powers after the founding of Palenque, Pacal Votan had communication with, if not actual travel back via the Kuxan Suum to, Valum Chivim. At Palenque there is another structure unique among Mayan architecture, the so-called Tower of the Winds or Observatory. Facing the Pyramid of the Inscriptions, this tower refers to the tower encountered by Pacal Votan in the legend. Since the tomb of Pacal Votan is the only one that can be compared to the tomb within the Great Pyramid of Egypt, it is most significant that, architecturally, the Tower facing the Pyramid enclosing the tomb bears a strong formal resemblance to the King's Chamber in the Great Pyramid. Both the Tower and the King's Chamber possess four levels rising above a high foundation or coffer. In any case, the tower represents the aspiration enclosing mortality, while the confusion concerning it is our failure to understand our inherent deathlessness or immortality.

Finally, the reference to the underground passage leading to the rock of heaven signifies the tomb itself, located within the Temple of the Inscriptions. Concluding the 52-year cycle of Pacal Votan's terrestrial manifestation in A.D. 683, *harmonic 13 85 54*, the tomb is only one in name. From the temple atop the pyramid, which is itself 52 feet high, 26 steps lead down, taking a sharp turn, descending another 22 steps, and then arriving at the chamber. The 26 steps refer to the number 26 (13×2), the fractal of the galactic constant, 260. The 22 steps refers to the number representing the sum of 13—the thirteen dwelling serpent or the *Oxlahuntiku*, the thirteen divinities of the higher heavens—and 9—the Nine Lords of Time, the *Bolontiku,* the nine divinities or original galactic masters who preceded Votan on his mission to planet Earth. The total number of steps, 48, is the equivalent of 6 octaves (8×6).

In actuality, the symbolism of the Nine Lords within the crypt and the "tree of life" adorning the lid of the sarcophagus give the clue: Pacal Votan, Galactic Agent 13 66 56, though appearing mortal, had actually "returned" to his starry homeland, Valum Chivim. There, he was able to report that the terrestrial Maya were ready to receive select numbers of their galactic kin and finish in earnest the harmonic activity concerning planet Earth in its passage through the 5,200-tun galactic synchronization beam begun August 13, 3113 B.C. Interestingly, a "speaking tube" goes from the crypt to the temple atop the Pyramid of the Inscriptions.

Clearly a manifestation of Kukulkan/Quetzalcoatl, the coming of Pacal Votan in A.D. 631 was indicated by the completion of the 36th Venus great cycle from the initiation date, 3113, B.C. The Venus great cycle represents the conjunction of 104 solar years of 365 days each, with 146 sacred calendar cycles of 260 days each and 65 Venus cycles of 584 days each. The total number of days or kin in such a cycle is *37,960*. The fractal *3796* represents the number of tun elapsed between 3113 B.C. and A.D. 631, and the number of solar years elapsed between 3113 B.C. and A.D. 683. The 52-year cycle—A.D. 631-683—representing the duration of Votan's life activity on the planet corresponds, of course, to the "calendar round:" the conjunction of 52 solar years with 73 sacred calendar cycles. The next significant Quetzalcoatl avatar, 1 Reed Quetzalcoatl, also lived 52 years, from A.D. 947 to 999.

In consideration of the harmony of the numbers that encompass the life-mission of galactic master, Pacal Votan, agent 13 66 56, we can appreciate that his "tomb" is unique and comparable only to that of Cheops in the Great Pyramid of Egypt. If the Great Pyramid, the construction of which supposedly began in 2623 B.C., stands toward one end of the harmonic spectrum marking the current cycle of civilization, then what are we to say of the meaning of the appearance of Pacal Votan, commemorated by his pyramid tomb, approaching the other end of that cycle? Is it too preposterous to consider that there could be a connection between these two "funerary" monuments?

With the passing of Pacal Votan in A.D. 683, and the completion of the Temple of the Inscriptions in A.D. 692, came the second wave of galactic Maya and the commencement of a seven-katun cycle—A.D. 692-830 (140 tuns) or seven generations of fantastic, unparalleled harmonic activity: architecture, art, and above all, the precision harmonic-calibration record keeping. The process spread from Palenque back through Tikal and southward, especially to Copan and finally to Quirigua. By A.D. 810, 9.19.0.0.0, and the dedication of the Great Temple at Quirigua, the job was finished.

The "zoomorphic" sculptures of the late period of Quirigua, culminating in the great "Zoomorph P" (a full ten meters wide) commemorate the return of the Maya to their homeland among the stars. In reality these "zoomorphs" are representations of galactic cocoons, double-headed serpent/etheric transform units facilitating change from one galactic form to another. This is why a human form, often depicted in seated meditation, is seen emerging from the front jaws of one of these "monsters."

If we could take ourselves back to A.D. 810 Quirigua, we might see a gathering in the courtyard before the great temple, called Structure 1. The last of the galactic masters, seven of them perhaps, each accompanied by a large quartz crystal, seated in intense meditation on the grassy plaza, suddenly become surrounded by a humming vibration—a resonance that is part sound, part vision. Materializing into view are the luminous galactic cocoons. The cocoons first hover above the galactic masters, then slowly enclose them; the vibratory hum increases, blending with the ceaseless symphony of the omnipresent jungle. At first imperceptibly, then as if it were a scene changing in a dream, the vibratory cocoons fade and disappear. A hushed awe overcomes the small gathering, which then disperses with an air of solemn purpose and dedication.

By the time the tenth cycle, Baktun 9 drew to a close, A.D. 830, the galactic masters had already gone. The word had been given to withdraw, to take the secret *Book of the Seven Generations* and retire. The time of darkness was swiftly approaching. The cities were quickly abandoned. One wave of invaders would come, and then after them another, and finally still another, until pestilence and plague would wrack the land. What the harmonic patterns indicated was a period of increasing *density*. From the perspective of harmonic resonance, density is the inability to perceive with the whole body the harmonic

GALACTIC AGENT,
PACAL VOTAN

frequencies and their overtones. What this amounts to is the advent of materialism, a belief system supported by a powerful fear of death.

Despite this coming time of darkness in which the Nine Lords of Time would become perversely identified with the fearful powers of the night and the memory of the galactic masters would be viewed as a childish dream, the numbers of destiny would remain— the thirteen numbers and the twenty signs. These numbers would persist as a clue, a sign, that yet a third phase of the Mayan project was to be completed. Somewhere in that far and distant time, when armies clashed with metal and chemicals released the fire of the Sun, the wonder of Maya would burst again, releasing the mystery and showing the way that marks return among the patterns of the stars.

BAKTUN 10, A.D. 830: DEPARTURE & PROPHECY

4

THE LOOM OF MAYA:
THE HARMONIC MODULE REVEALED

Leaving for the moment the departure of the galactic masters at the end of the 9th baktun, let us look at what they left behind. Their achievement, their actual calling card, was a series of monuments which recorded in a very precise manner the correlations between the galactic harmonic pattern and the terrestrial solar calendar. The current 5,125 year cycle—3113 B.C.-A.D. 2012—is a precise calibration of the galactic fractal, 5,200 tun in diameter. This 5,200-tun (or 1,872,000 kin or 260 katun or 13 baktun) cycle literally acts like a lens focussing a beam through which information from galactic sources is synchronized via the Sun to the Earth.

Of course, the galactic masters left clear enough teachings and instructions when they departed, teachings carried on by the prophetic traditions of the later Maya. Written in the language of the Zuvuya, these teachings that describe the katun cycles are, without proper preparation, of little help. Indeed, they have actually given rise to great confusion among those trying to understand the mystery of the Classic Maya. But then, by no means was it the purpose of the galactic masters to be remembered. It was their purpose, however, to leave a legacy, the Tzolkin, that would aid in the retrieval of galactic information. The retrieval of this information has but one goal: to assist in the alignment to the whole which leads to conscious operation within the greater community of galactic intelligence.

Of course, to our progressive world-view the notion not only that the Maya were smarter than us but that they were here on a mission to help us on this planet become coordinated with a larger galactic project may seem ridiculous or terrifying. Plot lines that smack of a larger plan or purpose boggle our little egos. It is easier to dismiss them as the paranoid projections of soap-box philosophers or science-fiction fantasies than to admit them into the forum of proper intellectual discussion.

And yet, there is a persistent little voice that keeps saying, "Why not?" After all, the universe is vast, and who is to say that we have in our possession the secrets to all of the mysteries? And in the history of civilization as we know it, if there is any mystery that dogs us to this day, it is the mystery of the Maya. As the greatest Mayan scholar, J. Eric S. Thompson, said in his monumental *Maya Hieroglyphic Writing*: "One is amazed at the mastery over tremendous numbers implied in the various terms for higher units which have survived. Surely no other people on a comparable level of material culture have had such a concept of vast numbers, and a vocabulary for handling them" (p. 53). The cause for amazement either disappears or is intensified when we consider the inadmissible: the Maya and their "system" were of galactic origins.

Letting rest for a moment the extra-terrestrial origins of the Maya, let me also remind the reader that my purpose in presenting the Mayan Factor is twofold. First, to open our eyes to the possibility of the galactic mission of the Maya and its implications for us at this moment in history; and second, to present, in as simple and practicable terms as possible, the Mayan Harmonic Module, or Tzolkin. While archaeologists and astronomers, art historians and mathematicians pore over and ponder the meaning of the sculpted stones and temple cities of the Classic Maya, the key unlocking the whole of it, the 13 x 20 matrix of the Harmonic Module, is user-friendly and lies within our reach.

As I suggested in the previous chapter, the Tzolkin or Harmonic Module bears a strong resemblence, by analogy, to the I Ching. Like the I Ching, the Tzolkin at first appears to be an archaic relic in code language from a far earlier era. Yet, even before the I Ching had left the hands of the philologists and archaeologists, philosophers and psychologists were seeing that rather than being archaic, the I Ching is timeless, and hence of use to us today. In addition to renewed popular use as an oracle, the timelessness as well as the timeliness of the I Ching have been verified by correlations with the genetic code (Schön-berger, 1973) and with far-reaching mathematical-historical correspondences in my own *Earth Ascending* (1984).

The I Ching is based on a set of binary mathematical permutations, which also underlie what I call the "pure" progression of the Mayan number harmonics—2, 4, 8, 16, 32, 64. As it is presented to us, however, the I Ching is actually comprised of the combinations of eight symbols (trigrams) of three lines, either broken or unbroken, in all possible combinations with each other. By doubling the trigrams, the permutations yield 64 more complex symbolic possibilities of six lines each (hexagrams). By comparison, the Tzolkin is based on permutations of thirteen numbers and twenty symbols or Sacred Signs which yield a possibility of 260 permutations. At minimum, each one of the 260 permutations is a combination of one of thirteen numbers, one of twenty signs, and one of four directional positions.

Finally, like the I Ching, the Tzolkin is a system for revealing information relating to a deeper or larger purpose. While the I Ching is precisely synchronized with the *genetic code*, the Tzolkin is synchronized with the *galactic code*. As the genetic code governs information concerning the operation of all levels of the *life cycle*, inclusive of all plant and animal forms, the galactic code governs information affecting the operations of the *light cycle*. The light cycle defines resonant frequency ranges of radiant energy, inclusive of electricity, heat, light, and radio waves that inform the self-generative functions of all phenomena, organic or inorganic. The two codes are obviously interpenetrating and complementary.

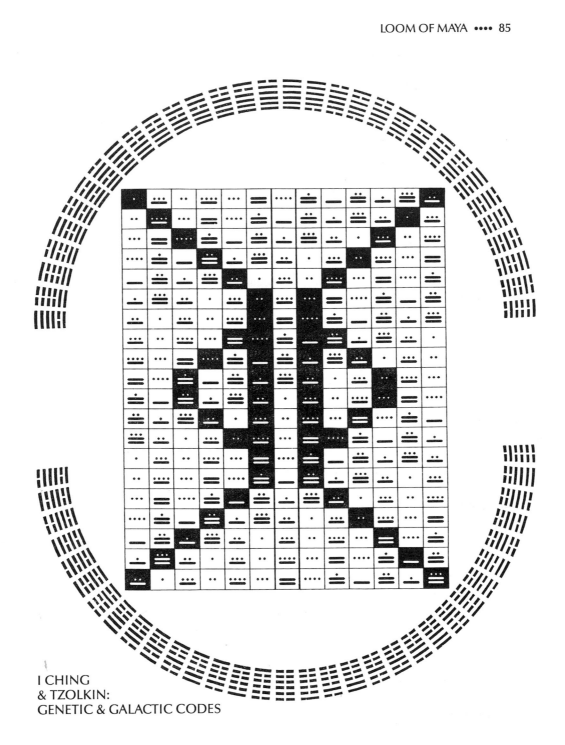

I CHING
& TZOLKIN:
GENETIC & GALACTIC CODES

In speaking of a galactic code analogous to a genetic code, what do we really mean? When we speak of the genetic code we can point to the obvious manifestations of its functioning, be they the organization of colonies of plankton in the sea or the differentiation of functions in a complex organism like ourselves. But to speak of the galactic code, of light cycles and radiant energy—how are these manifested in ways that are obvious, and what information processes does a galactic code govern?

Without bogging down in technicalities, let us consider the nature of life itself. Though we may know the molecular and chemical make-up that is necessary for construction of the nucleic acids that form the building blocks of life and which can be articulated as the 64-word genetic code, where and what would all this be without light? In a word, the genetic code describes but half the picture. Light—radiant energy— provides the other half. Indeed, if we were to say which is more primary, which comes first, light or life, then we must say "light." If we observe the simplest phenomena, flowers opening and closing in their daily cycle, we see that all of life not only depends upon light but actually aspires to light.

We know that "light," the spectrum of radiant energy, runs the gamut from radio waves to ultra-high-frequency cosmic radiation. In simple terms, radiant energy is a range of wave-functions, inclusive of electricity, that transmits information as well as transmutes energy. The power to bear information—transmission—and to transmute energy—transformation—is inherent in radiant energy and, like DNA, is governed by a code. It should also be recalled that DNA possesses a vibratory infrastructure that parallels the molecular structure. It is this radiant, vibratory infrastructure—the *light body*—that corresponds to the radiant-energy spectrum governed by the Tzolkin code, the Mayan Harmonic Module.

If we take radiant energy to its "source", we return to Hunab Ku, the galactic core. Emanating in spiralling spin/counter-spin pulsation streams from Hunab Ku, is the code governing the self-transmitting and self-transforming power of radiant energy. As described by the Tzolkin, the Mayan Harmonic Module, the galactic code governing radiant energy, is the primary source that informs and vitalizes the code of life, DNA, represented by its symbolic counterpart, the I Ching. In other words, the Tzolkin is to the I Ching what light is to life.

I realize that this discussion of genetic and galactic codes may require a leap of faith as well as imagination. Keeping in mind that the discovery of the identity of the 64-codon DNA with the I Ching was itself late in coming, let us turn to a consideration of the Tzolkin as a symbolic template or metaphor and see what we may learn.

As a template of the code governing the functioning of the entire spectrum of radiant energy, in its simplest terms, the finite components of the Tzolkin reduce to an easily remembered set of constants. These constants, a coherent system of symbols and numbers, have but a single, all-encompassing purpose: to assist us both in the retrieval of galactic information and in the attainment of a condition of galactic alignment.

**LOOM OF MAYA
GENERATED FROM
BINARY TRIPLET**

Such in its bare-bones essentials is the Tzolkin, the *galactic constant*: thirteen numbers, twenty symbols, and four rotating directional positions always coming back to itself, repeating, pulsing endlessly. The Tzolkin, or Harmonic Module, presents itself as a perfect metaphor of the self-generating and self-renewing galactic circuit.

While the combinations of the thirteen numbers and twenty positions or symbols produce the 260 units comprising the entire matrix, the 52 (13×4) *directional* position possibilities are reflected in the pattern unifying the matrix. If you look at this pattern carefully you will see that it occupies 26 units on the right side of the seventh or mystic column and 26 units the left side of that column, for a total of 52 units.

In *Earth Ascending*, out of deference to its strictly geometrical symmetry, I call this 52-unit unifying pattern the "binary triplet configuration." While I admit that this is not an entirely evocative description, I also refer to this pattern as "the primary resonant structure common to all processes and systems. It is the visible form of the cosmic code."

Out of respect for its function of weaving together the thirteen numbers and the twenty symbols, it seems altogether appropriate to call this 52-unit pattern the Loom of Maya. A loom is an instrument for weaving at least two different "threads." While Maya here refers to the Maya who left us the Tzolkin as a guide and a tool, Maya also refers to the term in Hindu philosophy often defined as the world of illusion, the *apparent* reality of the phenomenal world.

What is woven by the Loom of Maya is the matrix of possibilities that correspond to our experience of the world. This woven matrix is a texture of 260 components or symbols that inform our senses and mind with the informational keys necessary to relate to and work with the larger world around us. While these 260 symbols describe the larger world as a cyclical composite of symbols, they also define our internal capacity to perceive this world as being of the same nature as the world we perceive.

But what then are the threads woven by this Loom of Maya? The vertical threads are represented by the thirteen numbers, the horizontal threads by the twenty symbols. But what do these represent? As I have already suggested, the thirteen "numbers" represent primary patterns of radiant energy, which we could call *radio-pulses*. The twenty symbols represent the cycle of frequency-range possibilities for transformation or evolution that each of these radio-pulses may undergo. The combination of any one of the thirteen numbers and twenty directional positions creates a symbol or radiant pulsation pattern that contains a particular kind of information. The 260 symbolic pulses woven by the Loom of Maya create the entire resonant field which we experience as reality.

But let us talk for a moment about symbols. What is a symbol? A symbol is a resonant structure, the reverberation of a particular quality of radiant energy that takes form in our senses. Obviously, our sense faculties possess a form-receiving capacity; that is, the sense organs function as reverberatory receivers. Like different kinds of radar stations, the senses continuously receive the in-rush of resonant wave-forms that comprise our universe. It is the purpose of mind to "make sense" of the symbols or resonant structures informed by our sense faculties. Our various conditionings further affect the "interpretations" of the mind.

Plato and Jung called the resonant structures "archetypes," form-constants that exist in and define a field of consciousness that transcends both time and the individual. According to the Mayan Factor, these form-constants are the stuff woven on the Loom of Maya, while the Loom of Maya itself is the magically self-existing instrument created from the stuff it weaves. Self-created and self-creating, the Loom of Maya weaves the symbols into the whole tapestry which we experience through our mind and senses as our mind and senses. Not just as metaphor, but in truth, the world is a weave of symbols, and it is through symbols that we weave our understanding of the world.

When we understand that symbols are actually resonant structures, vibratory form-fields, and that we ourselves are resonant to our very core, then we can see that symbols are not something aery-faery but are completely vital to our functioning as whole beings. Asleep and unconscious to the potency of symbols, our dreams become nightmares, and we live in hostage to a world which is in reality the eclipse of symbolic knowing. As we know, we do not live by bread alone. Though we may feel that spirituality is a vague concept and transcendence a remote aspiration, it is really our own belief in the separation of science, spirituality, and art that keep us from a full comprehension of symbols and symbolic knowing.

As resonant structures, symbols literally create, work with, and inform our *light body*. The *light body* is the electro-resonant galactic code bank that informs the genetic code bank. It is the stuff of imagination, insight, all true understanding—and more! While the foundation of our light body corresponds to the vibratory infrastructure of the DNA, it can only be activated through a knowing use of symbols. Nor should this symbol-thriving light body be seen as separate from what we call our physical body. Rather, the resonant light body underlies and interpenetrates all of our functions. It is not poetry alone that commands us to declare that just as a flower cannot live without light and water, we cannot live without symbols.

If the thirteen numbers are the light that arouses the mind and body, then the twenty directional positions are the water that nourishes this very same mind and body. In the interplay of thirteen numbers and twenty symbols lies the in-dwelling galactic code-bank that informs the resonant structures comprising the symbol-woven tapestry of our reality.

Let us look more carefully at the Loom of Maya, for its very structure containing the meaning of the thirteen numbers and the twenty signs is the loom of our existence. It is important to actually *see* the pattern of the Loom of Maya as the unifying structure of the 260-unit matrix. If we look at the permutation table of the matrix, pure and simple, it seems like mere numbers, albeit an interesting series of patterns. Being the essential visual construct contained by the 260-unit matrix, the 52-unit Loom appears to us as the frame of a body. We can further think of the 52-unit pattern as the *resonant galactic frame*, enclosing and providing opportunity for the weaving of a total pattern—the 260-unit matrix.

In Chapter 2, we spoke of the identity of resonance and information. In its enclosing and framing capacity, the resonant galactic frame fulfills the minimum requirements for a definition of information. Information encloses or encapsulates—hence, in-forms. What is encapsulated is like a resonant seed, filled with potentiality. The purpose of information is to provide the opportunity for new growth, expansion, or fleshing out of the resonant seed contained in the information.

This being the case, what is the information encapsulated within the 52- unit resonant galactic frame? If we examine the Loom of Maya, we see that it spans all twenty positions that provide the horizontal structure of the Harmonic Module. Vertically, the seventh or middle column is distinctly devoid of any of the resonant frame units. At the same time, the seventh column provides the hinge for and actually defines the two sides of the resonant galactic frame. The invisible seventh is the mystic column. Unmirrored, it mirrors all.

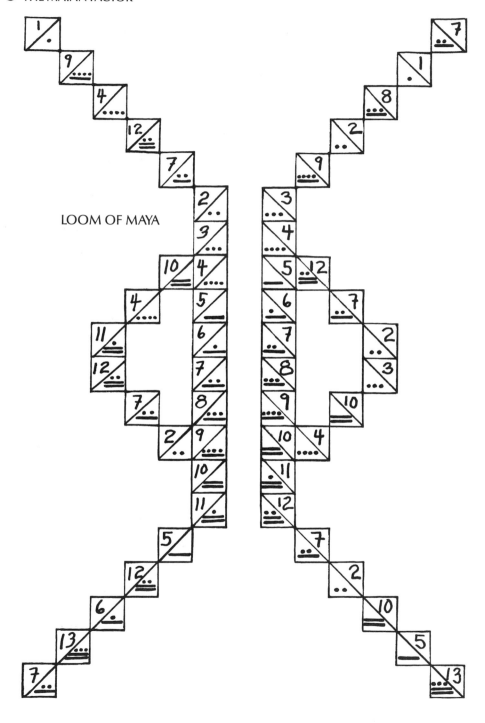

LOOM OF MAYA

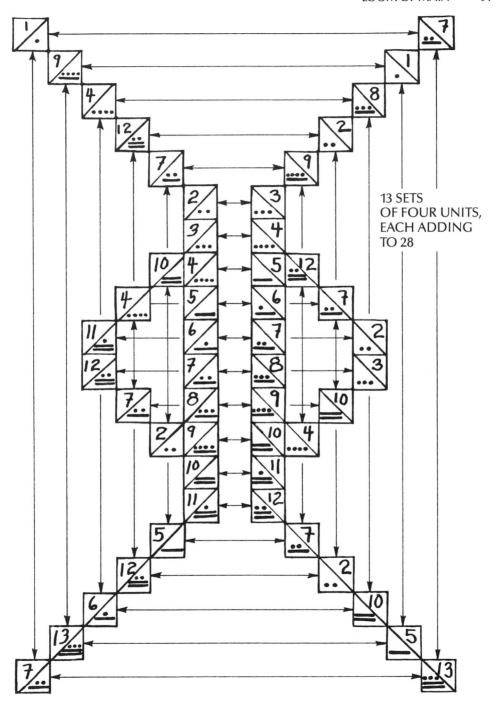

13 SETS
OF FOUR UNITS,
EACH ADDING
TO 28

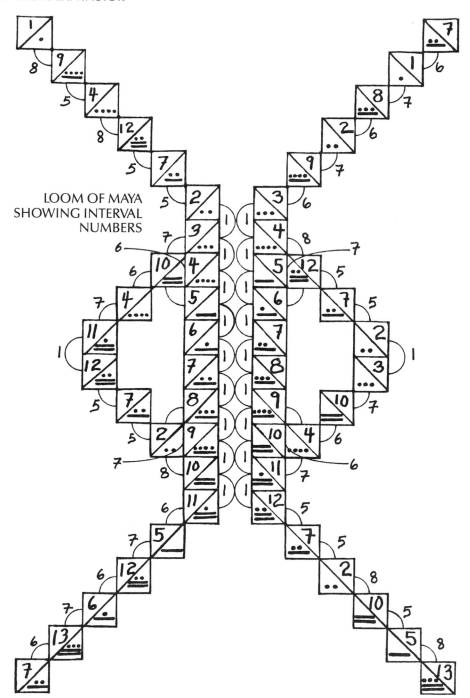

LOOM OF MAYA
SHOWING INTERVAL
NUMBERS

Also, when we look carefully at the individual frame-units, we see that each of the thirteen numbers is contained at least twice. We also note that the frame is 26 units per side—fractal of the total 260—while the total number 52 is a fractal of the 5200-tun diameter of the galactic synchronization beam. We also see that the Loom can naturally be broken down to its components of thirteen sets of four units each, starting with the corners and moving inward. Thus the first set of numbers is 1, 7, 13, 7; the second set is 9, 13, 5, 1; the third set is 4, 6, 10, 8; until we get to the center 6, 7, 8, 7. Each of the thirteen sets of four numbers adds up to 28, the number of days in a vague lunar month. $28 \times 13 = 364$, the number of days in a vague lunar year. 364 can also be factored as 7×52.

Of the 52 units in the Loom of Maya, 7 is contained eight times. Indeed, where the 7 appears an almost perfect symmetry pattern is disclosed. The positions of 1 and 13, which each appear twice, also create a complementary pattern to each other. Finally, if one counts the *intervals* between the 52 numbered units of the Loom, one finds that there are 60 such intervals. If one starts at the upper left corner, for instance, the intervals are between 1 and 9, 9 and 4, 4 and 12, 12 and 7, 7 and 2, 2 and 3, etc. Noting the *differences* between the numbers that create the intervals, we arrive at the interval numbers.

Thus, starting with the upper lefthand corner, we find the interval numbers to be: 8, 5, 8, 5, 5, etc. Indeed, if we look carefully we see that the interval numbers on the axis that runs from upper left to lower right are either 8 or 5, which add up to *13*, while all of the interval numbers on the axis running from upper right to lower left are either 6 or 7, again adding up to *13*. Finally the interval numbers of the vertical axis of the 52-unit galactic Loom are always *1*. If one adds the possible interval numbers, 1, 5, 6, 7 and 8, the total is *27*. If one adds all of the 60 interval numbers, the total is *270*, whose key factor is *9*. Thus, while *7* is the key factor of the sums of the *52*-unit Loom, *9* and *13* are the key interval factors.

Well, you may say, so what? All that is meant to be demonstrated here is the magical nature of a model or system that is reciprocally self-contained. The Loom is the analogue or hologram of the operating principle of the galaxy itself as a total self-contained system. Keeping in mind that the numbers represent symbolic qualities which describe the potential of our reality, then we see that everything is interactive, interdependent, that all cycles feed on themselves, that nothing can really be described without describing everything, that the whole indeed is contained in the part. The Loom of Maya and the Harmonic Module woven by it comprise a genuine resonant keyboard for our use in toning or dialing up galactic frequencies whose wave formations lie within our very being.

Let us turn, then, to the system of symbols and numbers that constitute the Harmonic Module, beginning with the thirteen numbers. As we saw in considering the Loom of Maya, we have a vertical frame of thirteen columns. The seventh column in the center creates a symmetry pattern with six columns on either side. As we noted, the seventh stands alone; unmirrored, it mirrors all. This is important to bear in mind when we con-

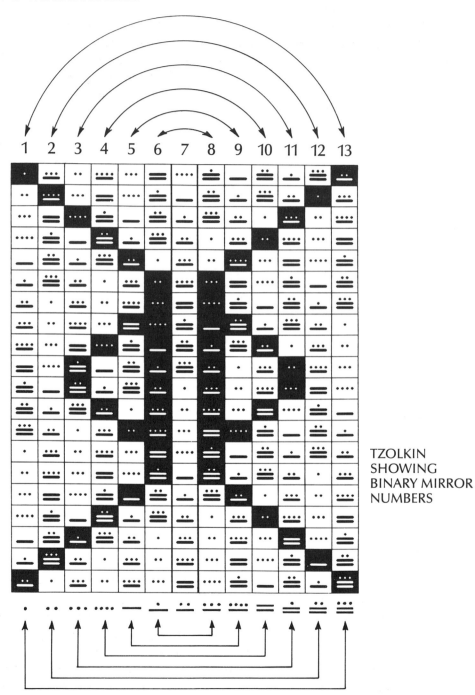

TZOLKIN
SHOWING
BINARY MIRROR
NUMBERS

sider the thirteen numbers or rays. With the exception of the number 7, the other numbers may be viewed as complementary pairs mirroring each other.

Thus we have as mirror symmetry numbers: *1* complementing *13*; *2* and *12*; *3* and *11*; *4* and *10*; *5* and *9*; *6* and *8*. The differences between the pairs recapitulate an even numbered progression: 12, 10, 8, 6, 4, 2. *7* has no mate, holds the center and reflects the total order. This is why we refer to *7* as the unmirrored whole mirroring the whole in all of its symmetry.

If we view the numbers as "pulsation-rays", each representing a particular radio-resonant function that simultaneously pulses and radiates, then we have the following designations:

1. The Pulsation-*Ray of Unity*

2. The Pulsation-*Ray of Polarity*

3. The Pulsation-*Ray of Rhythm*

4. The Pulsation-*Ray of Measure*

5. The Pulsation-*Ray of the Center*

6. The Pulsation-*Ray of Organic Balance*

7. The Pulsation-*Ray of Mystic Power*

8. The Pulsation-*Ray of Harmonic Resonance*

9. The Pulsation-*Ray of Cyclic Periodicity*

10. The Pulsation-*Ray of Manifestation*

11. The Pulsation-*Ray of Dissonant Structure*

12. The Pulsation-*Ray of Complex Stability*

13 The Pulsation-*Ray of Universal Movement*

A brief review of the qualities represented by the numbers reveals a progression describing the formal nature underlying the appearance of things. If *1* represents the inherent unifying principle in all manifestations, *13* represents the dynamic of movement present in everything and by which everything is ever-changing and at the same time vivified by the universal force of Hunab Ku. The numbers 1 through 9 represent the non-material principles of coherence immanent in and governing all phenomenal experience. While 10 represents the principle allowing manifestation to occur, based on the coherence of the preceding nine numbers, 11 represents the dynamic of dissonance accounting for randomness and non-stability. 12, on the other hand, represents the principle of complex stability which accounts for the conservative organizational force in nature.

If we look at the numbers in their mirror symmetry, we see an intimate set of reciprocal relations, the lower order number presenting the constituent principle of the larger order number. Thus, while 1, the principle of unity, is balanced by 13, the ray of universal movement, 2, the principle of polarity, is balanced by 12, the principle of complex stability. Reflection shows that any order of complex stability is held together— or torn apart—by a subtle balance of polar forces.

In the next mirror pair, we see that the principle of rhythm, 3, accounts for variability and introduces the possibility of randomness which plays such a role in 11, the principle of dissonant structures. 10, the principle that allows for manifestation to occur, is complemented by 4, representing the principle of measure. It is only through the operation of measure as wholeness and order that any manifestation can occur as a coherent organism.

The principle of the center governed by the number 5 allows the order of 4 to move, as the seasons move around a common solar center. The cyclic periodicity of movement organized about a common center, 5, is governed by 9. Finally, 6, the ray of organic balance, is so called because it represents a factoring of the polar principle, 2, with the principle of rhythm, 3. The product, 6, organic balance, represents the hexagonal ordering principle underlying crystal and cellular structures. This organic balance, 6, is complemented by 8, the principle of harmonic resonance which governs the octave frequency levels by which all organic structures, inclusive of crystals, vibrate.

With no mirror number to complement it, 7 has its unique symmetry relation to 1 and 13, the alpha and the omega, as it were, of the Mayan number harmonic. At the center of the pattern, 7 represents the magic by which the whole holds together.

Such, in brief, are the meanings of the numbers in their complementary relation to each other. Obviously, there are many more relations that can be explored intuitively through playing with the radially reciprocal relations the numbers all have to each other. Suffice it for the moment to say that the descriptions give some idea of the progression of the structural cycle underlying the operation of the galaxy—or any of its constituent members—as a self-sustaining, self-organizing whole.

The numbers take on a richer meaning when combined with the twenty positional symbols which describe the horizontal lattice of the Loom of Maya. If the thirteen numbers are pulsation-rays, the twenty Signs are the frequency range possibilities that allow for the primary harmonic structures to come into existence. While in *Earth Ascending* I compared the twenty symbols to the twenty amino acids which comprise the DNA, the nineteen intervals between the twenty symbols could also be compared to the nineteen twists that the complementary DNA strands take in order to complete a codon, one of the 64 six-part structures that constitute the genetic code. On our planet, the Maya translated these twenty positional places into the twenty symbols known as the twenty Sacred Signs.

It is often said that the Mayan signs are more ideographic than hieroglyphic. A

(E)	IMIX		NEPTUNE
(N)	IK		URANUS
(W)	AKBAL		SATURN
(S)	KAN		JUPITER
(E)	CHICCHAN		A-BELT
(N)	CIMI		MARS
(W)	MANIK		EARTH
(S)	LAMAT		VENUS
(E)	MULUC		MERCURY
(N)	OC		MERCURY
(W)	CHUEN		VENUS
(S)	EB		EARTH
(E)	BEN		MARS
(N)	IX		A-BELT
(W)	MEN		JUPITER
(S)	CIB		SATURN
(E)	CABAN		URANUS
(N)	ETZNAB		NEPTUNE
(W)	CAUAC		PLUTO
(S)	AHAU		PLUTO

TZOLKIN WITH SIGNS & PLANETS

hieroglyph uses images to depict words or sounds; an ideograph uses signs, often of an abstract nature, to convey ideas, without using particular words or phrases.

As ideographic symbols, there are many different ways in which these Signs can be read. Dense with meanings, the Signs demand an *analogical* understanding. Analogical thinking randomly floats and leaps to a conclusion by a like association linking seemingly dissimilar things. Analogical thinking is also that which creates form on the basis of like proportions. As we have already seen, the Mayan number symbolism is completely based on fractal harmonics which are based on like proportions. The twenty Sacred Signs, like the thirteen numbers, participate in the same fractal harmonic.

When we look at the twenty Sacred Signs, we see that they are elegantly, comically simple. Even more than ideographic they are iconic. They are simply images. Some are more abstract than others. Some appear like faces. One is like a hand. The ultimate in iconic simplicity, the Signs are as easy to imprint as any set of comic-book characters. Indeed, the Signs beg to be imprinted, for in essence they are memory triggers. Whether familiar, humorous, or enigmatic, the Signs are ready-made and without complication. In this lies their ease and their power.

EAST   NORTH   WEST   SOUTH

IMIX   IK   AKBAL   KAN

CHICCHAN   CIMI   MANIK   LAMAT

MULUC   OC   CHUEN   EB

BEN   IX   MEN   CIB

CABAN   ETZNAB   CAUAC   AHAU

20 SACRED SIGNS IN THEIR DIRECTIONAL MATRIX

The twenty Signs are associated with specific directions which further amplify their meaning. The directions run in counter-clockwise order, from East to North to West to South. This is so because this order complements the order of the numbers, 1, 2, 3, . . .13, which could be said to run in a clockwise direction. Remember, in the Zuvuya of Maya, time—and everything else—operates in at least two directions simultaneously!

The meaning of the directions is as follows:

EAST: Place of Light and Generation. Color: Red

NORTH: Place of Wisdom and Purification. Color: White

WEST: Place of Death and Transformation. Color: Black

SOUTH: Place of Life and Expansion. Color: Yellow

Like the numbers 1 through 13, the twenty Sacred Signs are reciprocal. They build on each other, and reference each other for meaning. On the other hand, a certain meaning is also gained by their relation to each other in the order in which they invariably appear. My initial presentation of the Sacred Signs is based on a somewhat cosmological description of the Signs from the prophetic text, *The Book of Chilam Balam*.

In this presentation, the Signs describe a process of development, the path of life itself. The first seven Signs represent the cycle of the lower body or physical being, while the remaining thirteen Signs describe the evolution of the higher mental body. However, it should not be thought that the evolution described by the later thirteen Signs in any way replaces the evolution described by the first seven Signs. Everything is congruent and interpenetrating. The second level of thirteen Signs is again divided into two stages. The first stage consists of seven Signs, inclusive of Signs 8-14, and the second stage consists of the six Signs from 15-20.

So, let us now present the Signs and their directional associations:

DEVELOPMENT OF PRIMARY BEING

1. IMIX: Source of Life, Dragon, Primal Water, Blood, Nurturance, Breast, Mother Energy, Power of Birthing. EAST

2. IK: Spirit, Breath, Wind, Cosmic Energy, Inspiration, Vital Principle, Respiratory System. NORTH

3. AKBAL: House, Enclosing Darkness, Night, Body, Place of Mystery, Heart and Internal Organs. WEST

4. KAN: Seed, Idea, Ordering Power of Growth, Generative Principle, Sex and Reproduction. SOUTH

5. CHICCHAN: Serpent, Nervous System, Reptilian Brain, Integration and Attainment of Autonomic Functions. EAST

 6. CIMI: Death, Revelation, Realization of Mortality of Physical Body. NORTH

 7. MANIK: Hand, Grasping, Closure, Knowledge of Power of Completion, Realization of Finiteness of Physical Being. WEST

DEVELOPMENT OF HIGHER BEING—*Generative Stage*

 8. LAMAT: Star, Harmony, The Octave, Intuitive Realization of Pattern of Higher Life, Love, Star-Seed. SOUTH

 9. MULUC: Raindrop, Cosmic Seed in Gate of Awakened Consciousness, Principle of Communication and Expansion of Higher Life. EAST

 10. OC: Dog, Mammalian Brain, Emotional Life, Guide and Principle of Loyalty, Faithfulness that Gives Strength in the Spiritual Journey. NORTH

 11. CHUEN: Monkey, Artist, Trickster, Principle of Intelligent Co-Creation of the Higher Life. WEST

 12. EB: Human as Vessel for Pentration of Higher Mind. SOUTH

 13. BEN: Sky-Walker, Pillars of Heaven and Earth, Aspiration for Uniting Heaven and Earth, Principle of Growth of Higher Mind, Reed. EAST

 14. IX: The Sorceror, The Jaguar, Feline Energy, The Night-Seer, Attainment of Magical Powers, Highest Level of Individual Conscious Development. NORTH

DEVELOPMENT OF HIGHER BEING—*Fulfilment Stage*

 15. MEN: Eagle, Higher Collective Mind, Planetary Mind and Consciousness. WEST

 16. CIB: Cosmic Force, Ability to Contact and Commune with Galactic Consciousness. SOUTH

17. CABAN: Earth, Earth Force, Synchronicity, Power of Intelligent Synchronization. EAST

 18. ETZNAB: Hall of Mirrors, Ritual Pattern of "No-Time," Ritual Stroke, Ritual Knife, Sword of Wisdom and Purification. NORTH

 19. CAUAC: Storm, Thunder Cloud and Thunder Being, Transformation that Precedes Full Realization. WEST

 20. AHAU: Solar Mind, Solar Lord, Mastery, Realization of Solar Body, Wisdom, Knowledge, Ability to Focus Galactic Whole, Ability to Encompass and Generate the Entire Cycle. SOUTH

The first Sign, *Imix*, is in the *East*; the last Sign, *Ahau*, is in the *South*. An entire circuit is completed, a circuit of life woven on the Loom of Maya. Everything is in it that pertains to being, not only as progressions of the light but as a ladder to be ascended by hero and heroine alike. The twenty Signs in their ever-revolving order define a path of life in which the physical being prepares and is a stage for the higher mental spirals of being. It is a path of being that is total and inclusive of human being, a path and a pattern of being that is universal, not merely of this life on this planet but for all life throughout the universe. In their glyphic, iconic, comic-book simplicity, the twenty Signs describe the destinal adventure as the Mayan navigators have successfully charted it in their light-crafted explorations of the galactic field.

Because of their directional order, the entire circuit of twenty Signs can be viewed as five sets of radial sprockets, each one turning counterclockwise from East to North to West to South. Each four-armed sprocket should be imagined spiralling in phase with the others, reciprocally and harmonically interacting in a simultaneous manner.

Let us further imagine that each of the five sprockets represents a direction in itself which also follows the fourfold counterclockwise movement characterizing the order of the Signs. Thus, the first four sprockets represent the directions East, North, West, and South, while the fifth sprocket represents the Season of the Center. In this manner a mandalic pattern is generated by the spiralling movement of the sprockets, each sprocket a fractal or hologram of the entire progression.

Here, then, follows the groupings of the twenty Signs into five Directional/Seasonal sprockets or cyclical families:

CYCLIC FAMILY OF THE EAST—*Generation of Light*
    EAST: IMIX. The Light Quickens into Forms
    NORTH: IK. The Wind Purifies the Forms
    WEST: AKBAL. The Forms Find Enclosure
    SOUTH: KAN. The Form Generates Its Own Seed

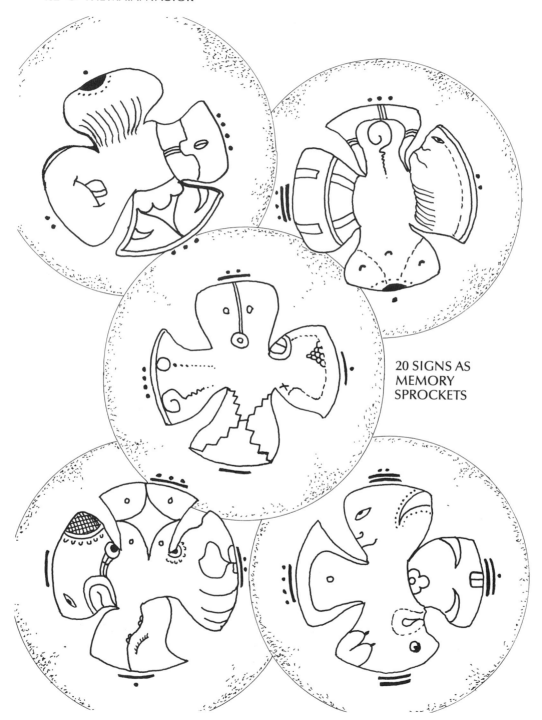

20 SIGNS AS
MEMORY
SPROCKETS

CYCLIC FAMILY OF THE NORTH—*Purification of the Light*
    EAST: CHICCHAN. The Form Takes on Specific Being
    NORTH: CIMI. Specific Being Knows and Transcends Death
    WEST: MANIK. Through Skill All Things Are Transformed
    SOUTH: LAMAT. Harmony Is Born Uniting All Things at Once

CYCLIC FAMILY OF THE WEST—*Transformation of the Light*
    EAST: MULUC. Through the Cosmic Gate the Creative Seed Is Sown
    NORTH: OC. Through Loyalty and Faithfulness the Creative Seed Is Guided
    WEST: CHUEN. Through Artistry the Creative Seed Is Empowered
    SOUTH: EB. The Creative Empowerment Penetrates, Making Fully Human

CYCLIC FAMILY OF THE SOUTH—*Expansion of the Light*
    EAST: BEN. Descent of the Sky-Walkers
    NORTH: IX. Star-Born Wisdom of the Magicians
    WEST: MEN. Attainment of the Planet-Mind
    SOUTH: CIB. Reunion with and Embodiment as the Cosmic Force

CYCLIC FAMILY OF THE CENTER—*Renewal of the Light*
    EAST: CABAN. Alignment of Planetary Force
    NORTH: ETZNAB. Ritual Entrance into Timelessness
    WEST: CAUAC. Transformation of Transformation
    SOUTH: AHAU. Attainment to the Mind of Light

Representing the power of the stages of the galactic ladder of light, the Signs constitute a lattice of the mythic voyage. For dwelling in the twenty Sacred Signs are the sources of all mythic structure. Myth is here understood as the frame of resonating points spun out from the galactic heart, informing every aspect of the galactic whole. The twenty anchor points of this mythic frame are the primary symbols whose spiralling power forms a fractal ladder connecting mythologies, worlds, and star systems.

In the process of unfoldment described by the twenty Signs, the 5th, 10th, 15th and 20th Signs represent key articulations of the evolutionary stages of mind passing into ever greater, more encompassing fields of being. Each of these four signs is associated with one each of the four directions, and so can be considered the ruler of that particular direction. These four signs, in their role as Evolutionary Directional Guardians, constitute an inner wheel of meaning:

    5th Sign. EAST: CHICCHAN. Reptile Brain. Autonomic System. Instinct.
    10th Sign. NORTH: OC. Mammal Brain. Emotional and Conceptual Mind.
    15th Sign. WEST: MEN. Planet Brain. Higher Resonant Mind.
    20th Sign. SOUTH: AHAU. Solar Brain. Starhood and the Mind of Light

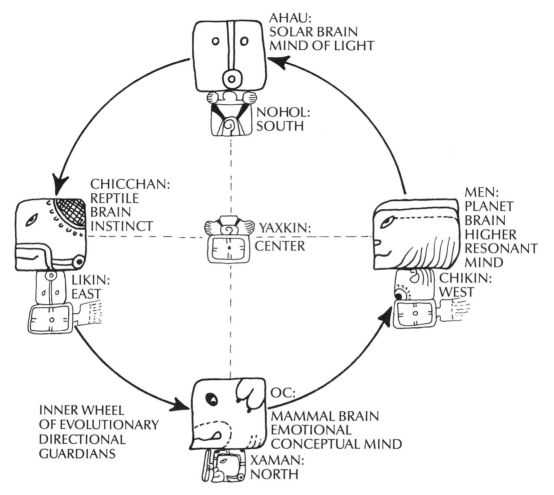

AHAU:
SOLAR BRAIN
MIND OF LIGHT

NOHOL:
SOUTH

MEN:
PLANET
BRAIN
HIGHER
RESONANT
MIND

CHICCHAN:
REPTILE
BRAIN
INSTINCT

YAXKIN:
CENTER

CHIKIN:
WEST

LIKIN:
EAST

INNER WHEEL
OF EVOLUTIONARY
DIRECTIONAL
GUARDIANS

OC:
MAMMAL BRAIN
EMOTIONAL
CONCEPTUAL MIND

XAMAN:
NORTH

When the twenty Sacred Signs are combined with the thirteen numbers, which can be visualized emanating from each of the signs, then the entire 260-unit mythic lattice is constructed. This lattice, called Tzolkin, the Harmonic Module, is a hologram and transmutation table of the different levels of information, knowledge, consciousness, and being. Through the understanding of the applications of this Module, different resonances can be pinpointed and the light body can be crafted and navigated. But these uses are for the advanced. The Maya knew that as a total organism we humans were not yet at the stage of fully crafting the light body, so they showed the use of the Tzolkin as a time-recording device.

Representing but one dimension of the Harmonic Module, the sacred 260-day calendar is nonetheless *the key* left behind by the Maya to unlock the other dimensions of the Module. As a hologram of the galactic process and pattern, the Sacred Calendar is still useful and needs to be understood for what it is: the fractal pattern demonstrating the twenty spiralling galactic vortices charged with their 13-pulsation-ray information beams superimposed upon a 260-day passage of our planet around the Sun.

The Maya further showed how this 260-unit pattern locks in with the solar cycle every 52 years. Being the fractal of the 5,200-tun cycle which describes the diameter of the current synchronization beam through which spaceship Earth is traversing, the 52-year cycle describes a period of time during which not one day was repeated—every day had a unique name and meaning. (See Appendix E. The 52-Year Cycle & Daily Calendar Round.)

As a fractal template applied to our planetary passage, the Tzolkin, or Sacred Calendar, is divisible into four larger patterns or seasons of 65 kin or days each. These four "seasons," holographically imprinted within every 260-day cycle, represent the unceasing galactic discharge of energy in a fourfold cyclical pattern. The fourfold energies correspond, among other things, to the four directions.

Thus, the larger 65-day "seasons of the Tzolkin" are functions of the four characters whom we just introduced as the Evolutionary Directional Guardians: CHICCHAN—

IMIX	1	8	2	9	3	10	4	11	5	12	6	13	7
IK	2	9	3	10	4	11	5	12	6	13	7	1	8
AKBAL	3	10	4	11	5	12	6	13	7	1	8	2	9
KAN	4	11	5	12	6	13	7	1	8	2	9	3	10
	5	12	6	13	7	1	8	2	9	(3)	(10)	(4)	(11)
CIMI	6	13	7	1	8	2	9	3	10	4	11	5	12
MANIK	7	1	8	2	9	3	10	4	11	5	12	6	13
LAMAC	8	2	9	3	10	4	11	5	12	6	13	7	1
MULUC	9	3	10	4	11	5	12	6	13	7	1	8	2
	(10)	(4)	(11)	5	12	6	13	7	1	8	2	9	(3)
CHUEN	11	5	12	6	13	7	1	8	2	9	3	10	4
EB	12	6	13	7	1	8	2	9	3	10	4	11	5
BEN	13	7	1	8	2	9	3	10	4	11	5	12	6
IX	1	8	2	9	3	10	4	11	5	12	6	13	7
	2	9	(3)	(10)	(4)	(11)	5	12	6	13	7	1	8
CIB	3	10	4	11	5	12	6	13	7	1	8	2	9
CABAN	4	11	5	12	6	13	7	1	8	2	9	3	10
ETZNAB	5	12	6	13	7	1	8	2	9	3	10	4	11
CAUAC	6	13	7	1	8	2	9	3	10	4	11	5	12
	7	1	8	2	9	(3)	(10)	(4)	(11)	5	12	6	13

CHICCHAN (E)

OC (N)

MEN (W)

AHAU (S)

TZOLKIN BURNER CYCLES

EAST, OC—*NORTH,* MEN—*WEST,* and AHAU—*SOUTH.* In the later prophetic texts, these Directional Guardians were associated with the image of "the Burner," the primordial, timeless fire-bringer, the hero of vision and light venerated everywhere by different names as the Promethean bestower of culture.

There are four Burners corresponding to the Four Evolutionary Stations, ruled by the Four Evolutionary Guardians. Each Evolutionary Station is divided into four stages, three of twenty days each, and one of five days, for a total of 65 days for each Evolutionary Station. Thus, there are four initiatory days per Station that are significant for the Burner Cycles.

The Sequence of Evolutionary Stations, Guardians and Burner Days is as follows:

STATION OF THE EAST. *Guardian:* CHICCHAN, The Serpent
  Burner Takes the Fire. 3 CHICCHAN
  Burner Begins the Fire. 10 CHICCHAN
  Burner Runs with the Fire. 4 CHICCHAN
  Burner Puts out the Fire. 11 CHICCHAN

STATION OF THE NORTH. *Guardian:* OC, The Dog
  Burner Takes the Fire. 3 OC
  Burner Begins the Fire. 10 OC
  Burner Runs with the Fire. 4 OC
  Burner Puts out the Fire. 11 OC

STATION OF THE WEST. *Guardian:* MEN, The Eagle
  Burner Takes the Fire. 3 MEN
  Burner Begins the Fire. 10 MEN
  Burner Runs with the Fire. 4 MEN
  Burner Puts out the Fire. 11 MEN

STATION OF THE SOUTH. *Guardian:* AHAU, The Solar Lord
  Burner Takes the Fire. 3 AHAU
  Burner Begins the Fire. 10 AHAU
  Burner Runs with the Fire. 4 AHAU
  Burner Puts out the Fire. 11 AHAU

In the imagery of the Burner, we may visualize the Four Sacred Stations of the Four Directions, each protected by its Guardian. It the first phase, Burner Takes the Fire, the Guardian takes the knowledge of fire from the previous Station to the new Station. The number associated with the first phase is 3, the ray of rhythm and synergy. In the Second Phase, Burner Begins the Fire, the knowledge of fire is actually applied to illumine the current evolutionary season. The number associated with this phase is 10, the ray of manifestation. In the third phase, Burner Runs with the Fire, the Guardian takes the Fire and spreads its influence. The number associated with this phase is 4, the Ray of Measure, of extension to the four directions. Finally, in the fourth phase, the Burner puts out the fire and seals the influence of the fire for the current evolutionary stage. The number associated with this fourth stage is 11, the Ray of Dissonance.

In this mythic structure commemorating the seasons of light, we begin to see some of the multi-leveled symbolic potentialities contained within the Tzolkin or Harmonic Module. Sprung from the Radial Matrix of Hunab Ku, the 13×20-unit template is merely the device for providing the focus that allows us to take in the whole. Ever mandalic, the Mayan Factor is a fractal harmonic whose wave-patterns describe a science beyond materialism and whose resonant matrices tune us into a mythic web directing us to the home which we never left.

Taking in the whole, the 260-unit Template can also be described as a *holoscanner*. Not only does such a device provide us with a view of the whole, but being a fractal or holographic chip off the old galactic block, it provides entrances to multiple realms of being and consciousness. With this challenging thought, let us take the Harmonic Module and see more precisely how it gives us a *holoscan* of the 5,200-tun synchronization Beam whose passage our planet is now preparing to conclude.

TZOLKIN
AS THE
HARMONIC
MODULE

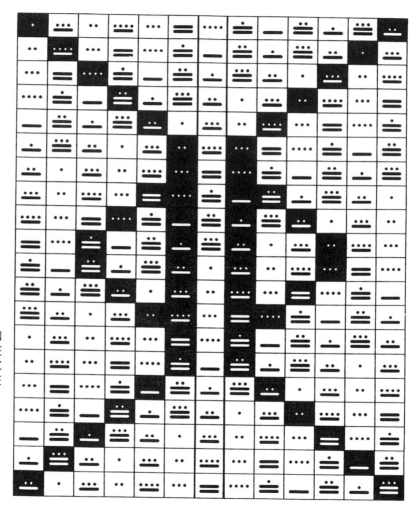

HISTORY &
THE SOLAR SYSTEM:
THE GALACTIC VIEW

5

The Mayan Matrix, the Tzolkin or Harmonic Module, bearing the code of the galactic harmonic, informs all systems with a common regulatory resonance called the light body. Just as each living organism possesses a light body—the DNA infrastructure—and even the entire species has its common collective light body, so the planet, as a conscious organism, is also characterized by its evolving light body.

Like the light body of individual and collective organisms, the planetary light body is the consciously articulated resonant structure that regulates and allows for the fulfillment of evolutionary destiny. It is important to bear in mind that the planetary light body, embedded in the planet memory program, can only be activated by conscious, cooperative effort. As we shall see, the key to the conscious articulation of the planet light body is in the science generically known as geomancy—Earth acupuncture.

As the radiant information bank of the planetary program, the 260-unit galactic code can be envisioned as primordially imprinting the electromagnetic ether of the *outer* planetary sheath, the upper of the two radiation belts that girdle the Earth. I say primordially, because the galactic core, Hunab Ku, like a powerful radio station, is endlessly generating the radiant light code.

The information flow between a planet body like Earth and the galactic core is maintained and mediated by the solar activity known as the binary sunspots. Both Sun and planet operate with the same galactic information bank. Whenever a stellar body, such as our Sun, begins its evolutionary course, it is imprinted with the 260-unit galactic code. Once a planet such as ours attains a point of resonant activation, the galactic information flow mediated through the sunspots imprints the outer electromagnetic sheath with the basics of the planetary memory program.

Once the planetary light program has imprinted and begun its functioning, the genetic information will also be imprinted in the planetary field. On our planet, the genetic imprinting is the function of the *lower* radiation belt, which can then be envisioned as impregnated by the light program of the upper radiation belt. The two radiation belts are like a vibratory loom, weaving resonance rather than cloth. The common resonance of the lower genetic and the upper galactic imprinting creates the total planet memory program, called the Psi Bank.

Functioning within the interactive membrane of the radiation belts, the Psi Bank engenders what Rupert Sheldrake calls *morphogenetic fields*—the memory-saturated resonant sub-fields whose functioning accounts for the continuity of the various organic life-forms.

What we are describing here is the intelligence structure of the planet considered as a living organism. In so doing, we are embroidering on James Lovelock's *Gaia hypothesis*, the notion that the Earth is indeed a conscious, evolving entity. Of course, virtually all prehistoric, that is to say, pre-technological peoples are/were aware of this fact. Through much of history, the belief that the Earth is sacred has commonly been held by peoples everywhere.

While we can say that the sacredness of the Earth as a living organism has long been a commonly held belief, it is another question altogether whether or not all people holding this belief shared their knowledge collectively or had as complete a view of the Earth as we possess today, thanks to our cumbersome but unifying space technology. Leaving aside arguments which declare that a common science was shared by the builders of Stonehenge, the Great Pyramid at Giza, and the Pyramids of Teotihuacan, let us assert, at the least, that by virtue of common resonance there was some such "universal" knowledge.

Given this perspective, let us introduce the Mayan Harmonic in its form as the Great Cycle—the Galactic Synchronization Beam. Let us go back some 5,000 years and describe a twofold situation. On the one hand is the situation of the Earth. On the other is the situation of the galactic navigators called Maya. First, let us discuss the Earth.

Following the last Ice Age over 12,000 years ago, a new cycle of life, a new solar age, began for the planet. Here and there we find remnants of an earlier cycle. This especially seems to be the case in South America. These outposts of earlier cycles remain hidden, discreet, watchful but uninvolved in the new cycle. Within 6,000 years, agricultural experiments begin to yield results in the river vallies of India, the Middle East, and North Africa. Galactic information infused through the Sun impregnates the mental fields of the agricultural peoples. Dim recollections of earlier cycles, other times, other planes of existence mingle with veneration of the Sun. A ripeness of thought and feeling builds up. Another cycle of civilization is about to commence.

At the same time, among the starry outposts of the Maya, none of what is occurring on planet Earth goes unnoticed. The word is out: another planet is gearing up for activation of its light body. Through collective effort of the larger community of galactic intelligence, the galactic synchronization beam is focussed through the Sun and its planetary system with special attention to the third planetary orbit, that of Earth. At just the right moment, through a collective mental intensity unheard of on our planet, the beam, 5,200 tun in diameter is activated; the Great Cycle commences.

Scholars quibble about the exact date that the Mayan Great Cycle began. Some say August 13, others August 11, yet others August 6, 3113 B.C. Of course, the date August 6 is

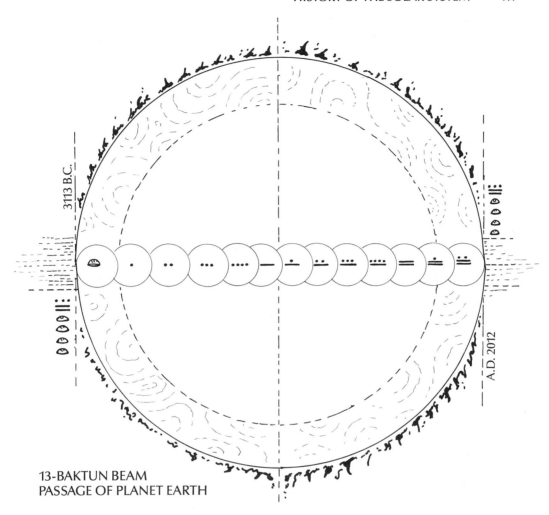

13-BAKTUN BEAM
PASSAGE OF PLANET EARTH

interesting because it is the date the Chinese commemorated as the midpoint between the summer solstice and the autumn equinox. It is also the acknowledged date of the atomic bombing of Hiroshima. In any case, it is almost exactly 5,100 years ago that the planet entered the galactic synchronization beam. It is only some 26 years from this writing that the planet leaves the beam.

But what is this beam? How do we describe it? What does it synchronize and how? In Mayan terms, this beam, the Great Cycle, measures 5,200 tun in diameter. In terms of kin or days, a tun consists of 360 kin/days each, or five days short of a vague solar year. An actual solar year is 365.2422 days. Thus 5,200 tun equals 5,125 vague solar years or 1,872,000 days.

As we have emphasized, the Mayan concern was with calibrating an equivalence between the calendar marking Earth's solar passage and the actual galactic harmonic. The 5,200-tun cycle represents a fractal of the 52-unit key, the Loom of Maya, synthesizing the galactic harmonic. As a fractal, the 5,200-tun cycle can be broken into 260 units of 20 tun each called katuns, and 13 units of 400 tun each called baktuns. While the key harmonic number of a tun is *360* kin and the katun is *7,200* kin, the baktun is *144,000* kin. It is very important to keep in mind that Mayan numbers are multi-dimensional. Their translation into days or years does not mean that the numbers cease being operational for other factors or values. The cycle of history as a 5,200-tun diameter harmonic wave-pattern is but one slice of a multi-dimensional galactic hologram.

As we also noted, when a schematic of the Great Cycle is presented as a set of thirteen baktuns arranged into twenty katuns each, thus creating the 260-unit grid, it is indistinguishable from the grid representing the 260-day Sacred Calendar, or Tzolkin. In other words, the Tzolkin and the Great Cycle are fractals of each other. But then, both being fractals of the 260-unit galactic harmonic, how else could it be?

Thus, in the schematic, *The Mayan Harmonic Module as the Great Cycle*, the vertical columns starting on the lefthand side represent the sequence of thirteen baktuns. Counting down from the top left, each column possesses twenty informational units, each unit repesenting a katun cycle. Since the count of informational units 1-13 also proceeds in unbroken sequence from the top left down, a further breakdown of cycles can be presented, that of twenty cycles of thirteen katuns, each of these cycles being represented by the number sequence 1-13. Thus, there are thirteen baktuns of twenty units each, and twenty subcycles of thirteen katuns each. The Maya called this overlay of twenty thirteen-katun subcycles *Ahau cycles*.

Summarizing then, the Great Cycle consists of: **1,872,000 kin**/days; **5200 tun** of 360 kin/days each (slightly less than one year per tun); **260 katun** of 7200 kin/days each (slightly less than twenty years per katun); **twenty Ahau cycles** of thirteen katuns or 93,600 days each (260 tun or approx 256 years per Ahau cycle); **thirteen baktun** of 144,000 kin/days each (400 tun or slightly more than 394 years per baktun).

The key unit to look at is the baktun cycle. Remembering that the tun is short five days of a vague solar year, then the formula, 400 tun = 20 katun = 1 baktun, rounds out to slightly more than 394 vague solar years. In other words, in its subdivision into thirteen baktun cycles, the Great Cycle or Galactic Synchronization Beam repeats the key galactic number sequence 1-13. With this set of thirteen baktuns represented by the thirteen vertical columns of the Mayan Harmonic Module, we can begin to construct the calendar of the Great Cycle, overlaying it on the time period 3113 B.C.-A.D. 2012.

First, let us list the thirteen baktun cycles in sequence. It should be noted that the first cycle is baktun 0, the second is baktun 1, etc., meaning that a cycle is not counted until its duration has elapsed one round. In contemplating each of the baktun cycles as represented on the module, attention should be paid to the Loom of Maya units occurring in each cycle. These Loom of Maya units, of which there are 52, represent periods of more

MAYAN
HARMONIC MODULE
AS THE GREAT CYCLE

3113 B.C.
BEAM ENTRY

3113 B.C. | 2718 B.C. | 2324 B.C. | 1930 B.C. | 1536 B.C. | 1141 B.C. | 747 B.C. | 353 B.C. | A.D. 41 | A.D. 435 | A.D. 830 | A.D. 1224 | A.D. 1618

A.D. 1618

IMIX	NEPTUNE — 1638
IK	URANUS — 1658
AKBAL	SATURN — 1677
KAN	JUPITER — 1697
CHICCHAN	A-BELT — 1717
CIMI	MARS — 1736
MANIK	EARTH — 1756
LAMAT	VENUS — 1776
MULUC	MERCURY — 1796
OC	MERCURY — 1815
CHUEN	VENUS — 1835
EB	EARTH — 1855
BEN	MARS — 1874
IX	A-BELT — 1894
MEN	JUPITER — 1914
CIB	SATURN — 1933
CABAN	URANUS — 1953
ETZNAB	NEPTUNE — 1972
CAUAC	PLUTO — 1992
AHAU	PLUTO — A.D. 2012

A.D. 2012
GALACTIC SYNCHRONIZATION

1. BAKTUN OF THE STAR PLANTING
2. BAKTUN OF THE PYRAMID
3. BAKTUN OF THE WHEEL
4. BAKTUN OF THE SACRED MOUNTAIN
5. BAKTUN OF THE HOUSE OF SHANG
6. BAKTUN OF THE IMPERIAL SEAL
7. BAKTUN OF THE MIND TEACHINGS
8. BAKTUN OF THE ANOINTED ONE
9. BAKTUN OF THE LORDS OF RED & BLACK
10. BAKTUN OF THE MAYA
11. BAKTUN OF THE HOLY WARS
12. BAKTUN OF THE HIDDEN SEED
13. BAKTUN OF THE TRANSFORMATION OF MATTER

intensified galactic activation. The names given to the 13 baktun cycles refer to the key event/qualities distinguishing that cycle.

1. BAKTUN 0 (=13). *Baktun of the Star Planting.* 3113-2718 B.C. 13.0.0.0.0
Entry of Earth into Galactic Synchronization Beam. Planting of "star-transmissions" of the galactic league among peoples across the planet. Consolidation of upper and lower Egypt, 3100 B.C. Expansion of Sumeria, 3000 B.C. Construction of Stonehenge begun, 2800 B.C.

2. BAKTUN 1. *Baktun of the Pyramid.* 2718-2324 B.C. 1.0.0.0.0
Construction/activation of Great Pyramid at Giza, Egypt, 2700-2600 B.C., marks anchoring of planet light body. Spread of Sumerian civilization, Akkad and Ur, and development of bronze. Beginning of Harappa, Indus civilization. Beginning of settled agricultural life, China, Mesoamerica, Andes.

3. Baktun 2. *Baktun of the Wheel.* 2324-1930 B.C. 2.0.0.0.0
Full establishment of wheel, initiation of transport technology and cyclical thought, written codes of law, and metallurgical technology in Mesopotamia. Sargon and first Babylonian empire. Beginnings of chariot warfare, territorial imperialism. Era of legendary emperors, China. Establishment of Minoan civilization, Crete.

4. Baktun 3. *Baktun of the Sacred Mountain.* 1930-1536 B.C. 3.0.0.0.0
Middle and New Kingdom in Egypt; relocation of center to Sacred Mountain of the West, Valley of the Kings, marks decision of Egyptians to perpetuate dynastic rule, consolidates pattern of defensive territorialism as norm for civilized life. Waves of invaders—Hittites, Aryans; destruction of Minoan, Indus civilizations.

5. Baktun 4. *Baktun of the House of Shang.* 1536-1141 B.C. 4.0.0.0.0
Establishment of Shang Dynasty, China, enunciation of yin/yang doctrine, advanced bronze metallurgy and pattern of Chinese civilization. Beginnings of Vedic civilization, India. Emergence of Chavin civilization, Andes, and Olmecs, Mesoamerica. Akhenaton, Egypt; Abraham and Moses, Israel; Hittite consolidation, Mesopotamia.

6. Baktun 5. *Baktun of the Imperial Seal.* 1141-747 B.C. 5.0.0.0.0
Babylonian-Assyrian empires. Iron weaponry and war machines. Rise of Mycenean Greeks in Mediterranean, sack of Troy. Chou Dynasty, China, emergence of I Ching. Spread of Olmec culture throughout Mesoamerica. Horse used for warfare, pattern of militaristic imperial rule and dynastic succession established as norm for civilized life on planet.

7. Baktun 6. *Baktun of the Mind Teachings.* 747-353 B.C. 6.0.0.0.0
Period of first wave of galactic Mayans in Mesoamerica. Persian Empire. Rise of philosophical individualistic thought supplanting earlier collective forms. Pythagoras, Socrates, Plato, Aristotle in Greece; six schools of Vedic thought, Mahavira and Buddha, India; Lao Tzu, Confucius, Chuang Tzu in China. Construction of Monte Alban, Mexico, beginnings of Mayan calendar systems.

8. Baktun 7. *Baktun of the Anointed One.* 353 B.C.-A.D. 41. 7.0.0.0.0
Hellenistic civilization, Alexander the Great; Rise of Rome, beginning of Roman Empire; Celts in Europe, advanced iron technology; Warring States' consolidation of China by Ch'in Huang Ti, beginnings of Han Dynasty, Great Wall of China; spread of Buddhism as cosmopolitan religion from India to Central Asia. Jesus Christ, gnostic religions of Middle East; diffusion of Olmecs and beginning of Teotihuacan.

9. Baktun 8. *Baktun of the Lords of the Red and Black.* A.D. 41-435 8.0.0.0.0
Completion of Pyramid Center of Teotihuacan, consolidation of Mesoamerican cultural regime, Lords of Red and Black, first teachings of Quetzalcoatl; Moche, Nazca, and Tiahuanaco in Andes; Easter Island; emergence of West African kingdoms; expansion and collapse of Roman Empire, rise of Christianity; collapse of Han Dynasty, spread of Buddhism in China, Southeast Asia.

10. Baktun 9. *Baktun of the Maya.* A.D. 435-830. 9.0.0.0.0
Second galactic Mayan visitation, Pacal Votan of Palenque and flourishing of Mayan cultural regime; Muhammed and rise of Islam; Roman Christian Western Europe and Byzantine Orthodox Christian Eastern Europe; rise of Hinduism, India; spread of Buddhism to Tibet, Korea, Japan; T'ang Dynasty, China; rise of kingdoms in Southeast Asia, Indonesia (Borobadur, Java); ascendency of Tiahuanaco, Andes; Polynesian civilization, Oceania; early flourishing of Nigerian civilization.

11. Baktun 10. *Baktun of the Holy Wars.* A.D. 830-1224 . 10.0.0.0.0
Collapse of Classic Maya and Central Mexican civilization, 1 Reed Quetzalcoatl and rise of Toltecs; Chan Chan and Chimu civilization Andes; rise of I'fe in Nigeria; flourishing and spread of Islam and confrontation with Christian civilization—the Crusades; rise of Tibetan civilization; Sung Dynasty, China, printing press, gunpowder; Khmer Dynasty, Southeast Asia. Great Zimbabwe, East Africa.

12. Baktun 11. *Baktun of the Hidden Seed.* A.D. 1224-1618. 11.0.0.0.0
Expansion of Islam to India, Central and Southeast Asia, West Africa; seclusion of Tibet; rise of Turks, Mongols, conquest of China; seclusion of Japan; rise of Zimbabwe, East Africa, I'fe and Benin, West Africa; peak of Christian civilization, West Europe, and rise of Orthodox Russian civilization, East Europe; Reformation and split of Christian Church; spread and triumph of European civilization in conquest of Inca and Aztec empires; beginning of European colonization, decline of sacred world view (hidden seed).

13. Baktun 12. *Baktun of the Transformation of Matter.* A.D. 1618-2012. 12.0.0.0.0
Rise and triumph of scientific materialism, European world conquest, Industrial Revolution, Democratic revolutions of America, Europe; colonialism of Africa, Latin America, Asia; industrialization of Japan; Karl Marx and rise of communism; communist revolutions of Russia, China; World Wars I and II; atomic bomb and nuclear era; rise of Third World powers, Islam, Mexico and India; global terrorism and collapse of technological civiliza-

GALACTIC SYNCHRONIZATION BEAM SHOWING 13-BAKTUN CYCLES AS 13 MORPHOGENETIC SUB-FIELDS

260-KATUN CYCLES 52-UNIT GAIA LIGHT BODY

3113 B.C. — 2718 B.C. — 2324 B.C. — 1930 B.C. — 1536 B.C. — 1141 B.C. — 747 B.C.

← 400 TUN →

BAKTUN OF THE STAR PLANTING · BAKTUN OF THE PYRAMID · BAKTUN OF THE WHEEL · BAKTUN OF THE WESTERN MOUNTAIN · BAKTUN OF THE HOUSE OF SHANG · BAKTUN OF THE IMPERIAL SEAL

3113 B.C.	13.0.0.0.0	1.0.0.0.0	2.0.0.0.0	3.0.0.0.0	4.0.0.0.0	5.0.0.0.0
IMIX	URUK, MENES	ZOSER, EGYPT, CALENDAR	SARGON	ABRAHAM	SHANG DYNASTY CHINA	KING WEN
IK	KILNS	GREAT PYRAMID,	BABYLON		AKHNATON	CHOU DYNASTY
AKBAL	UNIFIED SUMER	GIZA		CRETE	HITTITE	CHINA
KAN	EGYPT			EMPIRE		KING DAVID, JERUSALEM
CHICCHAN	OLD		CHARIOT	EGYPT: QUEEN	THERA, EARTHQUAKE	
CIMI	KINGDOM		WARFARE	HATSHEPSUT	OLMECS	VEDIC
MANIK				VALLEY OF	CHAVIN	CIVILIZATION,
LAMAT			EGYPT	KINGS		INDIA
MULUC	HEIROGLYPHS	AKKAD	MIDDLE KINGDOM			
OC		UR			JADE	HORSE WARFARE
CHUEN	CUNIEFORM				KING TUT	
EB		HARAPPA			RAMSES	
BEN		CIVILIZATION			ASSYRIA	JERUSALEM
IX		INDIA	ZIGGURATS			
MEN				HORSES		
CIB			BRONZE	CENTRAL ASIA	VEDAS	LA VENTA
CABAN			TECHNOLOGY	HITTITES		ASSYRIAN
ETZNAB			MENUHOTEP	EGYPTIAN	PHOENICIANS	IRON
CAUAC	STONEHENGE	PYRAMID	UR, NAMMU, LEGAL CODE	EMPIRE	MYCENEANS	WEAPONS &
AHAU	GILGAMESH	TEXTS	HAMURABI	ARYANS INVADE INDIA		WAR MACHINES
BAKTUN #	(shell)	•	••	•••	••••	—

13-BAKTUN CYCLE:

Top dates (left to right): 747 B.C. | 353 B.C. | A.D. 41 | A.D. 435 | A.D. 830 | A.D. 1224 | A.D. 1618 | A.D. 2012

Baktun labels:

- BAKTUN OF THE MIND TEACHINGS
- BAKTUN OF THE ANOINTED ONE
- BAKTUN OF THE LORDS OF THE RED & BLACK
- BAKTUN OF THE MAYA
- BAKTUN OF THE HOLY WARS
- BAKTUN OF THE HIDDEN SEED
- BAKTUN OF THE TRANSFORMATION OF MATTER
- GALACTIC SYNCHRONIZATION: NEW HARMONIC FIELD BEYOND DUALITY

6.0.0.0.0	7.0.0.0.0	8.0.0.0.0	9.0.0.0.0	10.0.0.0.0	11.0.0.0.0	12.0.0.0.0	
GREEKS	ALEXANDER	ROMAN	FALL OF ROME	BOROBADUR	GOTHIC	DESCARTES	NEPTUNE
KUSHITE	CELTS	EMPIRE	BYZANTIUM		EUROPE	SCIENTIFIC	URANUS
	ASOKA	TEOTIHUACAN	RISE OF	VIKINGS	MONGOLS,	MATERIALISM	SATURN
NINEVEH	SPREAD OF BUDDHISM		CLASSIC	HEIAN JAPAN	KUBLAI KHAN	CHING DYNASTY	JUPITER
PYTHAGORAS	ZAPOTECS		MAYA	CHIMU	MAYAPAN	NEWTON	A-BELT
BABYLON REBUILT	CH'IN DYNASTY	NA ZCA	BUDDHISM IN JAPAN	XOCHICALCO	AZTEC	BAROQUE MUSIC	MARS
	HUANG-TI	GERMANIC	TIKAL	CE ACATL	BLACK PLAGUE	INDUSTRIAL	EARTH
LAO TZU	EARLY	INVASIONS	POPE GREGORY	TOPILTZIN QUETZALCOATL	INCA	REVOLUTION	VENUS
PERSIAN	MAYA	MOCHE	MUHAMMED	RISE OF	MOGHAL/INDIA	AMERICAN &	MERCURY
EMPIRE	HAN		PALENQUE	TOLTEC	OTTOMAN TURKS	FRENCH REVOLUTION	MERCURY
BUDDHA, MONTE ALBAN		END OF	PACAL VOTAN	MAYA		ROMANTICISM	VENUS
CONFUCIUS	DYNASTY	HAN DYNASTY	COPAN	IFE	MING DYNASTY	EUROPEAN	EARTH
	TEOTIHUACAN	TIAHUANACO		ANGKOR WAT		IMPERIALISM	MARS
PLATO	RISE OF ROME		HEIROGLYPHIC STAIRWAY	CRUSADES	FALL OF CONSTANTINOPLE	ELECTRICITY	A-BELT
CHUANG TZU			SPREAD OF ISLAM	BUDDHISM IN	PRINTING, CONQUEST	RUSSIAN REVOLUTION	JUPITER
ZOROASTER	GREAT WALL OF	CONSTANTINE		TIBET	OF MEXICO, PERU	WORLD WARS	SATURN
	CHINA	BUDDHISM IN	T'ANG DYNASTY	SUNG DYNASTY	EUROPE EXPLORATION	HIROSHIMA	URANUS
BANTU, W. AFRICA		CHINA	MISSISSIPPI CULTURE, BAGDAD	RUSSIA/KIEV	BENIN	NUCLEAR & SPACE TECH	NEPTUNE
PELOPPONESIAN WAR	JULIUS CAESAR	GUPTA DYNASTY, INDIA	PADMASAMBHAVA	ANASAZI	QUEEN ELIZABETH	HARMONIC CONVERGENCE	PLUTO
ARISTOTLE	CHRIST		CHARLEMAGNE	ZIMBABWE	GALILEO, KEPLER	EARTH REGENERATION	PLUTO

Right-side spanning labels:
- SOLAR MOVING INHALATION (NEPTUNE through MERCURY)
- GALACTIC/LUNAR MOVING EXHALATION (MERCURY through PLUTO)

A.D. 2012

WAVE-HARMONIC OF HISTORY

tion; Earth purification and final era of global regeneration; information age and crystal solar technology; galactic synchronization.

What we witness in this summary review of the character and chief activity of the thirteen baktun cycles is an acceleration and expansion of activity, building up in a great wave formation reaching its climax in the thirteenth cycle, Baktun 12, the Baktun of the Transformation of Matter. The name of the final baktun, as well as of the initial one, the Baktun of the Star Planting, gives the clues. What appears as a process of history—the Great Cycle— is actually a planetary process, a stage in the conscious growth of Earth, the crafting of Earth's light body.

In this total planetary endeavor, humans are the sensitive atmospheric instruments galactically utilized in a process whose objective is the transformation of the "material field" of the planet. The end of this transformation is to raise the overall planetary field to a higher, more harmonic level of resonant frequency. In this way, the planet light body, the consciously articulated etheric sheath of Earth, is constructed. This is something of what is meant in the reference to the Great Cycle as the 5,125-year diameter of a Galactic Synchronization Beam.

In order to grasp the meaning of history as the galactically synchronized construction of the planet light body, it is necessary to understand the role of our planet in relation to the larger organism of which it is a participating member—the solar system. As we understand it, the solar system consists of a central star—the Sun—and its family of at least ten planets. This solar system is a self-contained organism whose subtle sheath or morphic field is called the *heliocosm*. Every 11.3+ years the heliocosm pulses outward and then for another 11.3+ years it pulses inward. These 11.3 year inhalation-exhalation cycles are referred to as the *heliopause* whose total movement occurs over a period of some 23 years. While sixteen 260-day cycles equal 11.3 years, 11.3 twenty-three year cycles amount to approximately 260 years.

The registering of the solar inhalation-exhalation by the heliopause corresponds precisely to the activity of the binary sunspot movements. In the sunspot activity, two "spots"—one negative, the other positive—pulse inward from positions 30 degrees north and south toward the solar equator. Approximately every 11.3+ years, the two "spots" meet at the equator, reverse polarity, and begin the process again at 30 degrees north and south of the solar equator. Cued to the heliopause, the total sunspot movement occurs in a period just under 23 years. In other words, the morphic field of the Sun has a breathing pattern some 23 years in duration.

Clearly, the sunspots, whose activity causes great disturbances to Earth's radio waves and the bio-electromagnetic field in general, are connected with the solar breathing process. If we can view the solar system as a colossal organism whose body, the heliocosm, encompasses the orbits of the planets, what is the role of the planets within the solar body, and how does the solar breathing process affect the planets?

In our consideration of these matters, we must also take into account another important variable. If the Earth is a consciously evolving, living organism, what about the Sun about which it orbits? Brief contemplation leads us to the inescapable position that the Sun, too, possesses an intelligence—but one that is vast and virtually incomprehensible to us. Nonetheless, our forebears of the ancient civilizations of Egypt and Mexico, Peru and Mesopotamia had some knowledge of this, and in this knowledge lies their so-called sun worship. Furthermore, the activity of the heliopause and binary sunspots yields some indication of the nature of the solar-intelligence energy process. From the accumulated knowledges, ancient and modern, we may give the following description of the intelligent solar organism.

Coordinated by a central star which continuously monitors galactic information through the cyclical pulsing of its binary receiver/transmitters, the solar body is articulated as a series of subtle waves corresponding to the orbits of the ten planets. As Kepler intuited, the planetary orbits possess a harmonic relation to each other. In this way, the Asteroid Belt was discovered orbiting between Mars and Jupiter, Uranus was discovered orbiting beyond Saturn, and Neptune and Pluto were later discovered orbiting beyond Uranus. What is important in this description of the solar field is the harmonic wave-pattern created by the planetary orbits in their movement around the Sun. What, then, of the planets themselves?

If the Sun is the central coordinating intelligence in the solar field, the planets represent *harmonic gyroscopes* whose purpose it is to maintain the resonant frequency represented by the orbit which the planet holds. Indeed, this is precisely the description of Earth, for instance, spinning on its axis.

Though the heliocosm, the total solar body, is a self-regulatory system, it is at the same time a subsystem within the larger galactic field. Thus, its inhalation consists of cosmic forces—galactic frequencies—monitored either directly from the galactic core and/or via other intelligent star systems. Its exhalation represents transmuted streams of energy/information returned back to the galactic core, Hunab Ku. The planets, orbital harmonic gyroscopes, assist in the mediation of the energy information flow to and from the galactic core. The inhalation represents a solar-moving flow; the exhalation, the lunar-galactic flow. As we shall see, there is a correspondence between the solar inhalation-exhalation, the ten planet gyroscopes, and the twenty Sacred Signs.

In the overall solar evolutionary process, which encompasses our own planetary evolution, let us say that the purpose is to arrive at a superior intelligent coordination of the various planetary centers to the central solar core and of the central solar core to the galactic core. The indices of the solar body's attaining new levels of conscious integration are represented by the increasingly harmonic frequencies of the planetary orbits in resonance with the Sun's own increased harmonic frequency.

Let us also assume that in the process of a star's attaining to such a level of conscious, intelligent coordination, it reaches a stage in which cooperation is solicited and received from other, more evolved star systems. The cooperation of the other star systems would be in the form of a resonant frequency synchronization beam focussed on the orbiting harmonic gyroscopes, the planets themselves.

The focussing of such a resonant frequency synchronization beam would naturally be attuned to the galactic harmonic and would represent a minimum fractal of the total galactic seasonal flow. As we have already seen, this galactic harmonic is 5,200 tun or 260 katun in diameter and contains and encompasses all the mathematical ratios governing the radiant and genetic properties of universal life. For reasons which will become more evident as this vision of solar intelligence and galactic community unfolds, the focussing of this beam, corresponding to Earth time, 3113 B.C.-A.D. 2012, has been of particular significance for the transformation of terrestrial intelligence. Let us just say for the moment that during this synchronized 5,200-tun beam, the resonant harmonics of the third orbital gyroscope, Earth, have been deemed pivotal in the establishment of a stage of intelligent coordination, allowing the solar system to enter fully into the community of galactic intelligence.

Within the context of morphogenetic fields, the 5,200-tun Great Cycle can be viewed as a galactically activated field of a purposeful resonance divided into thirteen cyclical subfields. As a total field of resonance, the purpose of the Great Cycle is to facilitate Earth's lift-off—the creation and realization of the planetary light body. Through human instrumentation resulting in the transformation of matter and the simultaneous creation of a species-transcending coordination of intelligence, a genuine planetary consciousness is attained. This acquisition of planetary intelligence, represented by the sign MEN, is the prerequisite for attaining conscious resonance with the central solar intelligence, represented by the sign AHAU.

To make all of this information more meaningful and useful, let us return to the thirteen baktun cycles as the wave-harmonic of history. Let us look at these thirteen cycles as a landscape of morphic resonance divided into seven mountains and six valleys. Each a discrete field of morphic resonance unto itself, these seven mountains and six valleys build up as a single, ever-gathering wave-formation to a climax which occurs toward the end of the thirteenth cycle. The purpose of this "climax of matter" towards the end of the thirteenth cycle, the Baktun of the Transformation of Matter, is to induce an increase in harmonic frequency. Remembering that the Earth is a harmonic gyroscope, this heightened harmonic resonance affected by a singular unification of human consciousness will assist, sooner than later, in the propelling of the solar body into the community of galactic intelligence.

In this consideration of the thirteen baktun cycles of the synchronization beam considered as thirteen morphic subfields, our attention is drawn to the ending and beginning of the cycles themselves. The points of transition between the subcycles are critical in our understanding of morphogenetic fields. For while the field holds the memory for

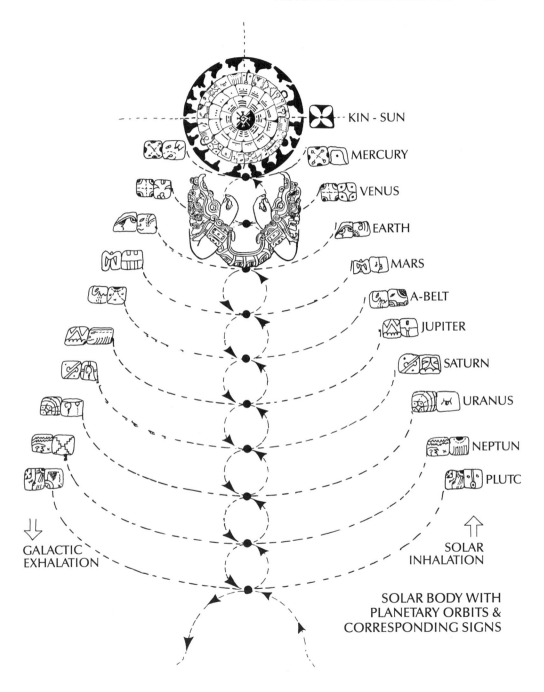

KIN - SUN

MERCURY

VENUS

EARTH

MARS

A-BELT

JUPITER

SATURN

URANUS

NEPTUN

PLUTC

⇓
GALACTIC
EXHALATION

⇧
SOLAR
INHALATION

SOLAR BODY WITH
PLANETARY ORBITS &
CORRESPONDING SIGNS

a species, it is at moments of cyclical transition that changes in the programming are introduced. Obviously the more minute the cycle, the subtler the program change; the larger the cycle, the greater the program change. In the human organism, these changes are experienced as shifts in the dominance of particular archetypal patterns.

Thus, each baktun cycle possesses a particular morphic resonance, represented by a particular archetype or set of archetypal symbols. In this regard, symbols can be considered as resonant capacitators. That is, a symbol, properly constructed, contains the capacity to evoke a particular resonance no matter where or when. In this way, particular archetypal resonances set in motion during one baktun may carry over into another, or several others. This situation is made more complex, given the human tendency to distort according to egotistic or territorial imperatives.

Representing a discrete field of morphic resonance, the baktun accounts for cyclic change. A cyclic transition describes the point at which one cycle ends and another begins. Every 394 years in the morphogenetic subfield called baktun, there is a pause or a break. During this break or cyclical pause, certain symbolic modes or cognitive dispositions are discarded and a certain new Psi Bank imprinting occurs. Naturally, there are lesser cycles in which this occurs, particularly the "generational" katun cycles of 19+ years. But the significance of the baktun cycles lies in their vastness in relation to the duration of a single human existence.

Thus, as we look over the map of the Galactic Synchronization Beam landscape, we see building up over 5,125 years the series of thirteen morphogenetic fields in their archetypal character, each subdivided into twenty katun subcycles. Though the transitions between the fields are not always marked by anything obviously momentous, we may nonetheless distinguish in each of the subfields, an overall marked change of character. As indicated, these changes of character are due to the generally unconscious discarding of certain symbolic/cognitive features and the imprinting of new information, the sum of which comprises the quality of the new morphic subfield. Thus, a transition between cycles marks an information transfer and imprint that affects and seals the overall memory-bearing quality of the new morphogenetic field.

Cyclical change is important, because it is the means by which creativity is introduced at a species/planet-wide level. Any change in a morphic field is preceded by a morphogenetic *subduction* prior to the transition. A subduction is a sudden pulling down of energy that precedes a somewhat later upheaval or discharge of new energy in the new morphic subfield. This subduction is usually occasioned by an event which presages what is to come. Thus, the construction of Stonehenge, with all of its astronomical and geodetic proportions could be viewed as the subduction event concluding the initial baktun of the Star Planting and presaging the following baktun, that of the Pyramid.

In any case, what is genuinely significant for us now is the subduction prior to the conclusion of the total cycle. If the changes between baktuns can be considered momentous, then the subduction and change occasioned by the conclusion of the entire Great Cycle must be of unprecedented proportions. This change, which has already been initiated, is signaled by a resonant frequency shift which will herald the conclusion of the Great Cycle or 5,200-tun Galactic Synchronization Beam, and will presage the brilliance of the post-A.D. 2012 phase of our galactic/solar/planetary reality.

In this general description of the thirteen subcycles of the Great Cycle or 5,200-tun Galactic Synchronization Beam, the patterns of human history become not only morphic resonances of a total planetary evolutionary process, but the planet itself plays its role in the larger morphogenetic harmonic of the solar system. Though, from a certain perspective, the human element is but the instrument of galactic purposes, this instrumentation is of necessity intelligent and purposeful. And if, at this stage in the harmonic calibrations of the Great Cycle, we are at the point of climax and the painful shedding of much that we have developed to get to where we are, the unconscious construction of our labors finally looms into view: the Light Body of Planet Earth—the raiment of Gaia, worn like a radiant garment from pole to magnetic pole.

Having sketched out the general morphic landscape of the thirteen baktuns of the Great Cycle, we may now turn to a consideration of the katun cycles. There are twenty katuns of something less than twenty years each to every baktun cycle. The significance or meaning of the katun cycles is derived from the symbolic attributes of the glyph associated with the katun. Thus, the first katun cycle is always associated with the glyph IMIX, the last with the glyph AHAU. The entire sequence of glyphs, then, gives a symbolic profile of the general unfolding of the morphogenetic pattern of any given baktun. The meaning of the katun cycles is further modified by the number accorded to the particular cycle.

The twenty-katun cycle, giving the general structure of the organic pattern of the baktun, may be constructed in the following manner:

1. **IMIX: Katun 0.** Morphogenetic Pattern Set
2. **IK: Katun 1.** Morphogenetic Pattern Receives Inspiration
3. **AKBAL: Katun 2.** Morphogenetic Pattern Receives Consecration
4. **KAN: Katun 3.** Morphogenetic Pattern Seeded into Daily Life Patterns
5. **CHICCHAN: Katun 4.** Morphogenetic Pattern Becomes Secondary Instinct
6. **CIMI: Katun 5.** Morphogenetic Pattern Provides Base of Revelation
7. **MANIK: Katun 6.** Morphogenetic Pattern Provides New Skill Base
8. **LAMAT: Katun 7.** Morphogenetic Pattern Realized as Cosmic Law
9. **MULUC: Katun 8.** Morphogenetic Pattern Established as Principle of Communication
10. **OC: Katun 9.** Morphogenetic Pattern Established as Social Principle
11. **CHUEN: Katun 10.** Morphogenetic Pattern Emerges as Dominant Artistic Force and Vision
12. **EB: Katun 11.** Morphogenetic Pattern Experienced as Inescapable Human Nature

13. **BEN: Katun 12.** Full Maturation of Cyclic Morphogenetic Pattern

14. **IX: Katun 13.** Beginning of Transcendence of Existing Pattern

15. **MEN: Katun 14.** Higher Aspects of Morphogenetic Pattern Pervade Total Educational Field of Cycle

16. **CIB: Katun 15.** Galactic Impulse toward New Cycle Begins to Be Felt

17. **CABAN: Katun 16.** Morphogenetic Pattern Reaches Climax of Power

18. **ETZNAB: Katun 17.** Morphogenetic Pattern Shows Self-Imitative, Self-Destructive Aspects

19. **CAUAC: Katun 18.** Morphogenetic Pattern Begins Transformation

20. **AHAU: Katun 19.** Morphogenetic Pattern Completes Transformation

Given this information of the thirteen baktuns and their twenty katun cycles, the 260-unit frame of the abacus of history may be constructed and contemplated. In addition to the symbolic glyph signs accorded to each of the katun cycles, there is also the harmonic number overlay—the twenty AHAU cycles showing the sequence of the numbers 1-13. Called by the post-classic Maya the AHAU Cycles, these twenty cycles, each thirteen katuns in length, provide a second harmonic galactic synchronization wave-pattern overlay, each 256 years in length. While the longer 400-tun baktun cycles bear the morphogenetic imprinting relating to the interaction of human and planetary consciousness, the shorter AHAU cycles, being 260 tun in duration—the number of the galactic code—represent higher galactic imprinting. This galactic imprinting is what infuses the total pattern of the Great Cycle/Galactic Synchronization Beam with the galactic momentum—the drive toward the resonantly transformative conclusion of the total cycle in A.D. 2012.

Thus, while the thirteen-baktun cycles may be envisioned as a gathering wave of seven mountains and six valleys, the twenty AHAU cycles may be imagined as the spiral of planetary DNA turning twenty times in a direction running parallel to and interacting with the baktun cycles but from a source above the baktun wave form. In addition to bearing their own discrete galacto-morphic quality, the AHAU cycles also account for the carryovers of morphogenetic information from one baktun to the next. In our rendering of these twenty thirteen-katun AHAU cycles, the name of the cycle is derived from the glyph to which the number 1 is affixed, initiating the cycle. In addition, a weave of mytho-poetic descriptions is woven describing the single, larger movement of the planet light body, the mind of the Earth, over the course of the 5,125-year Great Cycle.

1. **1 IMIX: 3113-2857 B.C.** The Seed Is Nurtured

2. **1 IX: 2857-2601 B.C.** Guarded by the Magicians

3. **1 MANIK: 2601-2344 B.C.** Given to the Builders

4. **1 AHAU: 2344-2087 B.C.** Offered to the Sun

5. **1 BEN: 2087-1830 B.C.** Watched by the Sky-Walkers

6. **1 CIMI: 1830-1574 B.C.** Concealed in Death

7. **1 CAUAC: 1574-1318 B.C.** Ripened by the Storm

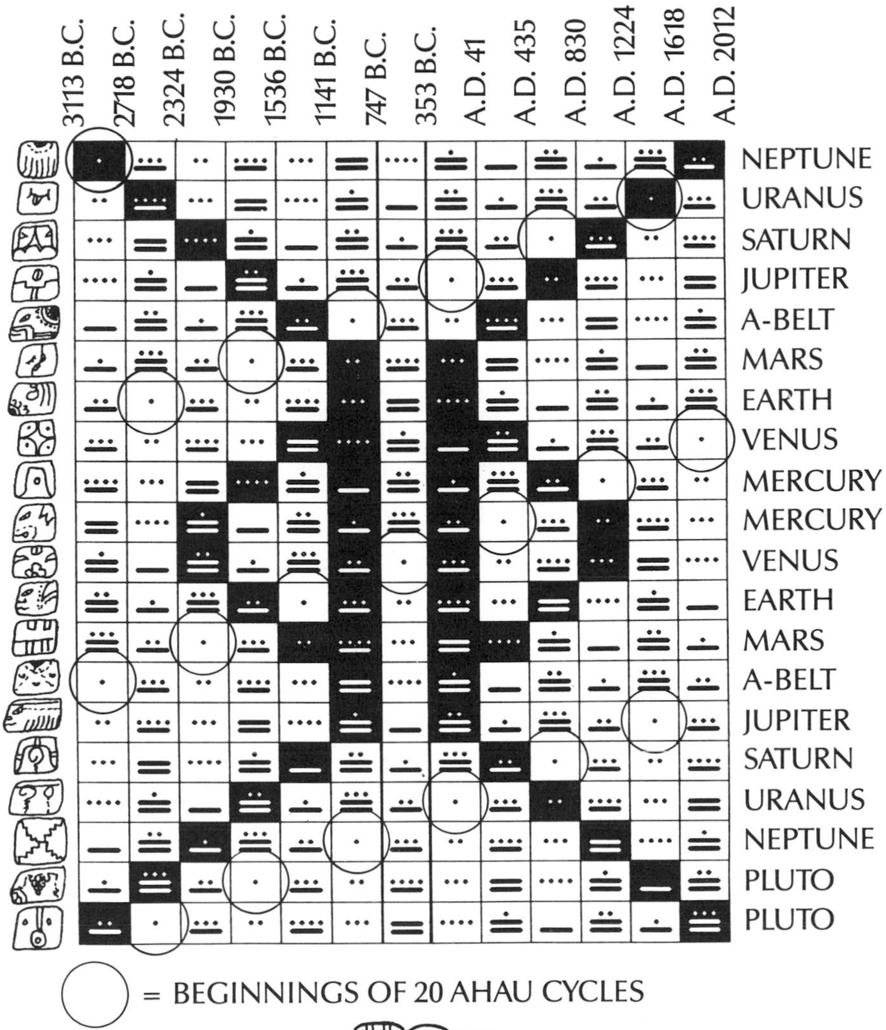
3113 B.C.
2718 B.C.
2324 B.C.
1930 B.C.
1536 B.C.
1141 B.C.
747 B.C.
353 B.C.
A.D. 41
A.D. 435
A.D. 830
A.D. 1224
A.D. 1618
A.D. 2012
NEPTUNE
URANUS
SATURN
JUPITER
A-BELT
MARS
EARTH
VENUS
MERCURY
MERCURY
VENUS
EARTH
MARS
A-BELT
JUPITER
SATURN
URANUS
NEPTUNE
PLUTO
PLUTO
= BEGINNINGS OF 20 AHAU CYCLES

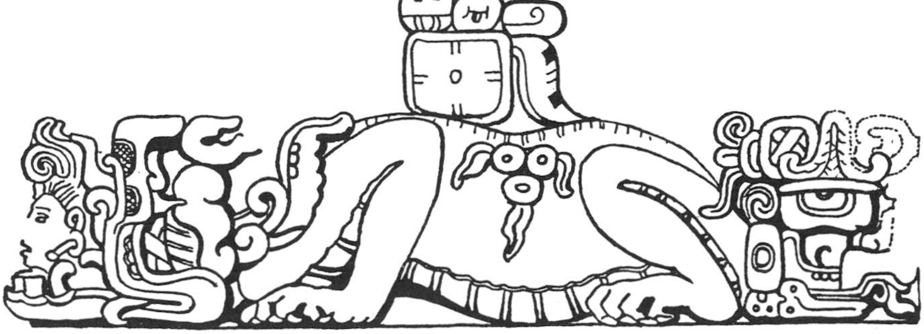

20-AHAU CYCLE OVERLAY

8. 1 EB: 1318-1062 B.C. Which Enters the Human

9. 1 CHICCHAN: 1062-806 B.C. Eaten by the Serpent

10. 1 ETZNAB: 806-550 B.C. Ritualized by the Sword

11. 1 CHUEN: 550-294 B.C. Mastered by the Trickster

12. 1 KAN: 294-38 B.C. To Be Sown Again as Seed

13. 1 CABAN: 38 B.C.-A.D. 219. Of the Force of the Earth

14. 1 OC: A.D. 219-465. By Loyalty Guided

15. 1 AKBAL: A.D. 465-731. Through the House of the Night

16. 1 CIB: A.D. 731-987. Illumined by the Cosmic Force

17. 1 MULUC: A.D. 987-1243. To Return through the Cosmic Gate

18. 1 IK: A.D. 1243-1499. As Spirit Pure

19. 1 MEN: A.D. 1499-1755. To Gather Whole the Mind of the Earth

20. 1 LAMAT: A.D. 1755-2012. And Seal It with the Star-Seed Harmony

Here the entire movement of the current cycle of history and civilization is seen as a unified movement, a wave harmonic, whose mythic end is in the conscious radiance of the Earth harmonized with the galactic force.

Contemplating the overlay of the twenty thirteen-katun cycles upon the thirteen baktuns comprising the two interactive fields of the 5,125-year diameter Galactic Synchronization Beam, a richness of meaning emerges. As the symbolic calculus of history, the bead game, the abacus of time, the Mayan Harmonic Module reveals a pattern or sets of patterns as mathematically precise as they are poetic. It is a pattern in which the human is integrally interwoven—not as the supreme ruler of a planet whose right it is to exploit, but as a mythic agent molded as much by galactic and terrestrial forces as by the karmic web that we have woven of our own collective actions.

As we shall see, adding to these overlays of katun cycles, numbers, symbolic associations, wave-patterns and historic fact, there are other planetary—harmonic gyroscopic—associations that also affect the meaning of each katun cycle. But for the moment, let these preliminary associations suffice. The point here is that we are given a view of the cycle of civilization matrixed according to the galactic code, the governing code of the light body. This light body, the vibratory infrastructure imprinted by the 260-unit galactic code, operates at all levels, whether that of a planet, a species, or an individual organism. In the development of a planet within a larger star system, it is of great significance, however, when this light body attains to a level of conscious radiance. This, of course, is the underlying purpose of the 5,125-year-diameter galactic synchronization beam that has now almost completely passed through our planet.

With this in mind, let us turn our attention to the construction of the planet light body. The vital form of the planet light body is the structure created by the 52-katun periods corresponding to the 52-unit resonant Loom of Maya. It is these 52-katun periods that are of particular importance in the galactic synchronization process. It is during these 52-katun cycles that the galactic force, though barely perceptible to everyday consciousness, is intensified with qualities that accord with the number and nature of the symbol accorded to that particular katun cycle, i.e., 12 CABAN, 7 IMIX, etc.

In presenting the 52-katun cycles, we are aware of the complete symmetry pattern constituted by the Loom of Maya and the Harmonic Module. Not only do we find that the mirror numbers are reflected in the cycles, i.e., cycle 1 and cycle 13, cycle 2 and cycle 12, etc., but that there is an inverse correspondence or counterpoint operative as well. This means that the first light-body katun unit corresponds to the last; the second to the second-to-the-last, etc. It is as if invisible webs connect the most distant points of the cycle, the one weaving forward from the beginning, the other weaving backward from the end. But then, that is as it should be, for a cycle or a circle is harmonic throughout, any given point has a symmetrical correspondence elsewhere in the cycle/circle. What is generated at one point is completed at a symmetrical other point. And in the whole, who is to separate the cause from the effect? Where we begin is where we end, and rather than there being anything like what we imagine evolution to be, there is only essence—there may be digressions from essence, and returnings to essence, but finally there is only essence.

Given this perspective, let us present here the 52-unit light body of history as a set of 26 Galactic Synchronization Beam correspondences:

CYCLE 1, Baktun 0
1. 1 IMIX: 3113 -3103 B.C.
2. 7 AHAU: 2737-2718 B.C.

CYCLE 2, Baktun 1
3. 9 IK: 2698-2678 B.C.
4. 13 CAUAC: 2363-2344 B.C.

CYCLE 3, Baktun 2
5. 4 AKBAL: 2285-2265 B.C.
6. 11 OC: 2146-2127 B.C.
7. 12 CHUEN: 2127-2107 B.C.
8. 6 ETZNAB: 1989-1970 B.C.

CYCLE 4, Batkun 3
9. 12 KAN: 1871-1852 B.C.
10. 4 MULUC: 1774-1754 B.C.
11. 7 OC: 1715-1695 B.C.
12. 12 CABAN: 1615-1595 B.C.

CYCLE 5, Baktun 4
13. 7 CHICCHAN: 1457-1438 B.C.
14. 10 LAMAT: 1398-1379 B.C.
15. 2 BEN: 1300-1281 B.C.
16. 5 CIB: 1242 -1222 B.C.

CYCLE 13, Baktun 12
52. 13 AHAU: A.D. 1992-2012
51. 7 IMIX: A.D. 1618-1637

CYCLE 12, Baktun 11
50. 5 CAUAC: A.D. 1578-1598
49. 1 IK: A.D. 1244-1263

CYCLE 11, Baktun 10
48. 10 ETZNAB: A.D. 1165-1184
47. 3 CHUEN: A.D. 1027-1046
46. 2 OC: A.D. 1007-1027
45. 8 AKBAL: A.D. 870-889

CYCLE 10, Baktun 9
44. 2 CABAN: A.D. 752-771
43. 10 OC: A.D. 654-674
42. 7 MULUC: A.D. 595-615
41. 2 KAN: A.D. 495-515

CYCLE 9, Baktun 8
40. 7 CIB: A.D. 388-357
39. 4 BEN: A.D. 279-299
38. 12 LAMAT: A.D. 181-200
37. 9 CHICCHAN: A.D. 122-142

CYCLE 6, Baktun 5

17. 2 CIMI: 1042-1022 B.C.
18. 3 MANIK: 1022-1002 B.C.
19. 4 LAMAT: 1002-983 B.C.
20. 5 MULUC: 983-963 B.C.
21. 6 OC: 963-943 B.C.
22. 7 CHUEN: 943-923 B.C.
23. 8 EB: 923-904 B.C.
24. 9 BEN: 904-884 B.C.
25. 10 IX: 884-844 B.C.
26. 11 MEN: 844-824 B.C.

CYCLE 8, Baktun 7

36. 12 MEN: 80-60 B.C.
35. 11 IX: 100-80 B.C.
34. 10 BEN: 119-100 B.C.
33. 9 EB: 139-119 B.C.
32. 8 CHUEN: 159-139 B.C.
31. 7 OC: 178-159 B.C.
30. 6 MULUC: 197-178 B.C.
29. 5 LAMAT: 217-197 B.C.
28. 4 MANIK: 237-217 B.C.
27. 3 CIMI: 256-237 B.C.

Of course, not included in any of the light-body units is the mystic seventh cycle, baktun 6. As the mystic column or center, the seventh-cycle, Baktun of the Mind Teachings, can be understood as pure resonace allowing for the galactic symmetry pattern to hold together.

Seen as a counterpoint, the 52-unit Light Body of Planet Earth is constructed or woven in two directions simultaneously. This corresponds to the Zuvuya principle—the simultaneous coming from and returning to source that characterizes all phenomena. The fruit is in the seed. Though at this moment in time it may not seem as though there is much order to things, it is simply that we participate in the darkness that precedes the full, effulgent brilliance of the light. The thirteenth baktun cycle, like the first, contains a strain of eighteen consecutive katun cycles between periods of galactic intensification. Our cycle, the 259th-katun cycle, is the conclusion of as long a period of "galactic" darkness as any known during the entire Great Cycle. That is, between A.D. 1637 and 1992, the heyday of materialism, there are no galactic activation light-body units.

In actuality, however, as we approach the final light-body katun, 13 AHAU, A.D. 1992-2012, it will soon be evident that we are joining the omega to the alpha. The star seed sown at the time Menes was unifying upper and lower Egypt in 3100 B.C. will bear fruit as the unification of the upper and lower hemispheres of Planet Earth. Leaving the galactic synchronization beam in A.D. 2012, the cycle complete will be the cycle begun, and it will be as if we have seen ourselves for the first time, and at the same time, we shall recognize ourselves as human no more.

In order to obtain a better grasp of the meaning of the beam and of the overlays of baktuns, AHAU cycles, and the functioning of the planet light body, we shall now undertake a more detailed review of Cycle 13, Baktun 12 of the Great Cycle, the Baktun of the Transformation of Matter.

52-UNIT
PLANET LIGHT BODY

SHIELD
OF PACAL VOTAN

6

THE END OF THE CYCLE: SYNCHRONIZATION WITH THE BEYOND

12.18.14.18.9
OR JUNE 20, 1986 A.D.

At the moment of this writing, it is not yet dawn. On the current calendar, reckoned by the birth of a particular individual, Jesus Christ, it is June 20, A.D. 1986. On the Mayan calendar, reckoned from August 13, 3113, B.C., it is 10 BEN, 9 KAYEB, 12.18.14.18. 9, meaning that we are in Baktun 12, katun 18, year 14, vinal 18, day 9. Or we could say it is kin 1862599, which is the number of days elapsed from the initiation point of the Great Cycle, or less than 10,000 kin from the conclusion of the Great Cycle.

Any way it is sliced, the Great Cycle or the 5200-tun/thirteen-baktun-diameter synchronization beam through which our planet is passing, is about to draw to an end. As we indicated in the previous chapter, during the passage through this beam the advanced DNA lifeforms on this planet undergo an acceleration, strangely mimicked by the acceleration to which we subject atomic particles in our large atom smashers. It is this process of acceleration, and ultimately of synchronization, that we refer to as the *wave harmonic of history*. This wave harmonic is a minute but exquisitely proportioned fractal of the galactic evolutionary process. Therefore, the conclusion of the cycle in A.D. 2012—kin 1872000, 13.0.0.0.0—bodes nothing less than a major evolutionary upgrading of the light-life—*radiogenetic*—process which our planet represents.

However, to speak of the end of the cycle in the morphogenetic field whose calendar is dominated consciously or unconsciously by the presence and vision of the historical figure called Christ is to raise the spectre of Armageddon—a Second Coming preceded by an awesome final conflagration that bodes extinction. And indeed, this is precisely the scenario that seems to be working itself out through the Christ-based time frame that now dominates the world. Armed camps with inconceivable world-destroying firepower unleashed through the probing of the atom—initiated and originally supported by the most brilliant scientists of the twentieth century—this is the climactic Armageddon-like moment at which humankind and our planet have arrived.

So trapped and immersed are we in this script that there is little in the public imagination that escapes it. Popular cinema and video future visions portray either a post-nuclear

war barbarism or a technological society so regimented as to be a living nightmare. Even movies about the future of space travel are gripped by colossal, galactic war-visions—Star Wars. No genuine alternative to the terror of living in an armed global nuclear plant has yet inspired the popular imagination—or that of the world leaders. Armageddon, it seems, shall prevail.

When we look at the source of the Armageddon script, the Book of Revelations, we find that it is both unrelentingly righteous, making black-and-white distinctions between the saved and the damned, and at the same time, as visionary a text as can be conceived. Most curiously, however, the number symbolism of the Book of Revelations possesses a profoundly Mayan overtone. The fact that Christ is the thirteenth in a group numbering twelve disciples is paramount. Then there is the incessant emphasis on the number seven repeated in any number of ways as the mystical underpinning of the entire revelation. And finally, there are the 144,000 elect, the same number as there are days or kin in a baktun.

Remembering that the baktun is a multi-dimensional harmonic term and that we are currently in the thirteenth cycle, Baktun 12, we may begin to wonder if there is not some deep bond between the Christian Revelation and the Mayan Factor that has been ignored or avoided in the orthodox ruling circles of the neo-Christian West. Could the New Jerusalem, New Heaven, and New Earth, be the same as the entry into the unimaginable realm of the new cycle, the post-galactic synchronization following A.D. 2012, Mayan calendar date 13.0.0.0.0?

If there is any single marked contrast between the orthodox Christian and neo-Christian, i.e., scientific, viewpoint and that of the Mayan Factor, it is in the matter of beginnings and endings. The current mental frame or paradigm is so saturated in a big-bang beginning and an equally big-bang ending that the notion of the cyclical nature of things is most difficult to grasp. While many, if not all, non-western perspectives emphasize a cyclical interpretation of things, hence avoiding any ultimate damnation, the Mayan Factor beckons because it most precisely attunes the present moment to the harmonic reckonings of a larger, history-encompassing cycle about to end. And yet, this ending is most clearly not an ending but an invitation to ascend to an even more vast scale of operations.

Let us seize the opportunity presented by the cresting of the Armageddon myth to insert the evaluation presented by the Great Cycle. From the perspective of the Mayan Factor, the peaking of the Armageddon myth coincides with the cresting wave not only of the thirteenth cycle, Baktun 12, but of the entire wave harmonic of history itself. No wonder the times are so momentous. If the purpose of the passage through the Galactic Synchronization Beam has been to accelerate and intensify the development of life and consciousness on this planet as focused through the human species, then nothing typifies this process so well as Baktun 12. Let us take a closer look, then, and see what we may yet learn.

Called the Baktun of the Transformation of Matter, Cycle 13, Baktun 12, represents both the creation of a structure of incredible complexity—global industrial civilization—and at the same time, an immanent movement of such synchronizing transcendence as to be almost inconceivable. When we look at the whole Harmonic Module of thirteen baktuns and 260 katuns and see that we are already approaching the end of katun 259, it seems almost impossible to imagine that in some 25 years the world could be ready for an order of life and civilization altogether different from what now exists. And yet, if we contemplate the step-by-step process of change which has characterized Baktun 12 thus far, we shall see that the very next step, the step of transformation itself, is precisely what shall induce the disposition to galactic synchronization.

Let us first set out the frame of Baktun 12, a morphogenetic field of chaotic richness. Spanning the years A.D. 1618-2012, Baktun 12 not only possesses its own discrete wave cycle but at the same time embodies the culmination of the wave motion of the whole of the 13 baktun cycles, the Great Cycle itself. Since the critical crest of a wave motion occurs toward the conclusion of its total cycle as the culminating subcycle, Baktun 12 is peculiarly charged with an acceleration of exponential potency. This is why it is referred to as the Baktun of the Transformation of Matter. Everything from the initiation point in 3113 B.C. is a buildup to this climactic cycle of transformation and, ultimately, of synchronization.

In this readout of Baktun 12, katun by katun, the interconnected development of scientific materialism, the Industrial Revolution, and the global expansion of a materialistic acquisitive way of life leading to the critical present moment should be obvious. Equally obvious should be the extent to which an irreversible transformation has already occurred. Everything in the transformation is complete except the final step: synchronization of the entire field of global resonance. It is toward the occurrence of this synchronization that this abacus of history is put forth.

First, we shall present the read-out of the katun cycles of Baktun 12, showing the overlay of the thirteen-katun AHAU cycles. Like the first Baktun cycle, which it mirrors, the last cycle is characterized by an overlay of seven katuns of one AHAU cycle and the full thirteen katuns of the final AHAU cycle. The nineteenth Ahau cycle, 1499-1756, which Baktun 12 completes is that of 1 MEN—"To Gather Whole the Mind of the Earth," while AHAU cycle 20, is 1 LAMAT, 1756-2012, "And Seal it with the Star-Seed Harmony." These poetic words are clues to the actual process occurring in the fitful cauldron of material exploration which Baktun 12 represents.

Here then is the schematic of Baktun 12, with the AHAU cycle correspondences, the 13 number and 20 Sign correspondences described in Chapter 4, the harmonic number indices, and the morphogenetic pattern qualities:

Baktun 12: BAKTUN OF THE TRANSFORMATION OF MATTER

AHAU CYCLE	KATUN CYCLE *Harmonic index and year*		MORPHOGENETIC QUALITY
MEN	A.D. 1499-1755		To Gather Whole the Mind of the Earth
Stage 7.	1. 7 IMIX: 172800, 1618		Pattern Set
Stage 8.	2. 8 IK; 17352200, 1638		Pattern Receives Inspiration
Stage 9.	3. 9 AKBAL: 1742400, 1658		Pattern Receives Consecration
Stage 10.	4. 10 KAN: 1749600, 1677		Pattern Seeds Daily Life
Stage 11.	5. 11 CHICCHAN: 1756800, 1697		Pattern Becomes Instinct
Stage 12.	6. 12 CIMI: 1764000, 1717		Pattern as Base of Revelation
Stage 13.	7. 13 MANIK: 1771200, 1736		Pattern Becomes Skill Base

LAMAT	A. D. 1756-2012		And Seal it with the Star-Seed Harmony
Stage 1.	8. 1 LAMAT: 1778400, 1756		Pattern Established as Law
Stage 2.	9. 2 MULUC: 1785600, 1776		Pattern as Communication
Stage 3.	10. 3 OC: 1792800, 1796		Pattern as Social Form
Stage 4.	11. 4 CHUEN: 1800000, 1815		Pattern as Artistic Vision
Stage 5.	12. 5 EB: 1807200, 1835		Pattern as Human Nature

	Stage 6.	13. 6 BEN: 1814400, 1855	Pattern at Full Maturation
	Stage 7.	14. 7 IX: 1821600, 1874	Beginning of Self Transcendence
	Stage 8.	15. 8 MEN: 1828800, 1894	Higher Pattern Sets In
	Stage 9.	16. 9 CIB: 1836000, 1914	Impulse Toward New Cycle
	Stage 10.	17. 10 CABAN: 1843200, 1933	Climax of Power
	Stage 11.	18. 11 ETZNAB: 1850400, 1953	Self-Imitative Climax
	Stage 12.	19. 12 CAUAC: 1857600, 1973	Begin Transformation
	Stage 13.	20. 13 AHAU: 1864800, 1992	Complete Transformation

0. 1 IMIX: 1872000, 2012   Galactic Synchronization

Looking at the entire baktun as the creative intensification of a particular morphogenetic field as well as the climax of the total wave harmonic commonly known as history, the dialectical action of two qualities colors the whole process. The first is the alchemical impetus to transform matter through the interconnected stages inclusive of scientific revolution, industrial revolution, democratic social revolutions, culminating finally in nuclear action. This is what characterizes the overall movement of the twenty katuns constituting the transformation of matter.

Dialectically counterpointing this overt transformation of the material plane is the overlay of the unified planetary intention: the creation of a coherent terrestrial field of consciousness. This second process is the function mirrored in the AHAU cycles, MEN and LAMAT. It accounts for the tendencies toward global expansion and communication, romanticism, space exploration, and the urge toward a unified global consciousness brought about through a critically inspired necessity for synchronization.

The tension between the qualities—the one of material transformation, the other of a planetary consciousness harmonically attuned—actually represents the climax of the entire 5,125-year historical process. While the tendency toward material transformation functions as the outer morphogenetic sheath producing the current, dominant paradigm of scientific materialism, the counterpointing tendency accounts for the actual paradigm which emerges through the tension—the paradigm of a resonant unified field of planetary consciousness.

This new and culminating planetary paradigm will be apparent by A.D. 1992. Indeed, in reviewing the entire baktun, it should be kept in mind that this baktun is a perfect mirror of the first baktun in that its first and last cycles, 7 IMIX, A.D. 1618-1638, and 13 AHAU, A.D. 1992-2012, are characterized as galactic activation katuns. This means that there is an unbroken interval of 354 years, A.D. 1638-1992, of unrelieved movement toward material transformation, resulting in the seemingly disastrous and dynamically chaotic materialism of global industrial civilization. And yet it is precisely at the climax of matter, A.D. 1987-1992, fateful moment of materialism's full ripeness, that the highest and culminating purpose of the entire historical cycle reveals itself.

In order to better grasp this self-engendered climactic moment that now engulfs the morphogenetic field of scientific materialism and its manifestation as global industrial civilization, let us take a katun-by-katun look at Cycle 13, Baktun 12. In so doing, the coming paradigm will only be the more natural to accept, and the current one the more obvious in its passing. Both are functions not only of the same baktun cycle but of the overall process of synchronization which characterizes the entire 5,200-tun, 5,125-year passage of Earth through the advanced galactic acceleration process. As we shall see, the journey which we have undertaken leads to a far more vast and yet more immediately accessible domain than all of our radio telescopes can encompass. Here, then, begins the narrative of the twenty katuns of Baktun 12.

Cycle 13, Baktun 12: THE TRANSFORMATION OF MATTER

Katun 0: 7 IMIX. Galactic Activation. Planetary Ruler: Solar Neptune. Stage 7. MEN Cycle. Harmonic Index 1728000. A.D. 1618-1638. *Morphogenetic Pattern Set.*

Katun 0 represents the seventh katun of the MEN Cycle—"To gather whole the mind of Earth." This seventh stage completes the developmental phase of the AHAU overlay cycle. Begun in A.D. 1499, the MEN AHAU Cycle lays the stage for Baktun 12. The period of A.D. 1499-1618, of course, represents the tumultuous period of the European Renaissance—the beginnings of global expansion, the initial impulse toward scientific materialism, the heyday of alchemy, the splitting apart of the Christian church, and the final transformation of the "medieval" mind, dialectically transiting from a paradigm of spiritual hierarchy to one of secular materialism. While this process is most obvious in split-Christianity, its effects are actually global and account for the decadent receptivity which allows European power to spread slowly but ruthlessly over the globe.

As a galactic activation katun, 7 IMIX, represents the powerful focussing of energies that catalyze the scientific materialistic world view. Ruled by the solar Neptunian force, the highlights of this katun include the publication of René Descartes' *Meditations* in 1618, Kepler's *Harmonica Mundi* in 1619, Francis Bacon's *Novum Organum* in 1620 and *New Atlantis* in 1627, Galileo's *Discourse on Two Worlds,* in 1632 , and finally Descartes' epoch-making *Discourse on Method* in 1638. Within a twenty-year span the key tenets and ideas behind the scientific method and revolution are galvanized and set in place. Culturally accompanying this profound ideological event are the triumph of antihierarchical, secular Protestantism, the handmaiden of scientific materialism; the Thirty Years War begun in 1618; the arrival of the Mayflower in 1620; the development of colonial companies by France and England; and just to keep everything straight and accounted for, the invention of the slide rule in 1632 and the adding machine, by Blaise Pascal, in 1637.

Katun 1: 8 IK. Planetary Ruler: Solar Uranus.
Stage 8. MEN Cycle. Harmonic Number 1735200. A.D. 1638-1658.
Morphogenetic Pattern Receives Inspiration.

The underpinnings of the scientific revolution firmly set and secular, acquisitive Protestantism launched, the second katun cycle commences with the self-enforced isolation of the Japanese, who, having taken some European ideas, prepare for a two-century incubation before bursting forth as one of the global industrial leaders. In China, the fall of the glorious Ming Dynasty (1644) and the rise of the Manchurian Ching Dynasty, the last of the great Imperial Chinese dynasties, assures that Chinese civilization will remain tradition-bound until well after the initiation of the Industrial Revolution.

In competition with the Iroquois League of Nations, the Protestant foothold in North America continues to take root, while Latin America, under the vassalage of Spain and Portugal, is already sprouting a genuinely Colonial culture. The whole "New World" is ironically being fed by the Benin Empire in Africa, which provides collusion with slave-trading European interests. The Mughal Dynasty in India and the Ottoman Empire in the Middle East mark the late stages of the medieval Islamic world. In Europe, the dichotomous mind-matter, atomistic tenets of scientific materialism receive further inspiration from the pen of Thomas Hobbes. His *Leviathan* (1651) discourses on man's natural selfishness, a necessary foundation for capitalism, while his *De Corpore* (1655) describes a void universe through which particles move blindly. Musically, the new universe of coordinate geometry and mathematically predictable particles is reflected in the development of the fugue.

Katun 2: 9 AKBAL. Planetary Ruler: Solar Saturn.
Stage 9. MEN cycle. Harmonic Number 1742400. A.D. 1658-1677.
Morphogenetic Pattern Receives Consecration.

It is through the genius of Sir Isaac Newton that the new field receives its full consecration. 1664-1666 is the period of Newton's research on the law of gravity—a must for a materialist paradigm—followed in 1666 by his work on the spectrum and optics and in 1671 by his invention of the reflecting telescope. The culminating consecration of the new morphogenetic field is the establishment of Greenwich Observatory in 1675, establishing the present uniform planetary time zones and meridians. In the same year, 1675, Roemer calculates the speed of light and, building on coordinate geometry, both Newton and Leibnitz develop modern calculus. Leibnitz is the first major European to be impressed by the I Ching and its binary mathematics, to which he was introduced by Jesuit missionaries returning from China.

While the British expand their seagoing supremacy farther into America and India, several notable emperors appear on the scene, including Kang Hsi of China, 1662-1722, and Louis XIV of France 1661-1714. While Versailles expresses the new secular rationalism on a grand scale, Kang Hsi powerfully consolidates the essense of conservative Chinese civilization in the Forbidden City, Beijing.

Katun 3: 10 KAN. Planetary Ruler: Solar Jupiter.
Stage 10. MEN Cycle. Harmonic Number1749600. A.D. 1677-1697.
Morphogenetic Pattern Seeds Daily Life.

While the refinements of Dutch realist painting triumph as the visual norm of the new Protestant merchant class in Europe, the isolationist Edo (Tokyo) Dynasty of Japan foments and furthers its new merchant class. In Russia, Peter the Great turns Russian interests to greater attunement with those of colonially expanding Western Europe. The climactic text of Sir Isaac Newton's *Principia Mathematica* is published in 1687, establishing as dogma the underlying tenets of the new scientific paradigm, i.e., that science deals with "observed regularities" that apply throughout a universe that runs like a clock. The staples of this mechanistic point of view lie in the laws of motion and gravity. By 1696, these principles give birth to the first steam engine.

In the New England colonies of North America, the Salem witch trials offer a Protestant counterpoint to the Inquisition in Spain; both reinforce the male rationalistic conquistador/puritan mind-set of the new, scientifically materialistic, morphogenetic field.

Katun 4: 11 CHICCHAN. Planetary Ruler: Solar Asteroid Belt.
Stage 11. MEN Cycle. Harmonic Index: 1756800. A.D. 1697-1717.
Morphogenetic Pattern Becomes Secondary Instinct.

The rigidly mathematical principles of scientific materialism having been worked out and enunciated and the globe being rapidly colonized under a uniform standard of time, measurement, and acquisitive material need, this katun sees the great expansion of the British slave trade with the Benin of West Africa and the rise of the Sikhs in India as a hybrid amalgam of Hindu and Islamic influences. 1697 also marks the final defeat and subjugation of the last of the feudal Maya in Central America. The application of the principles of scientific materialism produced the first iron-smelting mill in 1711, thus readying the way for heavy industrialization.

The publication of Newton's *Opticks*, in 1704, is followed in 1705 by Halley's confirmation of the 76-year periodicity of the comet named after him. The next return, in 1781, is to be marked by the discovery of the first "modern" planet, Uranus.

Katun 5: 12 CIMI. Planetary Ruler: Solar Mars.
Stage 12. MEN Cycle. Harmonic Index: 17640000. A.D. 1717-1736.
Morphogenetic Pattern as Base of Revelation.

As the British imperial hold in India grows stronger with trading concessions wrested from the Mughals in 1717, the development of silk machines and the beginnings of coal mining back home augur the initiation of the Industrial Revolution. In 1720, the Manchu Dynasty of China spreads its influence into Tibet, which, nonetheless, continues to remain isolated from the winds of change swirling through most of the rest of the world. Tibet remains the only major hierarchical center to hold to principles, stemming from the preceding morphogenetic field, until its collapse in 1959.

To supplement and expand the authority of the new scientific vision, thinkers like Voltaire and Ben Franklin are some of the first exponents of what comes to be called the "Enlightenment," the philosophical revelation and artistic expression that accompanies the ascendency of a secular rationalist world view. The triumph of rationalism notwithstanding, Franklin becomes the first Grand Master of the Masonic Order in North America in 1733.

Katun 6: 13 MANIK. Planetary ruler: Solar Earth.
Culminating Stage 13. MEN Cycle. Harmonic Index: 1771200. A.D. 1736-1756.
Morphogenetic Pattern Establishes Skill Base.

With the full deployment of coal mining and related crucible metal for steel smelting as well as textile technologies, Newton's England becomes the first base of industrial world civilization. This fact, coupled with England's unchallenged global naval and military power, assures that industrialism is to be the base for the development of a planetary civilization—the prerequisite for the attainment of a genuine planetary mind and consciousness. Attending this development, urbanization of the world also commences with increasing numbers of traditional rural folk pulling up their roots and resettling in the industrial slums of the great cities.

In France, in 1751, the group known as the Encyclopedists produce the first edition of the Great Encyclopedia, the prototype of all modern rationalist encyclopedias. In 1755, however, the great Lisbon earthquake stuns the minds of the optimistic rationalists, for Earth, excluded from the provinces of life and rationalism, can only produce irrational effects.

END OF 19TH AHAU CYCLE—BEGINNING OF 20TH AHAU CYCLE
To Seed the Whole with Star-Seed Harmony

Katun 7: 1 LAMAT. Planetary Ruler: Solar Venus.
Stage 1. LAMAT Cycle. Harmonic Index: 1778400. A.D. 1756-1776.
Morphogenetic Pattern Realized as Cosmic Law.

The ground having been established for the possibility of a unified global civilization, the start of the twentieth and final AHAU cycle of the 5,125-year Great Cycle is powerfully initiated by developments not only in the technological field—Watts' steam engine and carbon dioxide—but even more definitively in the economic and political arena. The new technologies and world view demand systems of governance commensurate to them. And so laissez-faire capitalistic economic thinking is born at this point, as well as industrial democracy, with its unprecedented socio-political structures that supercede the agrarian monarchies. The Lunar Society in England, as well as the Masons and Free Thinkers in America and Europe, forge ahead in pioneering new ways of assuring the spread of the new thought and technology. Borrowing from the Iroquois Federation, the Declaration of Independence, and the beginnings of the American Revolution inaugurate the next critical phase of the transformation of human society and of the material bases of the Earth itself.

Katun 8: 2 MULUC. Planetary Ruler: Solar Mercury.
Stage 2. LAMAT Cycle. Harmonic Index: 1785600. A.D. 1776-1796.
Morphogenetic Pattern Established as Principle of Communication.

Completed with the Constitution in 1787, the American Revolution establishes the model for overthrowing the old and asserting democratic power. In 1789, France follows suit with the first overthrowing of established monarchy. In England, *The Times* newspaper begins printing in 1788, establishing the norm for communication in the new industrial world.

In addition to hot-air balloons in 1783 and the great expansion of the cotton industry during the 1780s, in 1789 Lavoisier establishes the critical, rationalist principles of modern chemistry. As the crowning achievement of the era, in 1781 Herschel discovers the planet Uranus, the first "modern" planet, whose symbolic attributes include rulership over electricity and revolution. Finally, in 1795, Hutton wrote his *Theory of the Earth* establishing the modern science of geology.

In the meantime, artists like William Blake in England and the Japanese woodblock artists of Tokyo begin to find new forms of expression to articulate the wonder and psychic dimensions of the new secular order. In Germany, composers like Beethoven and writers like Goethe and Novalis herald the dawning of Romanticism as the artistic expression of the Industrial Age.

END OF SOLAR INHALATION CYCLE—COMMENCEMENT OF SOLAR EXHALATION CYCLE

Katun 9: 3 OC. Plantary ruler: Lunar Mercury.
Stage 3. LAMAT Cycle. Harmonic Index: 1792800. A.D. 1796-1815
Morphogenetic Pattern Established as Social Principle.

With the settling down of the new American democratic society and its turn toward a banking/industrialist economy—that of the Hamiltonians—the concept of wars for independence spreads to colonial areas of Latin America. By 1811, the Latin American wars for independence are being fanned by democratic liberationists, Hidalgo, Marti, and Bolivar. Such wars notwithstanding, the United States of America inaugurates its cross-continental neo-imperialist push with the purchase of the Louisiana Territory in 1803. The War of 1812 between the U.S. and Great Britain proves America as a power to be reckoned with. In Europe, Napoleon emerges from the French Revolution as the first of the modern egotists, spreading his vision of liberation across Europe in a series of devastating wars.

Scientific and technological improvements during this period include vaccination in

1796, the discovery of the Asteroid Belt in 1801-02, and the railroad locomotive in 1804, the latter assuring the first new form of industrial transportation. Lithography emerges as a rapid means of graphic communication for the new communication form, newspapers. The romantic vision of the nocturn—the powerful repose of night—in painting, poetry, and in music seems altogether fitting as the cycle of galactic energy for the baktun enters its ten-katun lunar exhalation phase.

Katun 10: 4 CHUEN. Planetary ruler: Lunar Venus.
Stage 4. LAMAT Cycle. Harmonic Index: 1800000. A.D. 1815-1835.
Morphogenetic Pattern Established as Dominant Artistic Vision.

The romantic temper, already fired by the contradictory forces of popular revolution and revulsion against the irreversible tide of material progress with its pitting of individuality against mysticism, and represented by geniuses like Goya, Blake, Beethoven, and Goethe becomes the stylistic norm. In Japan, which is cultivating its own secular mercantile society, this trend is reflected in the work of artists like Hiroshige and Hokusai. By this time, the Industrial Revolution is an established fact. The new industrial towns spread across England, the nostalgia for the medieval era, the romantic rallying point of the Greek War for Independence, the Populist Revolution in France in 1830, and the development of industrial architecture all spur the romantic, artistic imagination. In anticipation of the needs of the new urbanized society, scientific research in electricity continues apace; Ampere and Ohm develop the theory of electrical currents, while the elements of photography are being worked out by early pioneers.

Katun 11: 5 EB. Planetary Ruler: Lunar Earth.
Stage 5. LAMAT Cycle. Harmonic Index: 1807200. A.D. 1835-1855.
Morphogenetic Pattern Experienced as Inescapable Human Nature.

The socio-economic foundations of the global industrial order fully established, this stage represents a fitful step into advanced materialism exemplified by European imperialist expansion, as well as the carrying out of the American doctrine of Manifest Destiny and the Mexican-American War. The great Chinese empire is finally opened up for European exploitation, and despite the Taipei rebellion, through concerted efforts Europe maintains the upper hand. The development of Morse code and the telegraph as well as the emergence of photography assure the continuing acceleration of popular means of communication, thus establishing the notion of "mass media."

The discovery of Neptune, planet of the collective unconscious, in 1844; the emergence of the Ba'hai in Persia; and the philosophy of Karl Marx in Europe announce the potential for non-imperialist globalist visions. The revolutions of 1848 highlight the friction caused by the rapid spread of new technologies—the sewing machine, concrete, anesthesia—and their incapacity to be accommodated by proper social planning. In 1851, the first world's fair/technological exhibition hall opens in London, and Foucault demonstrates the rotation of the Earth.

Katun 12: 6 BEN. Planetary Ruler: Lunar Mars.
Stage 6. LAMAT Cycle. Harmonic Index: 1814400. A.D. 1855-1874.
Morphogenetic Pattern Reaches Full Maturation of Cyclic Path.

During this period, the tenets and principles put forth in the very first katun of this baktun attain to a level of unprecedented material power and expansion. Under Queen Victoria, England gains control over India, and in the same year, 1858, China fully becomes the pawn of European interests. In 1864, Japan opens itself to the West, while the 1867 Meiji Restoration assures that Japan is to pursue a course of rapid industrialization.

1855 marks the first development of synthetic plastics and celluloid, followed by the emergence of Bessemer Steel furnaces, dynamite, the typewriter, and conclusive experiments in electricity and the theory of electromagnetism. Materialist science also triumphs with Darwin's *Origin of the Species* in 1859, and Mendel's genetic theory in 1865. The rise and spread of Russian imperialism is countered in North America by the American Civil War, which, finally, is the leverage to open all of America to industrialization. The completion of the European rail system in 1870, the Franco-Prussian War in 1871, and the impact of photography upon popular art set the stage for Impressionist painting and intensified individual experimentation in art.

Katun 13: 7 IX. Planetary Ruler: Lunar Asteroid Belt.
Stage 7. LAMAT Cycle. Harmonic Index: 1821600. A.D. 1874-1894.
Self-Transcendence of Established Morphogenetic Pattern Begins.

Here, with the mystic seventh stage of the LAMAT Cycle corresponding to IX, the sign of the Sorceror, deeper invisible forces begin to subtly reshape the dialectics of the morphogenetic field. This era marks the dawning of "Modernist" culture; the work of the great electrical geniuses Tesla and Edison, the electrical technologies of light, telephone, and phonograph, the emergence of motor transport and the machine gun in 1885, advances in steel engineering, and the building of the Brooklyn Bridge, Statue of Liberty, and the Eiffel Tower are counterpointed by the teachings of Ramakrishna and Madame Blavatsky. The Chicago World's Fair and World Council of Religions in 1893 represent further openings toward global consciousness. At the same time, labor problems, strikes, the philosophy of anarchy and terrorism, and the final defeat of the American Indian in 1891 following the rise of the Ghost Dance religion further entrench and dispose the industrial powers toward policies of coercion and colonialist repression.

Katun 14: 8 MEN. Planetary Ruler: Lunar Jupiter.
Stage 8. LAMAT Cycle. Harmonic Index: 1828800. A.D. 1894-1914.
Higher Principles of Morphogenetic Pattern Pervade the Field of Thought.

Here we have the full emergence of Modernist culture: skyscrapers; cinema; X-rays; airplanes; automobiles; and the theories of radiation, the electron and proton, relativity, quantum theory, continental drift, and psychoanalysis—all elements pointing to unprecedented accelerated change and, ultimately, the foundations of a non-materialist world view. The 1894-95 Sino-Japanese War, followed by the 1906 Japanese-Russian War establish Japan's industrial and military power in the Western Pacific basin. In 1911, Sun Yat Sen seeks to rehabilitate and "modernize" China.

The final collapse of the Benin Empire in West Africa in the 1890s seals the bondage of Africa to European powers, leaving only the stagnant Ottoman Empire as the last outpost of non-industrialized, non-colonialized world civilization. Yet, despite rapidly advancing levels of material progress and scientific knowledge, the contradictory forces within the field precipitate what is to become known as World War I, "the war to end all wars."

Katun 15: 9 CIB. Planetary Ruler: Lunar Saturn
Stage 9. LAMAT Cycle. Harmonic Index: 1836000. A.D. 1914-1933.
Galactic Impulse Toward New Cycle Is Felt.

Accompanying the devastating effects of World War I, the Bolshevik Revolution in Russia, the subsequent conservative fascist re-entrenchments in Europe, and the economic collapse of 1929 are the initial developments in atomic theory and technology, including the Geiger Counter and cyclotron, the development of the Big Bang theory in 1927, and the discovery of neutrons in 1932. Technologically, the field of mass communications is greatly assisted by the development of radio and the "talking" movies. Clearly, during this era, global industrial civilization is at a crossroads. Grave questions concerning relentless industrialization are raised by the growing economic crisis. Gandhi in India and Roerich worldwide through the Pax Cultura movement articulate visions that question and go beyond industrialism.

The 1930-31 discovery of Pluto, ruler of the underworld and transformation, however, augurs the continuing drift into deeper levels of materialism and, ultimately, the transformation of matter itself. Complementing the crisis of industrial civilization are the first impulses toward a holistic world view, Jan Smuts', *Holism and Evolution* (1924), Buckminster Fuller's synergistic philosophy, Walter Russell's synthesizing wave principles in *The Universal One* (1927), and Carl Jung's comprehensive psychology of the unconscious.

Katun 16: 10 CABAN. Planetary Ruler: Lunar Uranus
Stage 10. LAMAT Cycle. Harmonic Index: 1843200. A.D. 1933-1953.
Morphogenetic Pattern Attains Climax of Power.

There is no question that events during this Katun mark the most irreversible moments of the entire baktun, sealing the destiny of the remainder of the cycle. The economic collapse and depression of world capitalism is artificially overcome by the turn to a war economy of unprecedented magnitude. Though catalyzed by the fascist revisionists, World War II and its ultimate instrument, the atomic bomb, is no surprise. Einstein first advised Roosevelt concerning the Bomb in 1939, the same year that radar was invented.

The development of plutonium, the first artificial element, in 1940, followed by the first nuclear reaction in 1942, the Manhattan Project in 1944, and the detonation of the first atomic bomb in 1945 are the critical stages sealing the destiny of the planet. After the bombings of Hiroshima and Nagasaki and the conclusion of World War II, military research becomes the paramount factor in the economy of the most powerful nations, the USA and USSR. Coincidentally, in 1947, the US Air Force begins its Blue Book study and investigation of UFOs and Britain attains nuclear power. This is followed in 1948 by Russian nuclear power and the U.S. counter-development of the H-bomb, thus inaugurating the arms race. The trend toward total war is offset by the founding of the still-to-be-fully-utilized globalist organization, the United Nations. Global radio is supplemented by television in 1948, thus assuring the implementation of a philosophy of consumerism to maintain the acquisitive mind-set and economy of the Western industrialized nations.

Katun 17: 11 ETZNAB. Planetary Ruler: Lunar Neptune.
Stage 11. LAMAT Cycle. Harmonic Index: 1850400. A.D. 1953-1973.
Morphogenetic Pattern Shows Beginning of Dissipative Structures.

With the atomic-fueled Cold War as a backdrop, this era is initiated by the powerful discoveries of DNA (1953), the Van Allen radiation belts (1958), and tectonic plates (1964). The new information technologies are established with the emergence of computers in 1955, while the space age is launched with Sputnik in 1957, the first manned space flight in 1961, the first Moon landing in 1969, and the first Earth satellites and launching of planetary space probes in 1971. Providing context for these events was the introduction of Teilhard de Chardin's concept of Earth's mental envelope, the *noosphere,* in 1955, and Oliver Reiser's Psi Field in 1966.

In the meantime, led by Japanese technology, the cultural ferment of global industrial civilization is triggered by the spread of Asian philosophies—Zen, Hinduism, and Tibetan Buddhism—and the emergence of popular electronic culture—rock-n-roll—in 1956, which becomes a global phenomenon with the emergence of the Beatles in 1964. The war in Vietnam, a popular anti-war movement, the civil rights movement, the rise of Third World powers, and the spreading prevalence of psychedelics and other drugs also contribute to the dissipation of traditional structures in the global industrial field. Student riots in Europe, Mexico, and the Eastern bloc countries complement the unrest of the Chinese Cultural Revolution.

The emergence of the ecology movement in 1970, signals the first popular response to the deteriorating condition of the environment due to industrial abuse. This is countered in 1971 by the world's largest underground H-Bomb test, the Amchitka blast which detonated the equivalent of ten billion tons of TNT, 6,000 feet beneath the sea off Amchitka Island in the North Pacific Aleutians.

Katun 18: 12 CAUAC. Planetary Ruler: Lunar Pluto.
Stage 12. LAMAT Cycle. Harmonic Index: 1857600. A.D. 1973-1992.
Morphogenetic Patterns Reach Maximum Entropy—Begin Transformation.

The development of oil politics (OPEC), marked by continuing war in the Middle East, the emergence of global terrorism, and the entrenchment of the superpowers in

MAD (Mutual Assured Deterence) nuclear policies, augur the final stalemate and collapse of petrochemical and armament-dependent world economy. The entropic disintegration of global industrial civilization is accompanied by space exploration which sees probes of Venus in 1975, Mars in 1976, Jupiter in 1981, Saturn in 1983, Uranus in 1986, Neptune in 1989, and Pluto in 1992; the rise of sophisticated global communications systems; and the decisive seismic and volcanic shifting of the Pacific tectonic plate through the 1970s and 1980s.

Culminating in the globally chaotic and irrevocably transformative events of 1987-92, including the resonant frequency shift of 1987, the concurrent collapse or regrouping of the major governments, and the emergence of the resonant field paradigm and a corresponding unified global communications network operating with bio-regional command bases, this era is pivotal in preparing for the conclusion not only of the baktun but of the entire 5,200-tun synchronization beam. During this era—the storm of transformation—the entire wave of history crests. Maximum acceleration and random entropy give way to ever-widening circles of synchronization.

END OF 10-KATUN, LUNAR-GALACTIC EXHALATION CYCLE—COMMENCEMENT OF SOLAR INHALATION CYCLE

Katun 19: 13 AHAU. Galactic Activation Planetary Ruler: Solar Pluto
Stage 12. LAMAT Cycle. Harmonic Index: 1864800. A.D. 1992-2012.
Morphogenetic Pattern Completes Self-Transformation.

As the 260th katun of the entire great cycle, the 52nd and last galactic activation cycle, as well as the first such galactic activation cycle since the inauguration of the scientific materialist philosophy in 1618-1638, this katun marks the final transformation and reversal of the total field. The emergence of non-materialistic, ecologically harmonic technologies, long-prepared-for by thinkers like Tesla, Fuller, and Russell, to complement the new decentralized mediarchy information society, and the understanding of the resonant relation of psychic and solar force fields and their effects on the understanding of health and disease are the chief illuminating contributions of this era.

The mobilization of global social forces for demilitarization and deindustrialization, though hampered by reactionary elements including the rise of China, are nonetheless successful by the time the cycle closes in A.D. 2012. At this point, the synchronization process of the entire Great Cycle reaches new peaks and the globalization of human society takes unprecedented turns toward galactic attunement.

The closing of the cycle is marked by a festive climate, a synchronization of mythic forms, and a tone of spiritual regeneration hitherto unknown in the historical phase. Signalled as the Mayan Return, the Mayan Factor provides the final touch as the planet attains conscious articulation of its light body, thus entering its next evolutionary stage and assuring thereby that the galactic community receives a new member.

0. 1. IMIX. Harmonic index: 1872000 A.D. 2012. 13.0.0.0.0.
Galactic Synchronization—Synchronization with the Beyond

To speak of galactic synchronization, synchronization with the beyond, is to surpass all fantasy and all of our wildest dreams. ETs, UFOs, the "space brothers"—these are not alien entities, but emanations of *being* itself. And being is, in its essence, light, radiant energy. From light we come and to light we shall return. During the time that we have spun our historical tale, we have been participating in the unfoldment of a larger being. But by the very nature of the phase of the 5,125-year/5,200-tun galactic synchronization beam in which we have been involved, we have lost sight of this fact.

Spun through the increasingly accelerated phases of the thirteen cycles of this beam, our planet has arrived at an advanced stage of conscious synchronization of component elements. This has been brought about by the most complex forms of DNA, inducing an artificial leap—the sprawl of civilization—which in actuality has had but one goal—the quickening and transformation of matter. This is the critical significance of the thirteenth cycle, Baktun 12, A.D. 1618-2012.

Once this critical transformation of matter was attained on July 16, 1945, two basic processes were set in motion. One involved the materialist aggrandizement of power represented by the entrenchment of the prevalent global industrial-social order; the other involved the dissonant quickening of the resonant field of the planet resulting in a wide spectrum of effects from UFO sightings and increased psychism to tectonic plate shifts and terrorism.

The reason for the intense subjective effects experienced by the human psyche lies in the overall impact of radioactivity and electromagnetic pollution on the infrastructure of DNA, causing increased randomness and entropy of behavior. But this response of DNA experienced as socially disruptive behavior in the human realm, inclusive of rises in the incidence of cancer and new diseases like AIDS, is actually only a complement of what is occurring in the larger host organism, Earth.

The resonant body of Earth, the vibratory infrastructure that literally holds together the sense-perceptible body of Earth, is in a condition of intense "fever" called resonant dissonance. Remembering that the planets function as gyroscopes holding the frequency pattern of their particular orbits, we see that environmentally impactful events since 1945 have actually set in motion a dissonant vibratory wave affecting the overall spin of the planet. If the dissonance is not checked, then, similar to an uncontrolled nuclear reaction, the end-result would be the development of a wobble in the spin and a consequent shattering of the planetary form. The Earth could be broken up into smaller bodies not unlike the Asteroid belt.

In order to accommodate the increased dissonance of frequency, wave adjustments are set off at the crystal core of the Earth until a new harmonic resonance of slightly higher frequency is attained, thus accommodating the dissonance and stabilizing at a new level

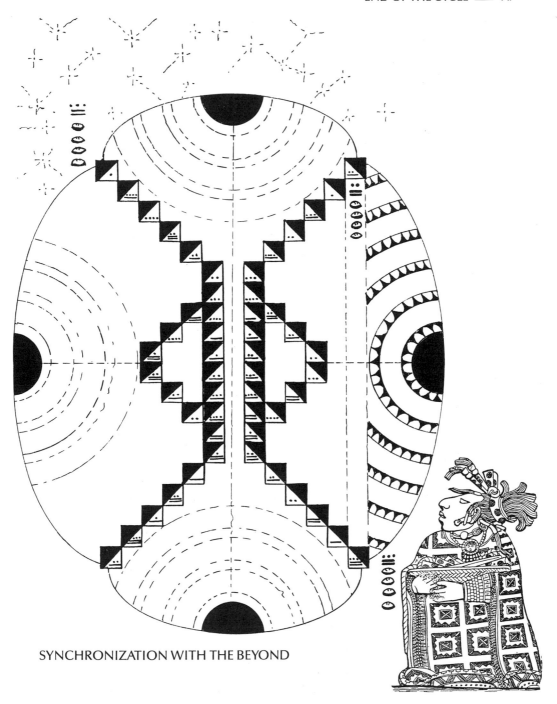

SYNCHRONIZATION WITH THE BEYOND

of resonance. If this new level of resonance can be attained before further destructive impacts are inflicted upon the planetary field—whether as increased carbon dioxide or further nuclear testing—then the planet will have successfully charted the 5,200-tun synchronization beam.

As can be seen, the acceleration of DNA through this beam is played out to the very last possible moment before a critical synchronization occurs. This synchronization, taking place at the peak of maximum acceleration and dissonant entropy, requires the interface of the infrastructure of DNA with the vibratory accommodations occurring through the self-organizing and self-healing processes of the Earth as a whole field.

To talk about the interface of the infrastructure of DNA with the vibratory accommodations of the Earth is to evoke the purified spiritual intentions of a synchronized collective of human beings who understand that their responsibility to the planet is taking precedence over all other allegiances and concerns at this particular time. Such an evocation is in the nature of a planetary mystery, a rite of passage that synergizes hitherto scarcely suspected force-fields into radiant manifestation. This is what is meant by "harmonic convergence" occurring at 1863022 and 1863023, August 16-17, 1987. Through such an event, the Armageddon script is short-circuited, yet the possibility of a New Heaven and a New Earth is fully present.

It must be kept in mind that from the perspective of the Mayan Factor, the acceleration of activity climaxing in the thirteenth cycle, Baktun 12, is but a phase in the larger playing out of the galactic resonant field. The 64-code-word field of DNA—the factor that is quickened and synchronized during passage through the 5,200-tun synchronization beam—is but the central parcel in a resonant plot of frequencies whose code form is 260 units. At this point in our densification into matter, not only have we lost sight of the total DNA field of which we are operants, but even more have we forgotten the larger matrix, the galactic harmonic module which completely enfolds us.

To understand even better the cathartic moment that now engulfs our entire being upon this planet, let us turn to a consideration of technology and transformation. For if it is the purpose of the Mayan Factor to lead us to the path beyond technology, it is also its purpose to transit us through the eye of the hurricane, the transformation of matter which technology has induced. To pass through the eye of the hurricane is to engage the counter-spin transcending history, the return ride on the Zuvuya of timelessness whose harmonic waves concentrically radiate from beginninglessness to endlessness—the single source, the always-now of being.

7

TECHNOLOGY & TRANSFORMATION

Maskull: ". . . but one thing puzzles me."

Panawe: "What's that?"

Maskull: "How it happens that men here are ignorant of tools and arts, and have no civilization and yet contrive to be social in their habits and wise in their thoughts."

Panawe: "Do you imagine then that love and wisdom spring from tools? But I see how it arises. In your world you have fewer sense organs, and to make up for the deficiency you have been obliged to call in the assistance of stones and metals. That is by no means a sign of superiority."

The conversation between Maskull, an Earthling, and Panawe, an Arcturian, in John Lindsay's fictional fantasy, *Voyage from Arcturus,* underscores the debate concerning the nature and purpose of technology, commonly understood as the material extension of our body and sense organs. What we think of as history or as historical progress is virtually synonymous with the history of technology. The same could be said of civilization. Indeed, the tendency is to view the improvement of creature comforts via some form of technology as the index of civilized life. A dangerous and subtle materialism is implicit in this definition of things. But what relation does technological improvement have to genuine creativity, or, for that matter, spirituality?

On the one hand, this line of thought places us in the untenable position of proclaiming the superiority of suburban automobile and television existence to that of the aborigine in the outback, daubed with ochre and cinnabar and chanting ageless resonances to the still-living rocks. Of course, it is heretical to voice the thought that the sensory awakedness of the aborigine is preferable to twentieth-century technological comfort, which, in actuality, is a closing off of the sense fields and a narrowing of the perceptions we have of life. Indeed, is it possible that the trap of technological development lies in our creating an environment in which all we receive is the limited frequency feedback of our own artificially devised improvements? What if the trap of civilization is a sensory shutdown that gravely impairs our ability to receive fresh information?

This situation would be compounded if the seductive frame of artificially induced environments might also condition our ability to appreciate new sensory input. We might then find the predicament of the collective human organism to be akin to that of a caged animal suffocating on the toxic residue of its own waste products. Indeed, when we survey the reality of the world at the present moment, this description seems á *propos*.

These considerations, however, still beg the question: what is technology? If it is so potentially disturbing to ourselves and our host environment, planet Earth, why did we develop technology in the first place?

To answer this question, and to recall the subtitle of this book—*Path Beyond Technology*—it is necessary to put forth a very simple equation:

Pre-History = Pre-Technological
History = Technological
Post-History = Post-Technological

In this equation, the Mayan Factor accounts not only for a comprehensive description of the middle term of the equation, but also for the relation between the first and third terms, the pre- and post- conditions of history/technology. From the perspective of the Mayan Factor, history, the exponential spread of communication in the form of material technology, is contained by and a function of the 5,200 to 5,125-year-diameter galactic synchronization beam. Indeed, technology as we now understand and define it could be described literally as a tool of the synchronization beam.

Technology, then, is a direct measure of the acceleration and synchronization of DNA in relation to the manifestation of the light body of the planet. This means that coincident to the increase in technological application and its feedback is a commensurate quickening of the DNA infrastructure. This quickening of the DNA infrastructure is paralleled by the activation of the planet light body, a process that remains imperceptible until the virtual conclusion of the acceleration process.

Through the first 12 baktun cycles the acceleration gradually increases, becoming dramatic in the final baktun cycle and climaxing in the 259th katun. Synchronization becomes stabilized only in the 260th katun, the final cycle. An index of the exponential climax of the acceleration process is the increase in human birth. The birth of the five billionth human was heralded on July 7, 1986. Yet it was only twelve years ago that the human population reached four billion.

Prior to entry into the sychronization beam in "pre-history," the human organism by and large remained in a symbiotic relation with the environment. Fire and chipped stone aside, it was agriculture that hastened the technological imperative that was to be quickened by the beam. As we entered the beam, the tendencies toward material improvement, task specialization, social stratification, and territorial expansion became affirmed as the dominant evolutionary impetus. The view of nature ultimately affirmed by history is anything but symbiotic, rather, it is that of master and slave.

As the rate of technological innovation increases through the 5,125-year cycle, so the human organism spreads its vast artificial communications and social systems in a tighter web over the surface of the planet. For several millenia, despite less technologically advanced barbarian populations that inhabited its border regions, civilization defined itself by the acquisition of fresh territory. By the onset of global industrial civilization, horizons began to dim. Yet, just beyond the self-destructive, artificial grandeur of global industrial civilization is the attainment of the goal: a condition in which acceleration of change phases into synchronization of wholeness.

Assuming the capacity to attain critical synchronization prior to environmental self-destruction—the Armageddon bypass—then we may enter the 260th katun in A.D. 1992-2012. Ruled by the exalted thirteenth pulsation-ray and marked by the sign AHAU, presence of the solar mind, this katun cycle will initiate the ascendance to the post-historic and hence post-technological condition in which the human organism "returns" to its symbiotic harmony with nature.

In no way should this return be seen as an abandonment of civilization, understood as the process of human spiritual refinement, but rather as a passing to a more evolved stage of our existence. Lest this view be construed as a neo-romantic utopian fantasy, let us review the relation of the wave harmonic of history to the galactic harmonic and consider the fundamental postulate of the Mayan Factor: what light is to life, so the 260-unit Tzolkin is to the 64-unit DNA.

This postulate defines *radiogenesis*: *radio* refers to the information-bearing capacity of light and all spectral-radiant energy; *genesis* to the capacity of light to transform itself

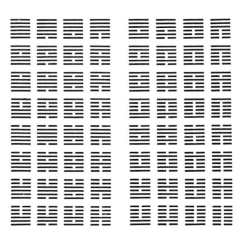

TZOLKIN SHOWING PLACE
OF 64-UNIT DNA CODE

into the palpably plasmic and mobile phenomenon called life. From the perspective of the Mayan Factor, the relation between light and life is not a linear, causal one—i.e. first there is light, then there is life—but one in which life is embedded in a matrix of radiant energy possibilities. This is literally depicted in the Tzolkin, where the 64 units representing the DNA code occupy the central grid corresponding to the 32 units on either side of the mystic column accommodating the Loom of Maya in its crossover pattern.

Let us assume that the remaining units around the central 64-unit grid represent stages of light and radiant energy unfoldment that simultaneously precede, follow, and at the same time interpenetrate the evolution of DNA. Since the 64-unit gameboard of DNA is contained within the larger radiogenetic gameboard of the Tzolkin, we may consider that DNA itself is a bridge from one domain of light or radiant energy to another. By fractal analogy, the stage called history, through technological acceleration, mimics this function of DNA as a link between two radiant realms. In the radiogenetic proposition, the term "history" represents an intensification of the capacity of DNA to artificially (technologically) bridge and hence leap from one level of radiant symbiotic understanding and fulfillment—pre-history—to another—post-history.

Allowing fractal harmonics their full play, the stage of accelerating technological leapfrog can be plotted within the 64 central units of the Tzolkin, the whole of which is understood as a representation of the entire radiogenetic gameboard. During passage through the 5,200-tun beam, it is as if the technology-extruding DNA is completing a circuit through the 64 central units of the gameboard. Though it is not apparent until the circuit is complete, once the 64 units have been traversed, the whole game board—let us say—lights up. The lighting up of the game board refers to the final circuit-completing synchronization of DNA, corresponding to the date A.D. 2012, 13.0.0.0.0. Enter post-history!

A further distinction between the technological middle and the pre- and post-phases is the distinction between *myth* and *history* understood as qualitative conditions of consciousness. Myth defines the capacity for simultaneous, multi-referential resonance that merges being with being; history is the tendency to limit, measure, and materialize in a uni-referential direction that separates being from being.

From the perspective of myth, the rays of light slanting through the leaves in the forest are the nourishing fingers of the dawn bringing solar morsels to our waiting cells. A response to the light in the form of a chant and an offering of smoke from a circle of stones, inviting the presence of ancestor beings and the great ones who guide all things, completes the experience. To the historic consciousness, in contrast, the light slanting through the trees, though representing a mystery to some, tells us that another day has arrived, and, depending on our needs and interests, whether or not we will need a coat and hat—whether or not it will be a good day for sunbathing.

In other words, the mythic condition constructs from the experience a sacrament or ritual that affirms the bond between light and the greater forces, ultimately the forces of light. The historic mind uses the experience as information that determines practical creature-comfort goals. However, the creature-comfort-seeking aspect of historic consciousness is in actuality the feedback effect of the impulse of DNA to extrude technology. Hence historic consciousness is but a by-product of the larger technological bridging process, moving us from one natural symbiosis to another—from one realm of light to another.

To gain an even deeper level of understanding, let us put forth one more equation: Myth = DNA × Light. In this equation, myth or the mythic condition is the self-sustaining capacity of DNA to directly utilize light—the spectrum of radiant energy—to attain its ends. In the mythic condition, therefore, the psychic resonance between organism and radiant energy is direct and provides both primary nurturance and primary reality. This resonance is dependent upon and intensifies a superior sensory capacity for radiant interactiveness. The experience of the senses—eyes, ears, nose, tongue, body—is not only primary, but attuned to nuances that both convey information and expand delight. In this condition, the need for artificial inducements to pleasure become obstructions to the untrammeled purity of sensory experience *per se*.

History and the historic condition, by contrast, represent the counter-spin capacity for DNA to artificially maximize its potential in relation to the totality of its host body, the planet, in our case, Earth. This accounts for the extrusion of technology—artificial extensions of the sense organs—to facilitate completion of the larger DNA circuit.

Naturally, to the individual cells of the larger organism, humankind, the greater purpose of the DNA circuit is, at best, dimly perceived. Consequently, most of the individual members tend to rely upon and become addicted to the sensory feedback that depends solely on the artificial technological extensions and environment. For this reason, at the far end of history where we find ourselves today, nature is hard-put to compete with television—in the words of the World War I song, "How can you keep 'em down on the farm after they've seen Paree?"

The historical intensification of DNA, the phase measured, accelerated and synchronized by the 5,200-tun beam, is only a transition. In attaining its goal of total technological relation to the host body, however, there is a shutdown of the sensory receivers, an immersion of the senses in their own artificial feedback loops. If the circuit is to be completed, there is a profound need to reawaken the sense fields to their own natural capacities. As anyone knows, it is no easy thing to break such artificial dependency loops. The immersion of an individual in such loops defines neurotic, addictive behavior; the immersion of a collective organism in such loops defines paradigm paralysis. Herein lies the drama of our times, the tension that accompanies the transformation from acceleration to synchronization. Fortunately, in this difficult process, Earth is a helper.

The critical tension which we are experiencing in our morphogenetic field is due to the inner contradictions of a paradigm bound by its own beliefs. Dominated by a white, male, neo-protestant priesthood defending its scientific "objectivity" through planetary political power plays—this paradigm paralysis is in reality a reflection of the dissonant shifting of the Earth. The technologically extruding DNA intensification called history, culminating in the sensory shutdown that forebodes Armageddon, is paralleled by Earth's own shifting field. We are not the sole authors of our experience, but players in a galactically amplified field whose principle character is Earth herself.

As a harmonic gyroscope holding the third solar orbit, Earth has its own subtle and powerful relationships to maintain within the plasmic field called the solar system. Responsive to the galactic harmonic, the imperceptible shiftings of the Earth interconnect with the shiftings of the other planetary bodies, and above-all, with the Sun itself. Just as the DNA has been quickened in response to the 5,200-tun synchronization beam through which we are passing, so Earth, too, as a whole resonant field is affected.

All the while the human DNA-pack has been asserting its capacity for artificially rearranging the environment according to its presumed needs, Earth has been experiencing a parallel development. Unwittingly, however, as the believers in the dominant paradigm have intensified their own materially limited and mechanistically contrived understanding of things, the resonant ripening of the Earth has increasingly escaped the attention of the ruling mentality. But this is of little matter, for consciously or unconsciously, all member organisms of Earth have been crafting the planetary light body. The passage through the 5,200-tun synchronization beam has been the culminating moment thus far of Gaia's galactic journey from primal solar spin-off to radiantly conscious light body. Little do subordinate humans realize how close they are to the moment when the genetic game board of their reality becomes the illumined design of galactic destiny.

Here is a picture of what has been happening. Slowly, over the aeons, at Earth's core, the iron crystal lodestone of her harmonic gyroscope has been emanating the resonant frequencies that keep it in orbit. These resonant frequencies have a particular shape or form, for form follows frequency. This is why Plato described the Earth as being like a leather ball sewn together from twelve different pieces, creating a dodecahedron or twelve interfaced pentagons. The vertices between the twelve pentagonal pieces define the structure of the resonant body of the Earth as the frequency emissions reach the surface.

As the core resonance continuously emanates out to the surface of the Earth and beyond, an etheric geomagnetic grid comes into being, forming the foundations of the planetary light body. Attuned through the frequency patterns of their DNA infrastructure, animal migration patterns and human settlements tend to conform to the lines and nodal points of the grid. Of course, this grid is warped and reshaped by tectonic plate activity, variable shifts in terrain and atmosphere, and solar-galactically triggered fluctuations in the electromagnetic field of the planet itself. Nonetheless, anchored at the poles, amplified at times by (to us) unforeseen and imperceptible shifts in the galactic program, the continuous pulsation of the grid slowly shapes the infrastructure of the planetary light body.

Now, just as the DNA received a counter-spin, technology-extruding impulse as the planet entered the 5,200-tun synchronization beam, so the resonant core of the Earth also received an impulse amounting to a jacked-up intensification of frequency. The neural pathways of the terrestrial grid that correspond to the resonant structure of the core became extra-active, corresponding to the more excited vibratory activity of the human DNA infrastructure. The restlessness of the human organism that is manifest in shipping lanes, causeways, silk routes, imperial walls, railroad tracks, freeways, airways, and radar amplified and eventually obscured the continuous pulsation of the grid. At nodal points temples, ziggurats, pyramids, cathedrals, pagodas, mosques, palaces, houses of parliament, airports and power-plants were erected, ultimately with little conscious regard for the Earth's invisible nexus.

As the final thrust into artificiality, the global Industrial Revolution swung into high gear, and the resonant frequency of the core of the Earth intensified to an unprecedented degree. What this intensification of frequency points to is an imminent stabilization at a higher frequency through a counter-spin movement that occurs just before exit from the synchronization beam. Indeed, the feedback signals to prepare for the counter-spin— the spin away from "history" corresponding to the return to post-history—have already been received in the form of nuclear radioactivity, industrial atmospheric disturbance, and random electromagnetic bombardment.

If you spin an ark (a specially constructed form in the shape of a simple ship's hull) clockwise, it will continue spinning until it stops. But if you spin it counterclockwise, it will slowly and ungraciously come to a halt, and then begin spinning clockwise. The Earth's passage through the synchronization beam is analogous to the counterclockwise spin. As the counterclockwise spin comes to a halt there is an increase in the wobble, a shake-up effect occurs, then—following a pause—the more harmonically congruent clockwise spin commences.

So we arrive at the moment when technology becomes transformation. This is initially experienced as a crisis, a crisis to which the dominant paradigm power holders are blinded. Though the present, scientifically materialistic power-holders believe that the world is the way it is because they have made it so, in actuality they are playing out roles specified by the harmonic wave phase of which the present era is a function. The belief they hold about the world, the dominant belief subscribed to and accepted by the governing institutions of the present world order, define the prevailing paradigm.

Belief in this paradigm, the scientific materialistic world view, can be described as a mental house. As we saw in Chapter 6, the foundations of the current mental house were laid in the seventeenth century during the initial katuns of the 12th baktun. By 1756 the walls of the mental house—belief in technological progress and industrial democracy— began to be erected. Between 1874 and 1953, the electromagnetic roof of the current mental house was emplaced. Finally, between 1953 and the present moment, the era of the launching of humankind and its artificial sensory intelligence probes into "outer space," the mental house began its internal dissolution. In this regard, it should be recalled that the notion of paradigm shift was first introduced by Thomas Kuhn in 1964.

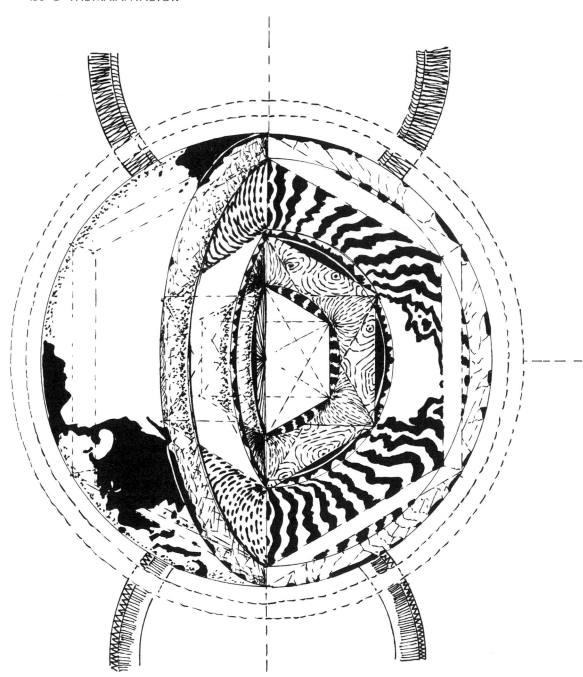

CRYSTAL EARTH CROSS-SECTION

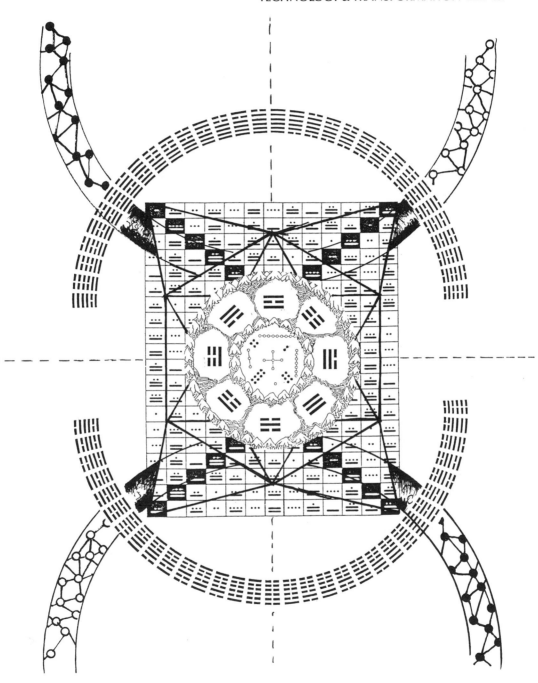

RECEIVING GALACTIC PROGRAM

Corresponding to this developmental frame is the climax in the counter-spin of the Earth's resonance. The signal for this climax was first received in 1945 with the detonation of atomic weapons. As a member of the solar-galactic order, Earth's response was first manifest in the UFO activity, which by 1947 could no longer be ignored. Without denying the *psychic* validity of the many people who have had encounters of the third kind, let us here define UFOs as Unified Field Organizers, an intelligent release of galactically programmed, psychically active, radiant energy simultaneously attracted to and emanated by Earth's resonant etheric body. They are referred to as Unified Field Organizers because they are a manifestation of Earth's intrinsically unified resonant field. Since this field is actually in solar-galactic resonance, UFOs also operate in conjunction with the harmonics of this field. In fact their "operations" are completely a function of resonant harmonics. Thus, the rapid shifts in direction attributed to UFOs are due to shifts in harmonic overtone alignment.

Following the discovery of DNA and the detection of the radiation belts in 1953, and the verification of tectonic plates in 1964, the internal dissolution of the current mental house had begun. All of these discoveries —DNA, radiation belts, tectonic plates—were necessary for the beginning of understanding of the coming paradigm, the new mental house of the unified resonant Earth. In the meantime, UFOs continued to accompany the era of massive nuclear testing, and with radar, television, radio and microwave radiation, the overall electromagnetic field of the planet entered a period of heightened dissonance. The etheric or light body of the planet intensified by this "bombardment," increased its signals through the morphogenetic field. In the wake of these signals came renewed interest in psychic phenomena, UFOs, psychedelic drugs, interspecies communication, and the ecology movement.

The counter-response of the dissolving mental house was space exploration, the extension of the materialist acquisitive paradigm into "outer space." The great era of space exploration, the "conquest of space," began with the Moon Landing on July 17, 1969, followed by probes to Mercury, Venus, Mars, Jupiter, Saturn and finally by January 24, 1986, Uranus. Two major inexplicables presented themselves through these "probes." The one was the finding of the officially suppressed, so-called Face of Mars on July 25, 1976; the other, the highly regular markings on the Uranian moon, Miranda, as well as the solar-oriented polar tilt and incredibly intense and erratic elecromagnetic field of Uranus.

While these findings presented paradigm-defying enigmas to the frame of the current mental house, space technology itself was still vaunted as the pinnacle of scientific achievement. Thus, it was particularly noteworthy that four days following the Voyager flight by Uranus, on January 28, 1986, the space shuttle Challenger exploded some 73 seconds following take-off. While follow-up investigations tried to pinpoint the "technological failure" contributing to the Challenger disaster, the next three NASA space launchings all exploded just following take-off. As if that were not enough, the European space launch Ariane also exploded shortly after take-off. This was all in a period between late January and mid-May, 1986. What was going on?

In resonance with the shifting foundations of the tectonic plates and over-saturated with electromagnetic dissonance, the roof of the current mental house had literally begun to collapse. Like flies picked off by a child in impish concentration, the space probes were flicked from their trajectories—by what? The answer is, by erratically triggered waves of dissonance set off by unwitting human desire to control and jam the electromagnetic field.

The Chernobyl nuclear disaster, occurring April 25-26, 1986, and the buzzing of the Brazilian Air Force by thirteen UFOs on May 23, 1986, were two further resonant field signals announcing the simultaneous failure and limits of technology and the rapid disintegration of the current mental house. Speaking with the voice of events whose origins and effects escape the modern consciousness, the resonant core of the Earth, attuned to the galactic harmonic, is readying for a harmonic convergence: the point at which the counter-spin of history finally comes to a momentary halt, and the still imperceptible spin of post-history commences.

By the time these words are read publicly, the event, Harmonic Convergence, will be but a few months away. Other events of a shattering, thought-provoking nature shall have recently occurred, demonstrating that not only the roof but even the walls of the current mental house are in a shambles. All that will be left is the dissolution of the foundations, the bedrock of scientific materialism that asserts the uniqueness and superiority of man in the universe. Meanwhile, the counter-effects of the new mental house, operating through the intensified resonant grid of Earth's light body, for the first time will become manifest as the networked thrust toward a unified moment of collective synchronization, Harmonic Convergence.

Through the trans-national grass-roots infrastructure of the new mental house and in collaboration with a cooperative global media conglomerate—a radio co-op—increasing numbers of humans are experiencing the reality of the global brain. The action of local collectives—art spores—operating through attunement to the knowledge that purpose is not an individual possession, will in all actuality be stringing beads of unified intention upon the planetary grid system.

And then it shall occur—Harmonic Convergence—the exponential acceleration of the wave harmonic of history as it phases into a moment of unprecedented synchronization. Like a shuttle on a loom shifting with lightning-like speed, the resonant frequency of the Earth grid will shift. In the shift, the foundations of the mental house imprinted with the names of Descartes, Newton, Galileo, and Copernicus will dissolve. Rippling ever more deeply through the consciousness of an aroused minority of the human race will be the realization of a larger, resonantly attractive force; a supersensible synthesis of mind and nature, hitherto undreamed of will dawn. The experience of reality as a unifying matrix— a synaesthetic blending of the senses brought about through light-sound sensory experience —will provide the first vibratory layers of the foundations of the new mental house.

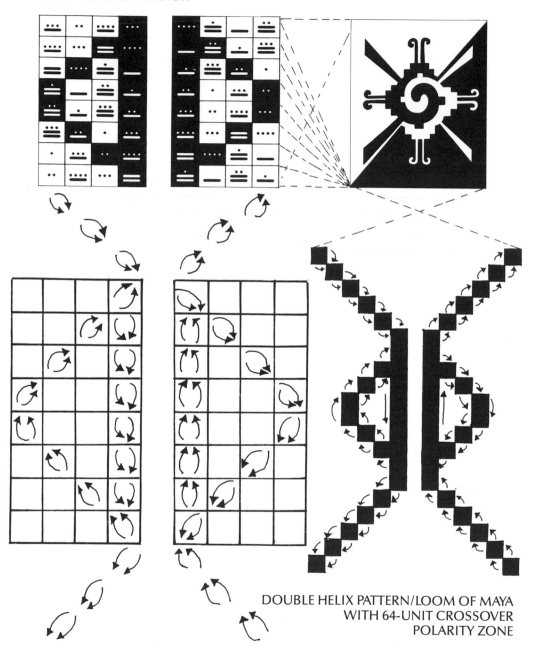

DOUBLE HELIX PATTERN/LOOM OF MAYA
WITH 64-UNIT CROSSOVER
POLARITY ZONE

This internal experience of unification—synaesthesia—will be understood as the inseparability of mind and nature, and in the power generated by the indissoluble unity of this experience, the edifice of modern civilization will disintegrate. As the climax and failure of the technology of the old mental house becomes increasingly apparent, obviously not without its difficulties and challenges, and amidst the chaotic backdrop of the collapsing old economic and political order, the transit to post-history shall begin. At the same time that the new mental house will be laying its foundations, the cumbersome, inert, mechano-chemical structure of the old will have to be dismantled. This synchronous activity—formulation of the new and cleansing and purification of the old—will be the single driving force as the final katun is entered, A.D. 1992-2012. Known as the Campaign for the Earth, the emergence of the psychically unified, media- connected, locally operative planetary society will slowly take form, emerging by A.D. 2012 as the evolutionary design plan of universally interactive intelligence.

While it is best to let forthcoming events tell their own story as the five-year span, A.D. 1987-1992, of the world revolutionary event of Harmonic Convergence unfolds, let us turn to the Mayan Factor for a structural description of the counter-spin harmonic of post-history. How can we envision post-history? What does it mean to speak of the crafting of the planet light body? How is the radiogenetic keyboard of the planet light body experienced at the human level?

Let us imagine that we are not extra- but super-terrestrials examining the resonant fluctuations of planet Earth. Our means of inspection is the 260-unit radiogenetic keyboard, the Tzolkin. Our focus is upon its 64 central units. Inscribed in this 64-unit matrix is the code and game plan of human destiny, the path beyond technology. Because of the design of the binary flow pattern, the Loom of Maya, this 64-unit matrix is referred to as the "Crossover-Polarity Zone." In other words, just as the chief feature of DNA is a double helix pattern by which a field is created for the crossing over of information from either molecular strand to the other, so the Loom of Maya pattern can be envisioned as a crossing over, to either side of the mystic central column, of the two symmetrical flows comprising the pattern of galactic activation.

The movement of this pattern of four units to the right and left of the central column defines the 64-unit symmetrical field. The 64-unit "keyboard" is the genetic matrix of transformation which unifies the entire 260-unit Tzolkin. The remainder of the Tzolkin, aside from the neutral-valued twenty- unit mystic column breaks down into 144 units of a four-phased radiant energy body, and 32 units of an eight-part crystal symmetry body. The total of twelve (four radiant energy and eight crystal symmetry) fields of the Tzolkin contain the code information describing the pre- and post-genetic radiance of galactic unfolding. The thirteenth field of the Tzolkin is, of course, at the center and represents the DNA.

Modeling the pre-and post-technological formula defining history, DNA is the transformational matrix holding together primordial and synthesizing phases of radiant

13-FIELD TZOLKIN

and crystalline energy activation. By its centrality in the overall matrix, the function of DNA is to vitalize the entire galactic activation pattern. As a fractal of the galactic whole, and of the geometry of DNA itself, the function of history/technology is to vitalize equally the radiant energy fields that define pre- and post-history.

How does this occur? The answer lies in following the pattern. This pattern, anchored by the fourteen galactic activation units on either side of the mystic column, describes the vibratory infrastructure not only of DNA, but of the universal light body. Holonomically registered at the cellular, individual organism, planetary, solar, and galactic levels, this vibratory infrastructure can also be read as the structural matrix supporting the wave harmonic of history as it passes through the 5,200-tun synchronization beam. Without the activation of the two-way flow during passage through the synchronization beam, the planetary light body would not be crafted. This two-way flow is the Zuvuya, the coming from and returning to Hunab Ku, the galactic core.

No different than the matrix of the etheric grid of the planetary light body, the struc-

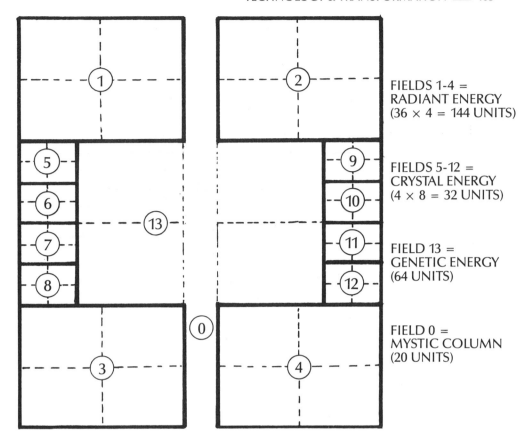

FIELDS 1-4 =
RADIANT ENERGY
(36 × 4 = 144 UNITS)

FIELDS 5-12 =
CRYSTAL ENERGY
(4 × 8 = 32 UNITS)

FIELD 13 =
GENETIC ENERGY
(64 UNITS)

FIELD 0 =
MYSTIC COLUMN
(20 UNITS)

tural matrix supporting the wave harmonic of history is a fractal of the universal galactic constant. The conscious activation of the Earth grid from its resonant core to its outer electromagnetic sheath is holonomically paralleled by the history-bridging, technology-extruding activation of DNA. Indeed technology is the scaffold surrounding the etheric grid of the planet. At the same time, it can equally be said that the galactic amplification of the resonant planetary grid defines the movement called history.

Remembering that "history" is the 5,125-year-diameter, technology- extruding phase of vibratory DNA acceleration, the bridge between the primordially radiant phase of prehistory and the resonantly synthesized phase of post-history, let us actually map out this historic passage on the 64-unit genetic keyboard.

As demonstrated in *Earth Ascending*, this 64-unit grid can be superimposed on the planet body. The horizontal dividing line corresponds to the equator. The vertical far left-hand row corresponds to the meridian running through the Great Pyramid in Egypt, some 30 degrees east of Greenwich. The numbering of the 64 units according to the number

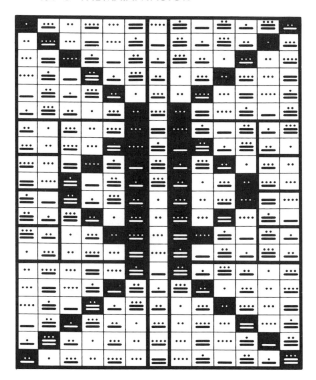

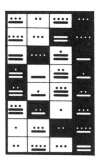
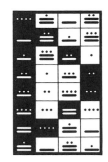

TZOLKIN WITH
64-UNIT CENTRAL MATRIX

pattern of the Ben Franklin magic square of 8 defines the actual pattern of movement uniting the genetic keyboard.

Following the numbering of the magic square, we see that the movement connecting numbers 1-16 and 49-64 is in the upper half of the grid, while the movement connecting the numbers 17-48 occurs completely in the lower half of the grid. Applied to our equation, numbers 1-16 correspond to pre-history, numbers 17-48 to history, and numbers 49-64 to post-history.

This means that the passage of Earth through the galactic synchronization beam corresponds to the movement through the entire lower half of the 64- unit genetic keyboard, the historic, technologically activated phase of genetic unfolding. When we speak of the counter-spin of history coming to an end and the return spin, the final synchronization of post-history commencing, we are referring to the passage from numbers 48 to 49. Since these 64 DNA code numbers also correspond to I Ching hexagrams, the passage from history to post-history is marked by the passage from the Well, 48, to Revolution/Moulting, 49. But this is revolution without guns; it is revolution by and for the Earth.

Initiated by the revolution of the Earth's resonant field, the final 26-year synchronization phase of the Great Cycle, A.D. 1986-2012, corresponds to the movement from 49 to 64. Once acceleration phases into synchronization—harmonic convergence—the increased harmonic frequency of the planetary field translates into a "speeding up" which is almost timeless. The result is a compression of "time" through the final quarter stage of the genetic keyboard. Conclusion at number 64, adjacent to number 1, the joining of alpha and omega, corresponds to passage from the synchronization beam 13.0.0.0.0, A.D. 2012, to New Heaven, New Earth, and entry into galactic synchronization.

But we may ask, amidst this profusion of numbers, where are the Maya in all of this? After all, what we are reading is a decoding of a multiple resonant system which they left behind—the Tzolkin, the Mayan Harmonic Module. Yes, where are the Maya when the world is ready to cash in its chips? What are the prophecies connected with the numbers, which, as we already saw in Chapter 6, dovetail with the numbers of the Book of Revela-

TZOLKIN WITH MAGIC SQUARE OF EIGHT ARRANGEMENT
OF DNA/I CHING CODE

tions? Is there a Mayan Second Coming, a Mayan Return? Is Kukulkan/Quetzalcoatl/Pacal Votan planning to check up on how things went once he and his galactic cohorts finished their harmonic calibrations on Earth, the third harmonic gyroscope out from the local star, the Sun?

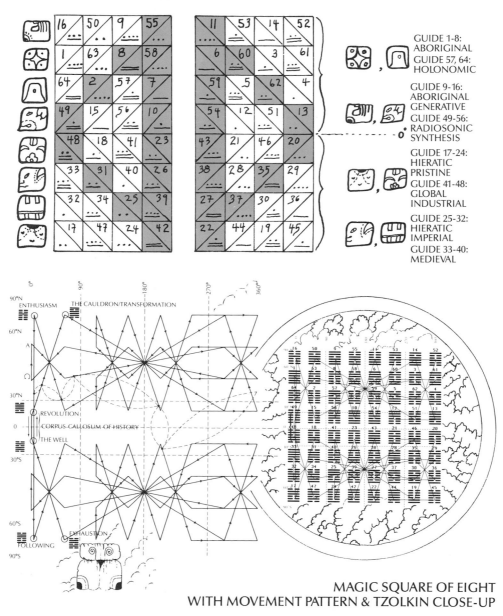

GUIDE 1-8:
ABORIGINAL
GUIDE 57, 64:
HOLONOMIC

GUIDE 9-16:
ABORIGINAL
GENERATIVE
GUIDE 49-56:
RADIOSONIC
SYNTHESIS

GUIDE 17-24:
HIERATIC
PRISTINE
GUIDE 41-48:
GLOBAL
INDUSTRIAL

GUIDE 25-32:
HIERATIC
IMPERIAL
GUIDE 33-40:
MEDIEVAL

MAGIC SQUARE OF EIGHT
WITH MOVEMENT PATTERN & TZOLKIN CLOSE-UP

Cosmic surfers that the ancient Maya were—and are—we cannot presume to know either their full capacities for what we would call interdimensional travel, or their whereabouts. True, the shamans of Highland Guatemala, the Daykeepers as they are called, keep the tradition, the knowledge that binds the Lightning in the Blood to the harmonic flow of galactic wisdom, and a few like Humbatz Men and Domingo Parédez translate that wisdom for us, while still others gather with the medicine people of the Americas for a last telling of the passage between worlds. But these are the remnants, the noble few who keep the beacon of incomprehensible timelessness aflame in their hearts.

Where are those whom we dubbed the galactic masters? What may we say of them following their departure at the end of Baktun 9? Or are their presences already here among us as the fateful days toward Harmonic Convergence march relentlessly? While we move forward, are the Maya coming back from the future on the return Zuvuya, ready to assist us in the playing out of the final katun of the Great Cycle? If the Tzolkin is a clue, a cosmic calling card left for a planet of humanoids, are there other clues elsewhere in our solar system?

The two chief planets referenced in the great, all-encompassing Mayan harmonic number, 13 66 560, are Venus and Mars. While our space probes showed Venus, so closely associated with Quetzalcoatl-Kukulkan, to possess a dense, vaporous, cloud-filled atmosphere too thick to see through to the bottom, Mars was waiting with at least one distinct clue—the Face of Mars, a massive humanoid face looking skyward a kilometer-and-a-half long. The fact that the face is looking straight up to the heavens is uncanny, and leaves the immediate impression that it was executed precisely for those like ourselves blundering into the universe with our nature-conquering pride and rocket-propelled sensing devices.

Though the Face was encountered on July 25, 1976, an even more uncanny clue, shot through the Mayan Zuvuya of time's trickery, was the unexecuted proposal for a monumental sculpture, a mile wide, had it been built, of a face looking skyward, to be entitled, *The Sculpture to Be Seen from Mars.* Uncanny, because the sculpture was proposed 29 years prior to the Viking probe in 1947—the Year of the UFO—by Japanese-American artist, Isamu Noguchi.

The coincidences—synchronicities of the most profound sort—involved in coming to terms with the Face of Mars and Noguchi's *Sculpture to Be Seen from Mars* are far too vast for the rational mind to comprehend, too immense for the little hook of scientific materialism to grasp, too inscrutable to be contained by the paltry net of the doctrine of the "non-prevalence of humanoids in the universe." But from within the resonant code of the Maya, masters of light and galactic travel, synchronizers of the wave-fractal that mobilizes molecules and engineers planets according to the same index, the Face of Mars, *The Sculpture to Be Seen from Mars,* and, yes, the chevron and oval markings of the Uranian moon, Miranda, are all of a piece, nodes in a resonant intergalactic web activated only by the mind wise enough to surrender the old paradigm and accept the new in unconditional terms.

FACE OF MARS:
TECHNOLOGY &
TRANSFORMATION

RETURN

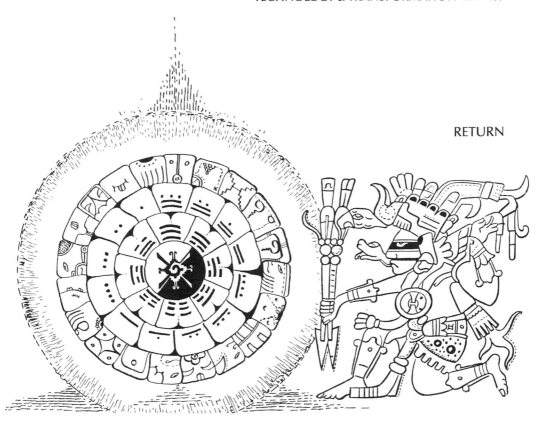

Pacal Votan and the holders of the lineage of the Quetzalcoatls of old and beyond foresaw all of this. Instantaneously releasing themselves through chromo-molecular transport into the farther reaches of the galaxy whence they had come, the Mayan sages nonetheless also prepared for a return. When? Well, most certainly during the last of the 52 galactic-activation katuns, A.D. 1992-2012, the katun signified as 13 AHAU, the most exalted number, the sign of Solar Mastery. But even in the immediate present, their return is imminent, for the moment soon arrives when the wave engendered by the Christian figurehead, Cortés, in A.D. 1519 will be turned around. That moment is August 16-17, 1987. Called Harmonic Convergence, August 16-17, 1987, kin 1863022 and 1863023, is the first Mayan-return entry point, a temporal planetary Tollan at which time their presence will be perceived by some as an inner light and by others as feathered serpent rainbow wheels turning in the air. Accompanying the resonant frequency shift, the luminous wave-forms of Quetzalcoatl will re-enter the atmosphere.

Signifying the commencement of the phase shift, when the rate of acceleration exponentially phases into synchronization, Harmonic Convergence will not only signal a return of Quetzalcoatl, but the elimination of Armageddon as well. To some it may even be as another Pentecost and second coming of the Christ. Amidst spectacle, celebration, and urgency, the old mental house will dissolve, activating the return of long-dormant archetypal memories and impressions. Synchronized with the descent of the new mental house, these "return" memories and impressions, corresponding to actual collective archetypal structures, will saturate the field and create the impulse toward the new order and lifestyle.

The chief feature of these return memories is the theme of *return* itself. Not just the return of Christ and Quetzalcoatl, but the return of all the gods and goddesses, heroes and heroines that have ever dwelled within the human imagination. For myth is no less real than history. And what is called the imagination is the function of the resonant structure called mind. Is it not this same mind of ours that we hold responsible for science and for myth? For on the Mayan Zuvuya, mental event, memory, and actual happening are all nodes in the same circuit. What some would call sacred geometry and others depth psychology are unified by their being informed by the same resonant structures. In this regard, Plato and Pythagoras, Goethe and Jung are numbered among the Maya, as are all those who readily accept the doctrine of harmony in whatever form it has been transmitted to them.

The Mayan return, Harmonic Convergence, is the re-impregnation of the planetary field with the archetypal, harmonic experiences of the planetary whole. This re-impregnation occurs through an internal precipitation, as long-suppressed psychic energy overflows its channels. And then, as we shall learn again, all the archetypes we need are hidden in the clouds, not just as poetry, but as actual reservoirs of resonant energy. This archetypal energy is the energy of galactic activation, streaming through us more unconsciously than consciously. Operating on harmonic frequencies, the galactic energy naturally seeks those structures resonant with it. These structures correspond to bio-electrical impulses connecting the sense-fields to actual modes of behavior. The impulses are organized into the primary "geometric" structures that are experienced through the immediate environment, whether it be the environment of clouds seen by the naked eye or the eery pulsation of a "quasar" received through the assistance of a radio telescope.

As the acknowledgement of our responsibility as humans of this planet reaches a critical mass, the moment of archetypal overflow will be triggered, releasing the fetters of the old paradigm and imprinting the new upon a critical mass of humans in one moment of resonant baptism. Then the past, the forgotten, and, yes, even the "what-is-to-come," will become conscious. The "return" is actually a making conscious of what has been storing up, and at the same time an increase in knowing. We shall see that events which the old paradigm refused to acknowledge had been turned into forms of fear in our mind. In that fresh moment of seeing, harmonic convergence, we shall know that fear no longer. For in consciousness is light. This is what is meant by the return of Quetzalcoatl. For others this moment will be the vision of the feathered rainbow serpent wheels turning in the air—

144,000, predicted by prophecy of the Zuvuya. Combined with the natural condition of things at the moment, a new zeal will be born into that ill-fated creature, "twentieth-century man." Through this zeal a signal shall come tumbling forth, releasing from the matrix a Campaign for the Earth, the opportunity for human self-redemption.

The Campaign for the Earth is the plan or design for the transit from one mental house to the next. By A.D. 1992, the plan initiated on Harmonic Convergence will have stabilized the world, though by no means shall everything be tamed. Like a gyroscope having gone into a temporary wobble and then restabilized, so Earth, on track once again, will chart its elliptical wave around the Sun. Inspired and illumined as a mobilized consciousness in resonance with itself and within the membranal walls of its solar system, Earth will be but a single synchronization away from entry into the Galactic Federation.

As the initial move back toward the central evolutionary stream from which plumb line the Late Industrial civilization represented a notable aberration, the Campaign for the Earth will be activated by archetypal characters, humans playing out impressions re-imprinted by galactic frequencies on Harmonic Convergence. Not only that, but many humans will also learn that they are playing out variations on the same imprinting. Common memory will possess the planet once again. Chief among the returning common archetypal memories and impressions will be those of King Arthur and the Kingdom of Shambhala. The archetypal resonance calls for a circle, a round table of twelve knights and a king—the magic thirteen once again—to restore the Kingdom of Avalon. Avalon is Earth, and the kingdom is our conscious resonant stewardship of this fair Earth. As a clan pledged to warriorhood, the Knights of the Round Table will be reborn as the willingness to mobilize and sacrifice on behalf of the cause of the Earth, which is the cause of the light. All true warriorhood is bound by service to the light.

While the Arthurian Round Table recapitulates the Mayan thirteen, the myth of Shambhala, the mystic kingdom of Central Asia, is an echo of the Nine Lords of galactic destiny, the Mayan Lords of Time, called in Tibet the Nine Great Lha. The Kingdom of Shambhala itself is the ninth and central feature in a valley surrounded by eight great mountains. Its inhabitants, inspired by the teachings of the Kalachakra Tantra, the Wheel of Time received through their Kings, all attained to a condition of collective enlightenment, whence they were no longer visible upon the Earth.

But, according to teachings left behind, a return is promised to help rid the world of the scourge of the "Three Lords of Materialism." This return is in the form of the release of a collective archetype known as the Warriors of Shambhala. The purpose of the return is to establish the Kingdom of Shambhala on Earth. But then, how different is this from the return of Avalon, from the injunctions of Christ regarding entry into the Kingdom of Heaven, or the return of Quetzalcoatl to restore a new reign of thirteen heavens? Each archetypal variation is strung out like a bead of insight upon the Mayan Zuvuya. As multiple resonance, myth opens the gates to a reality that is profoundly inter-dimensional.

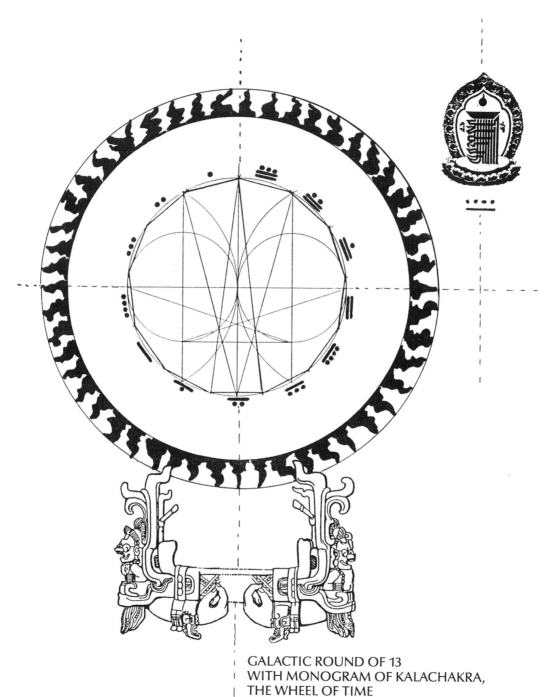

GALACTIC ROUND OF 13
WITH MONOGRAM OF KALACHAKRA,
THE WHEEL OF TIME

The great return of Harmonic Convergence, then, is like an awakening from cultural trance. It is the opportunity for all to engage the Mayan Factor, and, in a word, to receive the galactic imprint. Though at first we do not appear to be Mayan, by the time we reach the moment for galactic synchronization our way of life shall be in every regard a modeling after the lifestyle of the Maya who preceded us in Central America. Only we shall find ourselves as planetary Maya, possessing a brilliantly simple and sophisticated technology based on the matching of solar and psychic frequencies which harmonize the "ratio of the sense-fields." Creating a non-polluting technology, we shall allow ourselves to subsist comfortably in small bioregional groups, strung together as information nodes on a communications system that has finally dispensed with wires. And lastly, availing ourselves of the leisure time to which our genetic hardware had originally disposed us, we shall collectively come to know as one. In that knowing, our life shall pass into the greater life. The mystery of the unknown which has always beckoned us, by the light it contained in its question, will expand us into levels of being and knowing undreamed of by the strife-worn ego of the old mental house.

As the index of the rate of planetary acceleration, technology will indeed have transformed itself. Through synchronization, this transformation will show us that with all of our bio-electromagnetic hardware and galactic light-body programming, it is we ourselves, Maya returned, who in our own bodies are the best and most sophisticated technology there is—*we* are the path beyond technology.

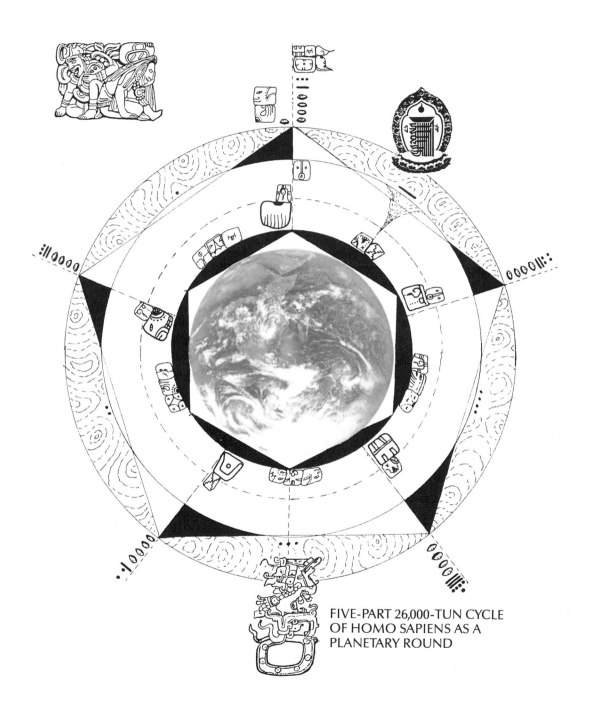

FIVE-PART 26,000-TUN CYCLE
OF HOMO SAPIENS AS A
PLANETARY ROUND

8

THE COMING SOLAR AGE

By means of the current 5,200-tun galactic synchronization beam, the Great Cycle, we have been focussing upon the climax of an evolutionary phase, one in which a planet gets hooked up with a technologically extruded circuit of self-reflective consciousness through a species called humankind. Yet, as Mayan measures go, a 5,200-tun cycle is a relatively brief one. Also, because we seem to be the center of the drama, it is easy for us to lose sight of the fact that our perspective is certainly not the only—nor necessarily the best—one for coming to terms with our situation.

As we have seen, Mayan science recognizes different coexisting levels of being, different coexisting dimensions of consciousness, which together pass through phases of interactive development during discrete evolutionary cycles. These dimensions of consciousness include: CHICCHAN—the reptilian brain or autonomic limbic system—the metabolic, vegetative physical garment; OC—the emotional-conceptual, strategizing, horizontal intelligence; MEN—the higher mind, the analogical vertical intelligence resonant with the evolutionary purpose of the planet; and AHAU—the solar mind, the mind of light, the realm of the evolutionary guides of the planet, whom the Maya call the AHAU KINES, the Solar Lords.

The emergence of humankind—*Homo sapiens*—represents a particular stage in the evolutionary cycle of a star system, a stage in which the purposive integration of the four levels of consciousness becomes a distinct planetary possibility. The stage, *Homo sapiens*, has a duration of 26,000 tun or five great cycles of 5,200 tun each. The 26,000-tun cycle is roughly equivalent to the so-called Platonic Great Year. The 5,200-tun cycle, which has been the focus of our book, is but the fifth or last stage of the current evolutionary cycle. What we are experiencing is the climax of our particular species and evolutionary stage—the very last 26 years of a cycle some 26,000 years in length!

What this advanced condition of humans represents is the skilled and witting use of physical, third-dimensional space suits to ply and tame a planet's physical plane. CHICCHAN and OC are highly interactive in the use of this space suit. The light body or etheric double, what the Egyptians call the KA, is the fourth-dimensional electromagnetic probe that instruments the third-dimension physical body. It corresponds to an outlet of MEN. Finally, there is AHAU, the solar mind, which is purely electromagnetic or fifth-dimensional and knows no time. It is activated by the galactic Zuvuya and processes inter-dimensional information on behalf of the planet. On our planet, the realm of the solar lords or guides constitutes the etheric body of the planet and is resonant with both the planet's electromagnetic field and its inter-dimensional, gyroscopic control at the crystal core of the Earth.

At the beginning of the present evolutionary cycle, almost 26,000 years ago, at the peak of the last Ice Age, the solar lords, the AHAU KINES, were endowed, courtesy of the Galactic Federation, with the evolutionary seed-pack for the activation of different stages of the present cycle. The elements of the seed-pack are the purely electromagnetic forms of the archetypes of the evolutionary cycle. As the synchronization of third- with fourth-dimensional need—the physical with the light body—reaches certain stages or levels of development, a triggering of suitable archetypal forms occurs.

The mythic name for the fifth dimensional planetary realm of the solar lords, the AHAU KINES, the custodians of the archetypes of the evolutionary cycle, is none other than Shambhala. Directly interfacing with the Galactic Federation, positioned in relation to the north magnetic pole of the planet, and in particular attunement with Orion and Arcturus, the Kingdom of Shambhala entered the third and fourth dimensions during one particular stage of the present cycle.

This manifestation corresponded to a time following the birth of Lord Buddha (born of Queen Maya at 6.10.0.0.0, the Great Cycle's midpoint), when King Suchandra of Shambhala requested that the Buddha give the teachings of the Wheel of Time, Kalachakra. These teachings Suchandra brought back to the Kingdom, where they flourished under the reigns of seven great dharma kings. After the reign of the seventh, actually a queen, Visvamati, the Kingdom returned to the inter-dimensional realm, where it remains up to this moment, pregnant with spiritual warriors ready to rain down upon the materialistic deserts of the present-day world.

In the meantime—before, during, and after this interlude—the AHAU KINES, the Lords of the Sun, have remained ever-vigilant and attuned. It is due to their influence, which descends from time to time in the form of electromagnetic seeds called archetypes, that human concern has been elevated, directed, or channelled through the religion of the Sun, the great planetary solar cult. Indeed, especially through the initial stages of the present and last 5,200-tun cycle, the planetary solar cult was the highest means for the mobilization of social energy. Above all, at the initiation of the present cycle in 3113 B.C., the cult of the solar lord, RA, in Egypt was elevated to a place of supreme prominence. Commemorated and consecrated in the secret thirteenth chamber of the Great Pyramid, the cult of RA was intended to pierce like a ray of pure light at the initiation of the cycle for the purpose of evoking in humanity a constant memory of the higher evolutionary purpose.

The planetary solar cult was powerful in mobilizing the initial energy of the present

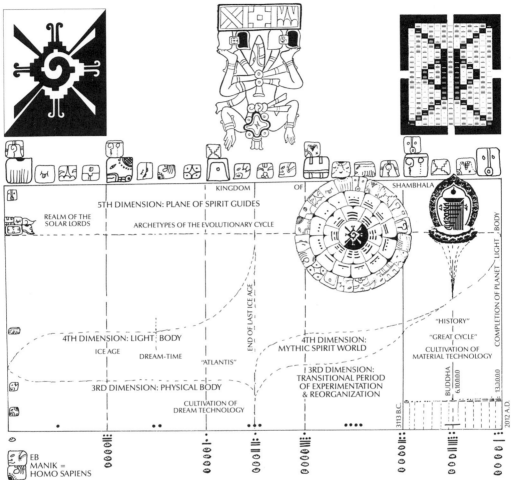

26,000-TUN CYCLE SHOWING RELATION OF THIRD, FOURTH, & FIFTH DIMENSIONS, GREAT CYCLE, AND KINGDOM OF SHAMBHALA

civilizational cycle, whether in Egypt, Mesopotamia, India, China, Mexico, or Peru. However, once the impact of the technological extrusion began to be translated into increasingly materialistic terms and forms, the power of the planetary solar cult began to diminish. As the influence diminished, humans began to rely more on their third-dimensional space-suit bodies, and less on their fourth-dimensional etheric or light-body doubles. As a result, contact and communication with the AHAU KINES, the great solar lords and guides, retrogressed. The advent of great teachers or avatars, most prominently the Buddha, Christ, and in the Americas, Quetzalcoatl, was for the purpose of keeping the higher evolutionary memory alive.

But, as we have seen, by the completion of the twelfth cycle, Baktun 11, the light of the planetary solar cult had dimmed to such a degree that the mental shadow called matter thrown by the eclipse of the solar religion was deemed the most appropriate beginning place for the new science. Hence, in a fever of shadow-begotten insight, the science of mechanistic materialism was born. At the time of the final Spanish conquest of the Maya in A.D. 1697, the eclipse was total. In its nocturnal intensity the principle of solar rulership in human affairs faded from the memory of increasing numbers of humans. This aftermath of the eclipse became known as the Age of Materialism. From it, the ultimate technological extrusion, global industrial civilization, was spawned.

As the triumph of man's infatuation with his own material inventiveness, global industrialization has had the singular effect of intensifying the blindness of modern humans to the actuality of the Sun as an *intelligence* to be factored into our every activity. The smoke churned by the dark mills of Satan, literally as well as metaphorically, has caused a forgetfulness of our solar heritage that has now brought us to the brink of self-destruction. Until we understand that the fatal fascination with our technological inventiveness represents a turning away from the forces of light and an actual disregard of our own potential as universal co-creators, we shall not escape the consequences of our ignorance. For the truth is that we turn to gadgetry, not willing to own up to the power that lies within our own internal circuitry, a bio-electromagnetic circuitry which is directly connected, through the Solar Lords, the AHAU KINES, to the Sun. So it is that we have come to labor in the pits of materialism. Cut off from the fifth-dimensional guides, blind even to the existence of the fourth-dimensional light body—the "soul"—identifying exclusively with the third-dimensional physical garment, materialistic humanity charts a shadow-course through a darkness of its own making.

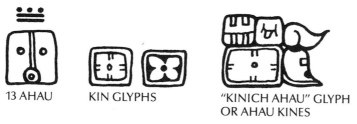

13 AHAU   KIN GLYPHS   "KINICH AHAU" GLYPH
OR AHAU KINES

Mythically, the Faustian development of global industrialization represents a turning away from the light—our guiding, inner "soul-light"— to pursue the immediate power gains of a facile technological mastery over our material means. In truth, this turning away is a surrender to the force of darkness, called by the ancient Mexicans, Tezcatlipoca, the Dark Lord of Time. It is Tezcatlipoca, the trickster counterpart of Quetzalcoatl, who, disguised as Cortés, arrived in Mexico in A.D. 1519 announcing the entry into the present 468-year "hell-cycle." Emboldened by the example of men like Cortés, aided and abetted by the raw might which technological mastery has brought certain of us—we have endeavored to build an entire civilization in ignorance of the principles of light and solar rulership.

It is significant that one of the last of the truly imperial monarchs of Europe prior to the triumph of the Industrial Revolution, Louis XIV, was called the Sun King. By the time the extravagant Louis XIV was in his grave, coal was being mined in Arthur's ancient Albion. And when it came time to express the awesome power of Faustian man's dominion over nature, it is equally significant that it was through artificial release of the power of the atom, the power that we believe generates the Sun, that we created our own stop sign, the atomic bomb. But to what end? Hiroshima, Nagasaki, and Chernobyl are mute witness to the oblivion to which our disregard of the Sun and the true principles of cosmic order consign us. And yet nuclear weapons are stockpiled in unceasing number, each one a deadly projection of our solar blind-spot.

Yet with the moment of technological transformation upon us, and with some five years prior to entry into the last katun of the 260-katun /5200-tun synchronization beam, we may still revive and awaken to the gift of the Sun. After all, the 260th katun of the Harmonic Module is the katun ruled by 13 AHAU. Thirteen, the movement immanent in all things, is the most powerful of the galactic pulsation-rays. Exalted in the sign of Solar Mastery and consciousness, AHAU, the culmination of the twenty signs, we should anticipate that the 260th katun would be an era of spiritual regeneration, heralding a planetary golden age. Indeed, despite the dehumanizing materialism of the age, we possess the knowledge and the timing to transform the 13 AHAU Katun, A.D. 1992-2012, into the New Solar Age, one far surpassing the solar golden ages of Egypt or, even more recently, of the Classic Maya. For this would be a genuinely planetary golden age, an age auguring conscious entry into the Galactic Federation. Assuming the best, assuming that Harmonic Convergence is the twist in the collective DNA that dissolves the old mental house and projects the foundations of the new, what will this be like? What is the path beyond technology? How is it that the "how of AHAU" is, in and through ourselves, connected to the Sun? First of all, let us paint a new picture of the world, one that includes our past but reframes it in a solarized context.

According to the Mayan Factor, we live at the bottom of an electromagnetic ocean. What we call the physical plane Earth is itself the ocean floor, while we, like squids or semi-blinded denizens, swarm about our little ways; only dimly aware that we swim and move across the bottom of a vast, multi-dimensional electromagnetic ocean. How odd we must seem to those who swim and delve in currents far above us, and what can we say about those beings who are beyond the surface? What must they see?

But to live, to survive in the dense, yet fragile bottom of the electromagnetic sea, we ourselves must be possessed of bio-electromagnetic circuitry. In truth, through our exquisitely woven sensory radar, we are capable of far more nourishment and direction from the electromagnetic field than we now allow ourselves. Indeed, at present we have capitulated all of our electromagnetic powers to privately owned or badly managed state utility companies to whom we must pay for what is naturally ours. Yet, as Nicholas Tesla proved in his laboratory in Colorado Springs, a single human being can co-generate an electromagnetic field of incredible intensity, while remaining calm and in resonance.

The elements of the circuitry connecting the third-dimensional physical garment to, and inclusive of, the fourth-dimensional light body are well known. First, there is the sensory radar—the five sense organs and "mind;" then, there are the neural canals which carry electrical impulses from sense organ to central computer, the brain, for processing; finally, there are the psychophysical centers associated with the glandular system called the chakras and their network of subtle energy flows. The circuit is completed by the subtle currents that flow as resonant transmission from the chakra system directly through the Kuxan Suum, the galactic fibers, to the main currents of the electromagnetic ocean which connect us to the plane of the solar lords and guides and thence to the Sun and the galactic hub.

The information-bearing currents of the higher—the fifth, sixth and seventh—dimensions of the electromagnetic ocean, flowing to and from the solar plexus, also have entry points at the crown of the head, the throat, the heart, the sexual organs, and the palms of the hands and soles of the feet. Thus, we see that the third-dimensional garment of the physical body, like any decent space suit, has its connecting points that provide the fourth-dimensional light body, coexisting with the physical body, its electromagnetic respiratory nodes.

The AH KINES, "Servant-Warriors of the Sun," are those humans who fully realize the dream light body within the physical body and—understanding the circuitry of the human organism—use the light body to navigate the electromagnetic waters which we call the universe. Through attunement of their sensory radar and skilled use of the Kuxan Suum, the "galactic umbilical cord" that emerges from the solar plexus, the AH KINES, the realized ones of the past and present, are able to become star-mediums, channeling galactic information directly into the terrestrial ocean floor of the great electromagnetic sea. In this way, they hop Zuvuyas and keep the sacred count. Possessing the same circuitry, we may do the same as the fabled AH KINES. Each one of us, returned to post-historic simplicity, may directly channel the alternating currents of the galaxy to suit our situation.

For this to occur, all we need to do is reverse our view. It is not the physical body that is primary, but the light body. The auto-kinetic physical body, like leaves to a tree, is the projection of our inner attainment. The light body, with its sensory radar, neural canals, central computer, chakra and subtle nervous system, and ultraradiant fibers, is the true skeleton of the physical body. Operating on the same 260-unit pulsation template as the Sun—the Mayan Harmonic Module—the functioning of our light body is amazingly simple. Yet disregard for it is what consigns us to what we call the realm of the beasts.

Using the template of the Tzolkin as the blueprint of the light body, we immediately identify the Loom of Maya as the electrical currents—the one positive, the other negative—that are the universal polar currents of any electromagnetic field. Using the physical body as a bio-electromagnetic battery, the universal electrical currents cross over each other in endless pulsation. This process occurs at the micro level with every nervous discharge and synaptic crossing. Indeed, what we call information is the "mental" processing of these discharges. It also occurs at the macro level and the entire physical unit, which each organism embodies, can be viewed as a single bio-electromagnetic battery accommodating the powerful crossing over of the two universal currents of energy.

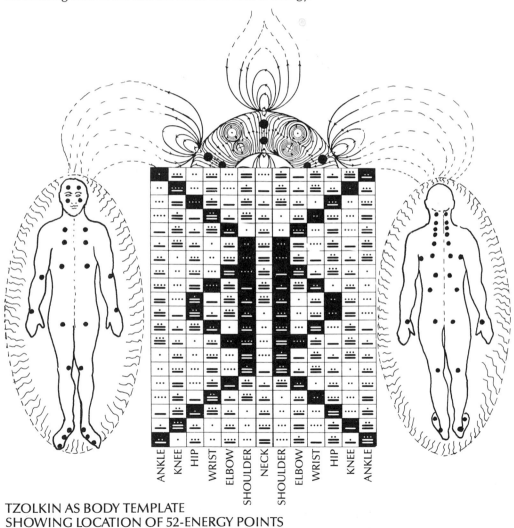

TZOLKIN AS BODY TEMPLATE
SHOWING LOCATION OF 52-ENERGY POINTS

The thirteen vertical columns of the harmonic template represent the thirteen major articulations of the body, which also divide the main neural canals running from feet and hands to brain, joined at and mediated by the central column. This central column—the mystic seventh column—represents the neck and spinal column as well as the alignment of chakras. On either side of the central column, the next two columns represent the shoulders, then the elbows, and finally the wrists. Continuing outward, the fourth columns out represent the hips, the fifth the knees, and finally the last columns out, the sixth, represent the ankles. These are the joints that articulate the flow of the neural canals to the palms of the hands and the soles of the feet, key entry points of subtle energy currents. The twenty Sacred Signs find their numerical counterpart in the twenty digits—the fingers and toes of the hands and feet.

The sense organs are also represented by the thirteen columns. The middle is the central channel—the greater mind opening to the universe, vast, fluid and open. Then following on either side, are the two columns each representing the local mind and the senses of sight, hearing, smell, taste, and, finally, touch. Clustered along the sides of the central channel, and represented by the ten units each of the Loom of Maya, are the neuro-cerebral radar receivers of the sense organs. The 26 galactic-activation points constituting either current of the Loom of Maya represent the 52 harmonizing points recognized in the pressure-point massage technique of Jin Shin Jyutsu. In truth, our present techniques of massage and psychic healing do not go far enough in their understanding and, hence, in their application of what we can rightly call bio-electromagnetic medicine.

Using the Harmonic Module as the template of the circuitry of the light body, and understanding the light body to be the true skeleton of the physical body, we can assert that the diseases and plagues which ail us—cancer and AIDS—are not cellular in cause but instead are the direct result of radical blockages in our collective bio-electromagnetic field. These blockages are the immediate result of immersion in and addiction to various feedback effects of our deleterious technological environment. The cure to these Late Industrial Age diseases, therefore, is not to be found in chemicals or radioactive treatment, but in a radical shift in disposition accompanied by the development of a genuine bio-electromagnetic medicine that accounts for the power of the mind, the reality of the light body, and the natural, organic restoration of intrinsic resonance as key factors in healing.

The clue to how this can be accomplished is again through the harmonic template, the 260-unit Tzolkin. As much as the Tzolkin gives us a blueprint of the individual light body that animates each one of us, it also describes the patterned flow of solar energy and intelligence, the ceaseless stream of universal creative spiritual energy itself. This, too, has been known by the AH KINES, the realized ones, for which reason they practice and are experienced in the arts of healing as well as those of resonant creative expression—music and song, color and form—all of whose harmonics are ruled or at least mediated by the subtle and all-pervasive frequencies of the Sun. Indeed, insofar as all of our senses are

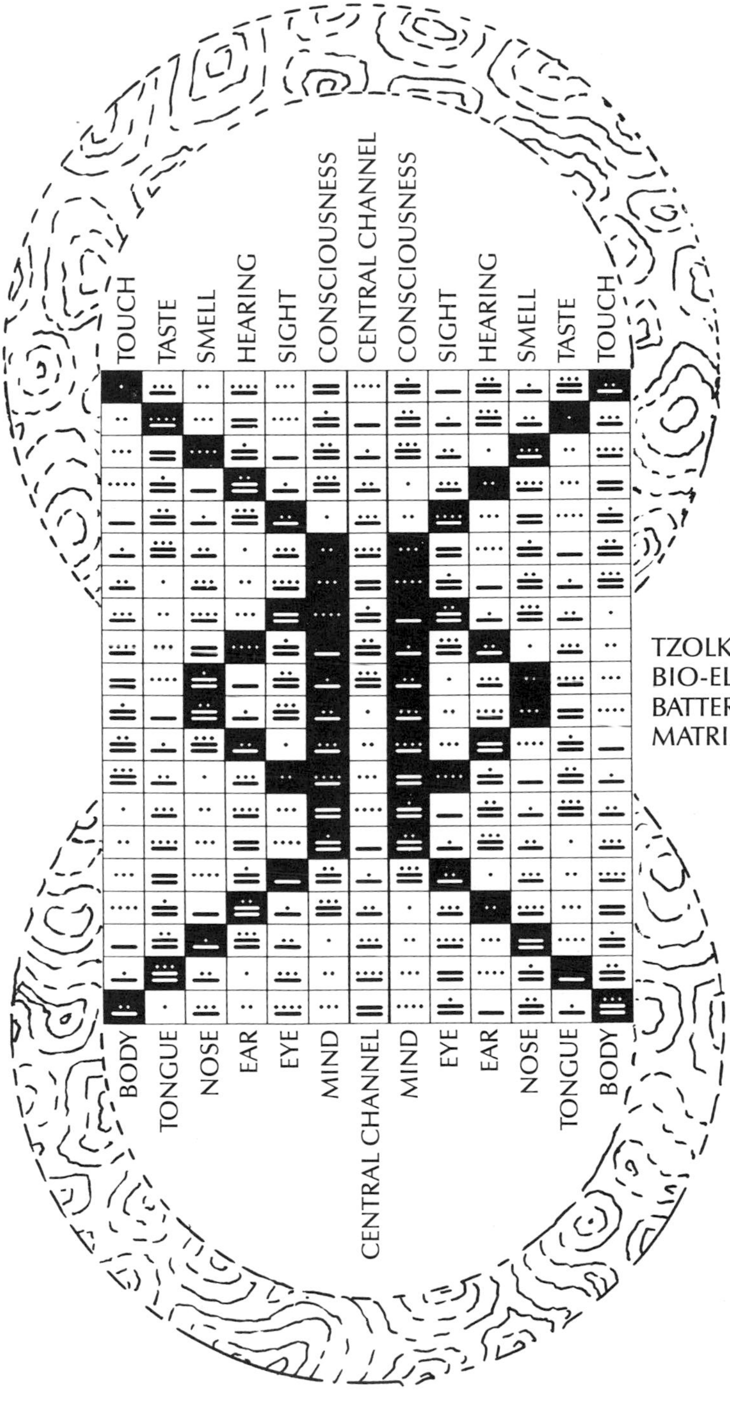
TOUCH
TASTE
SMELL
HEARING
SIGHT
CONSCIOUSNESS
CENTRAL CHANNEL
CONSCIOUSNESS
SIGHT
HEARING
SMELL
TASTE
TOUCH
BODY
TONGUE
NOSE
EAR
EYE
MIND
CENTRAL CHANNEL
MIND
EYE
EAR
NOSE
TONGUE
BODY

TZOLKIN AS
BIO-ELECTROMAGNETIC
BATTERY & SENSE-FIELD
MATRIX

informed by the solar-activated electromagnetic field, we may find heliotropic octaves in perfume and solar sunspot frequencies in what we taste. All this is literal and not just metaphorical, for the bio-electromagnetic battery of the individual human organism *through its sense organs* plugs directly into the planetary and solar electromagnetic batteries.

This is no new idea. The greatest visionaries of the era of scientific materialism have been attuned to the use of the senses in the attainment of light-body realization. Toward the beginning of the thirteenth baktun, in 1627, Francis Bacon's super-utopian *New Atlantis* speaks of the "miners of light" and describes a world filled with perspective houses, sound houses, perfume houses, and taste houses in which the refinements of the senses are synthesized and multiplied. The overseers of all of these activities are known as the Merchants of Light—the same as the AH KINES. Seeing past the industrial stage of civilization, Bacon asserts the unity of the senses as the basis of a benign and harmonic world order ruled by the Society of Solomon, called New Atlantis.

And Blake, too, speaks of the ending of the current industrial hell as being achieved by "an improvement of sensual enjoyment." But, Blake continues in his memorable *Heaven and Hell*, "First, the notion that man has a body distinct from his soul is to be expunged." It is this notion that body is distinct from soul, externalized as the belief that man is distinct from and superior to nature, that is the cause of the primary blockage experienced by the collective light body during the current mental house. It is the root cause of the diseases and terrors that plague us, from cancer and AIDs to fear of permanent death and nuclear winter.

The improvement of sensual enjoyment is inseparable from the capacity to realize our own electromagnetic potency. Through the circuitry of the light body we can directly hook up to the solar power house. The electromagnetic pulsations picked up by our sensory radar system, channeled by our neural canals, refined through our chakra system, and mediated by our higher planetary guides—the archivists of the archetypes—are one and the same with the pulsations of the solar body, the Sun, our local star.

The key to our flowering at this final stage of our evolutionary cycle lies in the simplicity of being in resonance. Even more, it is through remaining in resonance that the solar-psychic frequency, mediated by the terrestrial electromagnetic battery, is maintained; that the light body is nourished; and that we may discover the knowledge and energy necessary for our own individual maintenance. To say that we are knocking on the doors of magic is only to acknowledge our own lack of belief in what we are actually capable of through our own instrumentation, the sensory body. What has been demonstrated by shamans and wizards, yogis and spiritual masters, is—after all—everyone's evolutionary birthright.

But we are conditioned beings, trammeled by our own ignorance. For this reason the new scientists, "synaesthetic engineers," must erect houses of perspective and sound, perfume and taste, so that human organisms, long unaccustomed to the natural birthright of their

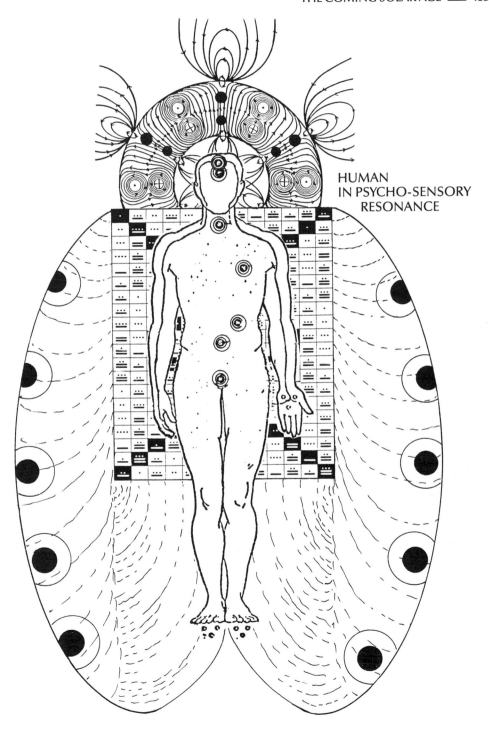

HUMAN
IN PSYCHO-SENSORY
RESONANCE

sense-fields, may learn again to navigate the electromagnetic ocean. In the circuitry of the light body are to be found those resonant laws of levity to offset the effects of bogging down in the neural ruts caused by following the material-bound laws of gravity too long. The law of levity is as real as the law of gravity and has everything to do with release from attachment to self-importance. For in the end, the joke is on those who cannot rise above themselves to dally in the vast luminosity which the narrow chinks of selfhood withhold from entering the sense-body's neural cavern.

In this process, control of the mind is paramount, for it is from the mind that the erroneous projections concerning our actual nature continuously stream. The clue to the process of mindfulness lies in the mystic column representing the greater mind. It is empty, an open channel, completely unencumbered. As long as the individual mind, represented by the two columns on either side of the mystic central column, remains open, empty, and free, accessing the greater mind, awareness is maintained and we act with natural spontaneity, entering a field in which we are ownerless. Like children endowed with the wisdom of the universe, we channel and receive our solar-galactic inheritance.

It is from this open, empty condition of mind that the new technology is sprung. Using the body as an electrically charged battery or tuning fork, the environment appropriate to the light body may be constructed. Solar cells, amplified and focussed by crystals, will be the electromagnetic field catchers. The energy caught will be channeled for heat or kinetic purposes, and will also be a source of superior sensual enrichment. Regulation of the energy will be through attunement to psychic frequencies. In this way will be achieved the dream of Nicholas Tesla, "free energy."

As Tesla observed, the resonance of the Earth functions like oscillations of a giant electromagnetic battery. The key features of this battery are the two shells of the ionosphere, the lower lunar and the upper solar shell, respectively 60 and 70 miles above the terrestrial bottom of the electromagnetic ocean. It is the currents of the ionosphere in direct resonance with the solar and lunar fields which moderate the wind and atmospheric currents of the lowest layers of the electromagnetic ocean. Oscillating at approximately 7.8 cycles per second, the ionosphere is in resonance with the human brain, which—when oscillating at 7.8 cycles per second—reflects a condition of samadhi or meditational absorption. This common neural-ionospheric frequency is a prime key unlocking the new technology.

Far beyond the ionosphere lie the next two components of the Earth's electromagnetic battery, the radiation belts—the lower, positively charged, proton lunar-galactic belt and the upper, negatively charged, electron solar belt. It is these belts, like a cellular membrane, that mediate the larger electromagnetic currents connecting the Earth to the Sun and the other systems of the galactic hub, Hunab Ku.

In polar resonance with the outer radiation belts lies the Earth's memory blanket: the PSI bank, the global brain, the noosphere, the realm of the archetypes of the evolutionary cycle, the mystic Kingdom of Shambhala. Corresponding to the interaction of the higher collective mind, represented by the sign MEN, with AHAU, the solar mind, the functioning of the planetary mind and memory field is inseparable from the planetary mediation of the electromagnetic energy of the vast galactic ocean. If we understand that energy and information are no different from each other, then we take a tremendous step into the light. The great streams of cosmic radiation that pour into the planetary field represent varieties of information. Encoded within the planet's memory bank and in resonance with the inter-dimensional chamber at the Earth's crystal core, this energy may be released through creative acts of ritual and ecstatic mystic attunement. The power to which such acts of attunement give rise—the power of poetry, dance, or music—is literally the same power as that which animates celestial phenomena like rainbows. In truth, we are woven of the stuff of the stars.

In the terrestrial field, "natural" discharges from the electromagnetic battery are numerous: the auroras emanated by the radiation belts and co-generated from either magnetic pole are chief among these discharges both in their beauty and the awesome energy which they convey. Lightning, spawned by the interactions of the ionosphere with the currents of the upper atmosphere and geomagnetic pulsations, is a further manifestation of the power of the Earth's electromagnetic battery. Interwoven with these phenomena are the radiant-energy being-emanations called thunderbirds, guides, or spirit beings of various sorts.

Resonating in common frequency with the ionosphere, our body, too, has its "lightning in the blood," and is defined by two polar currents and two polar generators. Regulated by the sex organs and the pineal glands, these two poles in resonance are capable of generating discharges that are the individual organismic equivalent of the auroras. When these discharges are consciously effected in resonance with the electromagnetic field as mediated by solar cells and crystals, the energy release may result in the "lighting up " of our environment. Directing these discharges to heat or kinetic needs, we may overcome the need for mechanistic contrivances and at the same time charge ourselves with a pleasure generally unknown in the present culture. In this way, we may begin to construct our houses of the senses that are at the same time temples of the solar body within and without. As Sir Thomas Browne wrote long ago, when the present science was yet in diapers, "We live as if by an invisible Sun burning within."

Thus constructing our houses of the senses, we shall come to know that our higher mind *is* the Sun. The new solar age shall dawn. Born will be the world view that is a textured interaction of resonant fields of greater and lesser magnitudes. Understanding energy and information as the transductions of universal constants plotted through the simple operations of wave harmonics, we shall create that technology which is planetary in scope and individual in operation. Forming ourselves into group cells bonded through techniques of sensory fusion artfully constructed, we shall learn as never before the skills

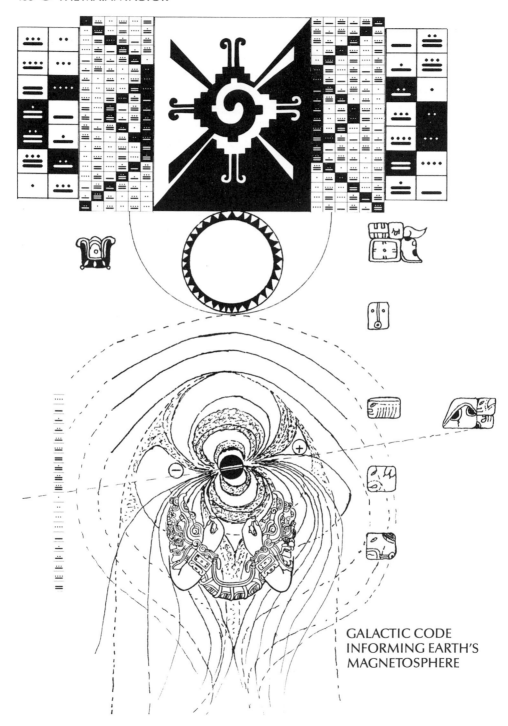

GALACTIC CODE
INFORMING EARTH'S
MAGNETOSPHERE

of navigating a universe as multiple in its dimensions as it is rich in its sensations.

As New Maya, having surrendered our cramped view of things and having crossed the threshold of history to post-history, thus receiving the imprint of the new, ultimately there will be no one exempt from the understanding of how to operate his or her own light body. For it will be understood that full utilization of Earth's electromagnetic battery is dependent upon the full participation of every last organism upon the planet. As the individual becomes more collective, the collective becomes more individual. As more merge their individual consciousness into the electromagnetic battery of the planet, so the bestowal of solar insight and intelligence will affect more individuals in their daily operations. In this way, the total synchronization augured by the 5,200-tun beam may be rapidly realized and galactic entrainment achieved by A.D. 2012, 13.0.0.0.0 on the beam.

The summons to compassionately incorporate all individuals, functioning up to their full bio-electromagnetic integrity into group cells each plugged into the Earth's electromagnetic battery, is a summons commanded by the Sun itself, AHAU KINICH, called by the Egyptians, RA, the supreme Solar Lord. Therefore we should not be surprised to find that after A.D. 1992 the emissaries of the Sun, the new bio-regional AH KINES, will be taking their positions among us in the establishment of the Kingdom of Heaven on Earth. In this way, the end of the 26,000-tun evolutionary cycle will be prepared for, and just as Menes unified Upper and Lower Egypt at the beginning of the Great Cycle, so the electromagnetic unification of the north and south planetary poles will mark its triumphant conclusion.

While I have described the general scientific aspects of the new Solar Age, it is also necessary to consider the spiritual creative lifestyle that will be mobilized through application of the new psycho-solar resonant field technology. Indeed, without spiritual creative foundations, the new Solar Age would flounder and become another abuse of cleverness. Organized into small cells, bio-electromagnetic spores, by A.D. 1992 the life of humans will begin to resemble more the extended family styles of the prehistoric phase than the attenuated and disintegrative nuclear families of the Late Industrial era. The emphasis on individual integrity will be balanced by individual and collective participation in the new fields created by the houses of the senses. Every cell will be a projection of the individual body, for one and the same circuit will animate individual, group cell, and planet light body. One function of the new science will be to assist in the exact location and alignment of cell-groups with planetary points to augment the resonance of the greater whole.

At the center of each local community will be a solar temple, a simple yet elegant construction for contemplation and energy regeneration. Adjacent to the solar temple will be houses of energy and information: solar-crystal light-sheds surrounding a computer-based nerve and education center, connecting the local bio-electromagnetic spore with every other cell group on the planet. Interspersed among gardens, where intensification agricultural techniques and light industry are practiced, will be radiantly constructed houses of the senses. And finally, spreading out in organically radial patterns, will be the residential neighborhood clusters.

Reflecting the radial pattern of the light body itself, the outer forms of the houses of the senses will vary from climate to climate giving rise to a rich diversity of style which is yet globally unified in purpose. Combining sensory enrichment, that we expect nowadays from stereophonic headsets and movie theaters, with the intense total involvement that comes from ritual participation and complete sensory engagement, the activities of the houses of the senses will be the action nexus plugging us into the electromagnetic battery of the planet. Instead of going to a job at nine o'clock every morning, we shall prepare each day for the celebratory task of ritual sensory attunement to solar galactic pulsations. Through sensory fusion—bringing together of various senses into the experience of synaesthesia—we will realize a synergistic amplification of energy and enjoyment.

The leisure for so doing will be the natural result of having divested ourselves of an unnecessary military economy and the production of wasteful and even toxic consumer goods that were in total disregard of the reality of the light body. Nourishing ourselves as simply and as locally as possible, we shall turn our surplus wealth into the research, education, and artistic production necessary for the establishment of a healthy collective organism in resonant attunement with the Sun and, through the Sun, with the galactic core, Hunab Ku.

In addition to the improvement of sensual enjoyment, there will be an equal improvement of the capacity for psychic or what are now termed paranormal powers. Indeed, everyone will be a channel—a medium—and what we understand today to be psychic impressions or channeling will be but child's play compared to our actual potential. Rather than dredge up dreary past-life archetypes announced in pseudo-spooky voices, we will channel the stars directly. We shall find that our excitement and our adventure is in collectively making inter-dimensional crossings that simultaneously enhance our growth toward the collective synchronization of the planet light body. Opening our long-disregarded sense fields at last for the nourishment of the light body, UFOs will finally be understood as inter-dimensional, Earth-generated, galactically programmed electromagnetic cells available to us for own educational purposes.

Like the Maya who preceded us, we shall understand that the path to the stars is through the senses and that proper utilization of our mind as the auto-regulatory control factor will help facilitate the passage to different levels or dimensions of being. These dimensions or levels of being, now frequented by what we call UFOs, are universally accessible, and hence the meeting grounds of intelligence from different sectors of the galaxy. Like a multi-leveled spore, the model of our "new" galactic home, as well as the means of "transport" to the different dimensions of the electromagnetic ocean, is the great single central channel along which the various levels of being are strung: individual, collective, planetary, solar, stellar, code matrix, and galactic core.

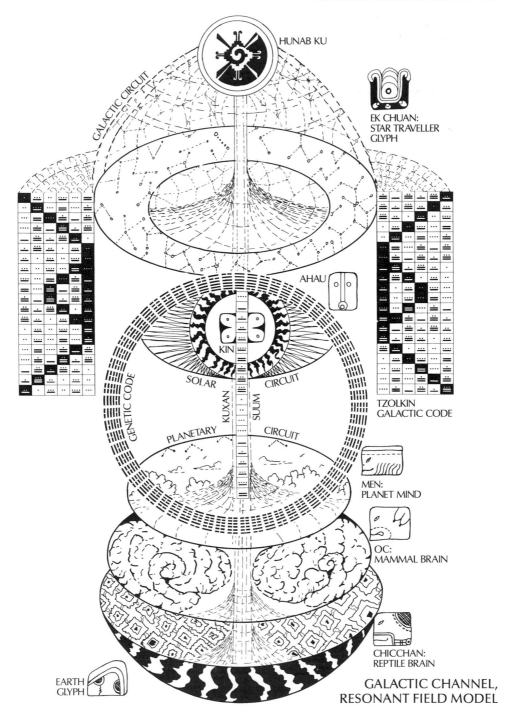

HUNAB KU

GALACTIC CIRCUIT

EK CHUAN:
STAR TRAVELLER
GLYPH

AHAU

KIN

SOLAR CIRCUIT

KUXAN SUUM

GENETIC CODE

PLANETARY CIRCUIT

TZOLKIN
GALACTIC CODE

MEN:
PLANET MIND

OC:
MAMMAL BRAIN

CHICCHAN:
REPTILE BRAIN

EARTH
GLYPH

GALACTIC CHANNEL,
RESONANT FIELD MODEL

As more and more of us learn to navigate the galactic median through skilled use of resonant harmonic frequencies, we will merge into the greater life. Direct psycho-sensory encounters with vistas more real and vast than those hinted at by our radio-telescopes will naturally dissolve those values that now bind us, by fear, to name and place. As we experience instead the fullness of the meaning of the universal life, selflessness and compassion will draw us on. As resonant navigators, we shall encounter the great ones of our myths, and the dream-time will envelop us in all its subtle richness. Techniques and insights developed by the great mystic traditions will be at the forefront of our activities, and where once we sank in dread for fear of death, we shall come to know again that continuity of being that makes the same wholeness out of each and every one of us.

In attaining to our universal being, we cannot underestimate the power of what we now call music, song, and harmonic sound. Through collective sound dwellings of the senses—radiosonic temples—the harmonics shall emerge that cause us to realize the Kingdom of Heaven on Earth. Understanding navigation as the function of a superior harmonic to which we are collectively attuned, we shall at the same time unlock ever-deeper levels of memory. As primary patterns of resonance, memory shall come to be known as the radial pattern that unifies all levels of being and consciousness. Through this knowledge, rung as the sonorous tones of collective synchronization, the palace of universal memory will open. Star-fields will merge, and the breakers of cosmic creation will wash across the consciousness of humankind.

Living through our senses, we shall make conscious at last the collective dream-time venerated by the aborigines. As we ride the pulsation waves of our neural circuits, communion will be re-established with the other kingdoms: the mineral, the plant, the animal, and the higher orders of the electromagnetic sea. Functioning again within the context of a greater natural hierarchy, our life will merge the shaman's environmental resilience with the pageantry of medieval court life, and all of this will be illumined by an intrinsic bio-luminescence at which present-day electricity can only hint. Humanity will be a kingdom once again, but a kingdom in liege to the Sun, and the entire Earth its single realm.

As we are chastened and made wise by our brief encounter with the machine and the horrors of nuclear experimentation, nobility in the New Kingdom will be a universally recognized trait. The democratic value of the individual will not be lost, but, rather, a new understanding of the individual in the galactic hierarchy will be established. The example of the warrior-shamans who first crossed over from history to post-history will spread as the life example for all. Chronicles of lyric beauty and epic proportion will spontaneously unfold through daily collective attunement. And at the market, theater, dance, and song will enliven the exchange of information and goods carried on by the merchants of light.

And if it be asked how all of this shall be ruled and regulated, then let us not underestimate the role of common sense and ordinary human insight directed and informed by a Council of Solar-Planetary Affairs. Charged with monitoring the alignment of the terrestrial electromagnetic battery with the solar frequencies and pulsations for the greater

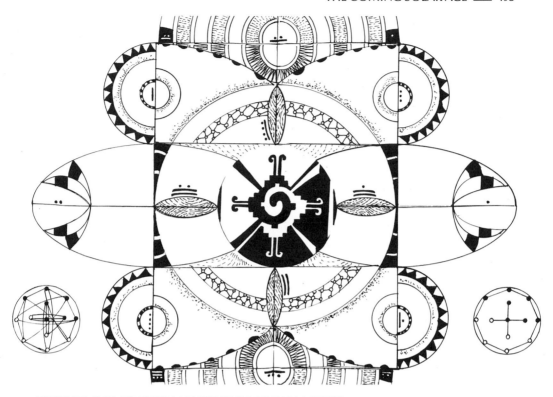

PSYCHO-SOLAR RESONANCE PULSATION MATRIX

harmonic resonance of the whole, the operations of this Council will naturally affect all other activities and actions on the planet.

Operating closely with the High Council of Solar-Planetary Affairs will be the Council of the Mediarchs and the Council of the Geomants. The former will be charged with globally disseminating information and education through the computer-video network; the latter will be charged with the harmonic, artistic interface of human and planetary fields of resonance. The conjoined action of these two councils will be to bring about ever greater synchronizations of the human race. The vast patchwork of bio-regionally organized locals will send emissaries to the Council of Solar-Planetary Affairs for annual conferences, solstices, and equinoxes among them. The primary event and focus of all activity will be the sponsoring of semi-annual, planet-wide Solar/Earth-Day celebrations.

Following the major task of divesting the old military establishment of its wealth and taking down and cleaning up of toxic facilities, economics after A.D. 1992 will be freely regulated. Economic arbiters or overseers, functioning closely with the Council of Solar-Planetary Affairs and the Council of the Mediarchs, will travel from bio-region to bio-region gathering information in order to equalize the production and distribution of global wealth. Indeed, wealth will be information distributed as information units appropriate to local bio-regions. Exchanges will be set up between representatives of different groups, effecting cultural as well as informational and economic cross-pollination. Voyaging under the banner of the great Solar Being, the traveling economic arbiter teams will be joyously accompanied by minstrel bands, artistic troupes assisting in the planetary cross-breeding.

Criminal activities, including theft, hoarding, plunder, rape, and murder, will be dealt with by the Council on Creative Rehabilitation. Operating closely with the Council on Global Health, the Council on Creative Rehabilitation will remand all "criminals" to Creative Rehabilitation Units overseen by geomantic ritualists who, following diagnosis, will then consign the offenders to creative problem-solving tasks connected with the Houses of the Senses.

With the need for war abandoned and the citizens of planet Earth awakened to a higher purpose through the Campaign for the Earth, the face of global society will change rapidly over the next generation. As the year A.D. 2012 approaches, the planet will be humming and vibrating as never before. The final five-year period, A.D. 2007-2012, will be singularly directed to the emplacement of galactic synchronization crews at all the planetary light-body grid-nodes.

Utilizing harmonic information patterns that inter-connect individual, planetary, and solar light bodies attuned to galactic frequencies, collective psychic-solar navigation teams and synchronization crews will help see that no one individual is left out of attunement. Education and rehabilitation teams will work in the last of the prisons and hospitals. Bio-electromagnetic medicine teams will see to it that every last bio-regional local is brought into alignment with the template of the planetary light body. Monitoring signals from the Galactic Federation, advanced units from the Council of Solar-Planetary Affairs will seed the last instructions to the synchronization crews.

Then it shall be ready. The unique moment, the moment of total planetary synchronization, 13.0.0.0.0 on the beam, will arrive—the closing out not only of the Great Cycle, but of the evolutionary interim called *Homo sapiens*. Amidst festive preparation and awesome galactic-solar signs psychically received, the human race, in harmony with the animal and other kingdoms and taking its rightful place in the great electromagnetic sea, will unify as a single circuit. Solar and galactic sound transmissions will inundate the planetary field. At last, Earth will be ready for the emergence into inter-planetary civilization.

Then, as if a switch were being thrown, a great voltage will race through this finally synchronized and integrated circuit called humanity. The Earth itself will be illumined. A current charging both poles will race across the skies, connecting the polar auroras in a single brilliant flash. Like an iridescent rainbow, this circumpolar energy uniting the planetary antipodes will be instantaneously understood as the external projection of the unification of the collective mind of humanity. In that moment of understanding, we shall

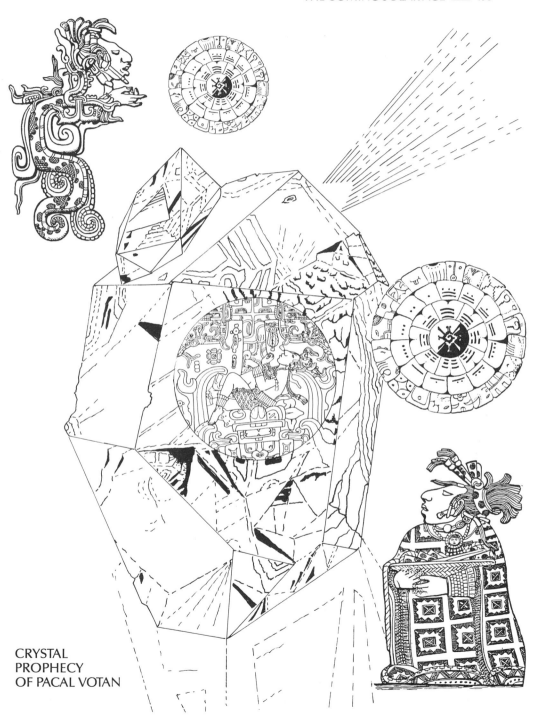

CRYSTAL
PROPHECY
OF PACAL VOTAN

be collectively projected into an evolutionary domain that is presently inconceivable.

And yet, we shall know. Like infants in a vast new playground, we shall retain the highest and most exalted vision. Purpose will be illumined to new levels of spontaneity. Everywhere shall be heard the Voices of the Galactic Federation: the Elders, the Ancestors, the great Bodhisattvas and Saints, the Maya returned, our deepest Selves, the Cosmic Mirror, the Raiment of Space and Time made One. As one voice, the announcement shall be made, heard by one ear: And now the adventure begins!

Now, some will say that I have woven a fantasy, a utopian tale that is unrealizable in such short time. But I have only woven from that which the Maya left behind and which the teachings of mind's vastness make accessible to all. According to the prophecies of Shambhala, following the final conquest of the Three Lords of Materialism by the spiritual armies released for the closing of the cycle, there will be a 500-year Golden Age. As we ride the final baktun fractal through this dark moment of Faustian denouement to ultimate planetary release from our self-created bondage, let those warrior-shamans among us take heart. For it is through the open portals of the heart that the future returns in all of its radiance.

Humbly presented as a gift to the children, I close with the Mayan code of honor: *In Lake'ch*: I am another yourself.

Completed 1 Imix, 12 Zotz, October 6, 1986, the Eastern Year 7 Muluc Boulder, Colorado, Central Rockies, North America.

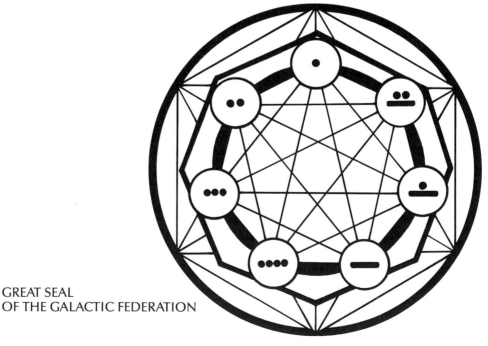

GREAT SEAL
OF THE GALACTIC FEDERATION

A RESONANT PARADIGM PRIMER:
A GLOSSARY OF KEY MAYAN TERMS & CONCEPTS

The Mayan Perspective, though often characterized as being obsessed with time, actually does not possess a specific word for time, or words for space or matter. For this reason, the Mayan Perspective is uniquely qualified to be a paradigm that is resonant and matrix-based, as distinct from the current paradigm which is atomistically anchored in calibrations of space, time, and matter.

The following glossary of terms, inspired by and loosely derived from Domingo Martinez Parédez' *Parapsicologia Maya* (Mexico, 1981), is intended as a *Resonant Paradigm Primer*. Its purpose is to provide the seeker with a basis for considering a view of reality distinct from the prevailing world view yet within the framework of a post-quantum physicalistic view of reality. This view of reality, like the Mayan, is a paradigm based on wave harmonics and resonant fields. The terms are arranged, as much as possible, to present a coherent cosmological unfolding of this dynamic non-materialistic perspective.

The Glossary is followed by several paragraphs extending the meaning of the Tzolkin by placing it in the context of holonomics—the law governing whole systems.

MAYAN GLOSSARY

HUNAB KU. The One Giver of Movement and Measure. The principle of intelligent energy that pervades the entire universe, animate or inanimate.

HUYUB CAAN (HURUCAAN). Heart of Heaven. Heavenly builder, cosmic design principle.

KIN. The Sun. Chief mediator of HUNAB KU for our planetary system. Day. Basic harmonic unit or wave property.

KINAN. Solar Force. Higher spiritual energy. Solar mind as the universally available means of transmitting higher psychic energy on this planet.

TIN KINANTAH. Quality of spirit-transmitting energy, solar-related higher energy accounting for different kinds of psychic or paranormal phenomena.

KINICH AHAU. Lord of the Sun. Galactic overseer, the realized solar mind, or mind of light.

AHAU KINES (Also AH KIN, AH KINES). Solar Lords. Priests of the Sun. Diviners of harmony, seers.

BAAXTEN. Capacity to project energy, as well as the effect of projection of energy.

PAX. Cosmic break or rupture, the power of music.

PIXAN. What manifests within form, "spirit."

TIN UILA LUUN TUL PIXAN. To see a soul, a spirit. To perceive the manifest.

KUXAN SUUM. Road to the sky, leading to the umbilical cord of the universe. Invisible galactic life-blood threads mediated by KIN, the Sun.

CAAN. Heaven.

CAN. Serpent, energy, four. Fourfold energy wave functions: gravitational force, electromagnetic force, strong force, and weak force (the latter two combined create the biopsychic field or psi). (In the I Ching, the four energy wave functions correspond respectively to Young Yin, Young Yang, Old Yang, Old Yin.)

NAC. Reverse of CAN: limit, form principle.

CANNAC. Principle that there is no form without spirit and vice versa. Complementarity of energy and form. Also, that which has to be learned.

TUMEN. Cause and effect. Principle of causal relatedness.

CUXTAL. To arrive at oxidation (CAXUM). Life-generating principle.

CANIL CUXTAL. Serpent of life. Energy arriving at oxidation or taking on form, limiting of energy; hence, suffering as primary quality of existence.

WINCLIL. Human being. WINC, tuber, root, LIL, vibratory, hence human. Cosmic vibratory root or resonator.

CI'ZIN. Radiation, ray, psyche. Particular energy projection, personality.

ET P'IZ. Our measure. Law of karma, compensation.

K'OCHIL. What we are born with, what we die with. Karmic residue modifying individual existence.

YACUNAH. Love, at the same time suffering. Inescapable poignancy of existence.

IN LAK'ECH. I am another yourself. Principle of universal love, compassion.

CHAN. Quality of intelligence. Intellect.

CHICCHAN. Reptile. Instinctual mind. Primary intelligence.

CHANES. First children of the Sun. Galactic messengers.

ITZAES. First children of the water. Atlanteans.

HOB, HOOL. Head, idea. Mind or mental faculty.

NENHOOL. Mirror of mind. Everything is reflection of oneself. Principle of NAGUAL, or light-body spirit double.

PANCHE BE. To seek the root of truth. Natural path of existence.

MEN. To believe, to create, to do. Higher mental force, expressing PIXAN, spirit energy, mediated by KINAN, higher solar mind.

H' MENES. Sorcerors, magicians, healers. Those versed in MEN.

H'PULYAHES. Lancers of evil. Misusers of energy.

DZAC. Medicine, poison.

OL, OLAL. Animatedness. Will, quality of spirit (PIXAN) as animated forms of expression.

OL UOLAH. Spirit of will exercised in accord with the law of cause (TUMEN) and effect (ET P'IZ).

LUK'AN TUMEN CAN. Bearers of the serpent. The initiates.

TUCU'T. To think, to venerate.

THAN. Drop of water. Power of the word.

HEL, GEL. Egg, zero, basis of transformation.

CANHEL. Self-transforming serpent. Dragon. Totality of fourfold energy manifest as self-transforming energy-being.

CHE, TE. Tree. TE-OTL. Tree spirit. Divine energy.

YAX. Green. Power of Renewal.

YAXKIN. The Center. Sourceless source. Place of Renewal

YAXCHE. Primal tree. Axis of the universe. Mystic column. Human being as channel.

BAAL CHE. Thing of the tree, i.e., animal, animal power.

TOK'ZAH. Acupuncture.

HUP KIIX. To puncture with needles.

XICH. Nerve. Electrical network.

ZUVUYA, ZUYUYA. Circuit by which all things return to themselves. Thirteenth or highest heaven. Planetary point of entry. Language of the KATUNS, the grammar of harmony.

TZOLKIN. Count of days. Sacred Calendar, cosmic matrix. Universal harmonic module accommodating every possible permutation of HUNAB KU—One Giver of Movement and Measure.

Movement—the life-giving principle of energy—is represented by the number thirteen, OXLAHUN. Each number, one through thirteen, is considered to be a pulse-emanation of a specific quality of energy which gives inherent structure and meaning to the possibilities of being. Inclusive of the preceding twelve numbers, thirteen is the force immanent in all things, the number of the highest heaven, the source of galactic information.

Measure—the form-giving principle of energy—is represented by the number four, CAN. To this number are accorded the four primary wave functions: gravity—attraction; electromagnetic—radiation; strong force—(psychic) transmission; and weak force—(psychic) receptivity.

The 4, representing Measure, multiplied by 5, the number descriptive of the primary matrix structure—the center and four cardinal points— yields 20. The TZOLKIN—the Universal Harmonic Module—is actually a matrix created by the permutations of the two key numbers, thirteen and twenty (4×5). Thus, the TZOLKIN pulsation-matrix consists of 260 permutation units.

The thirteen vertical columns of the TZOLKIN represent the principle of movement; the twenty horizontal columns represent the principle of measure considered as five rotating sequences of four stations or matrix positions.

Though the Tzolkin is generally considered as the 260-day Sacred Calendar—the numbers one through thirteen repeating twenty times in conjunction with twenty Sacred Signs—in actuality it is much more. Because it is the Universal Harmonic Matrix, it is also the module for the PSI BANK, the planet memory field. (See *Earth Ascending*, Maps 1, 2, 3, 9, 29, 30, 31, 32, 40, 41, 42, 46, 47, 48). Eight of these modules constitute the PSI BANK, four per polar field, the four again recapitulating the principle number of measure. Taken as a count of days, sixteen Tzolkin correspond to 11.3 years, the mean number describing the periodicity of binary sunspot cycles from inception of movement to polar reversal. 11.3 times 23, the mean number of years for a total movement of sunspots, yields 260, the number of units in a Tzolkin, the Universal Harmonic Module.

Taken as a grand calendar, the Tzolkin describes the MAYAN GREAT CYCLE, or Hologram of Time. This Cycle corresponding to 5,125 Earth years, runs from the Earth year now reckoned as 3113 B.C. through the Earth year now reckoned as A.D. 2012. It consists of thirteen baktun cycles of twenty katuns each for a total of 394 years per baktun. It also consists of twenty AHAU Cycles of thirteen Katuns each, totaling 256 years per cycle.

In speaking of the Great Cycle, the word calendar should be taken advisedly. Hologram of Time is much more in keeping with the Mayan Perspective. That is, just as the Tzolkin is the Universal Harmonic Module accommodating all permutations of movement and measure, so the Great Cycle should be understood as the hologram of civilizational possibility, providing the harmonic calibrations that link terrestrial evolutionary process with the galactic program. The purpose of the Hologram of Time is that intelligent manifestation construct the MYSTIC BODY OF THE PLANET. This Mystic Body of the Planet is the 52-UNIT BINARY TRIPLET CONFIGURATION or LOOM OF MAYA contained within and giving unique structure to the Tzolkin, the Universal Harmonic Module.

Since the Hologram of Time, the 5,125-year Great Cycle, is no different than the key module of the planetary Memory Field, the Psi Bank, the Hologram of Time can be seen as the field in which certain universal memory patterns are played out. The skillful playing out of these memory patterns results in the successful construction of the Mystic Body of the Planet. This Mystic Body is the aspect of KINAN, the Solar Mind, or Higher Mental Force as it unifies itself with one of its children, in this case, planet Earth.

It should be carefully noted that in terms of the Great Cycle, the planet is about to enter the 260th Katun (A.D. 1992), which is also the 52nd Katun of the Mystic Body, a Katun manifesting the thirteenth pulsation-ray, and ruled by the twentieth Sign AHAU, the Solar Mind. The understanding of the hologram of time, resonant structures, and planet memory patterns in general is critical if the Mystic Body is to be completed and KINAN or Higher Mental Force is to be established on planet Earth.

Understanding the Hologram of Time and resonant structures in terms of the Tzolkin is not difficult. As the Universal Harmonic Module, the Tzolkin is no farther away than our genetic composition and the functions of our own body—WINCLIL—cosmic vibratory root.

Because each of the eight modules of the Tzolkin Psi Bank Matrix can be divided into eight equal parts, the entire Psi Bank matrix accommodates the 64 (8×8)-unit generative field of the DNA, the planetary genetic information bank. Furthermore, thirteen, number of movement, corresponds to the thirteen chief articulations of the body: shoulders, elbows, wrists, hips, knees, ankles, and, corresponding to the mystic column, the neck and spinal column. To four, number of measure, correspond the two arms and two legs, while to the twenty (4×5) correspond the twenty digits—ten toes, ten fingers. The 52 units of the BINARY TRIPLET CONFIGURATION correspond to the 52 meridian points—26 each side of the body.

Since the code structure of the 64 DNA codons is identical with the binary code language of the I Ching, an intimate relation is established between the eight-part Tzolkin/Psi Bank key and the I Ching understood as the code of life. The reason this connection exists is that Tzolkin is the self-existing Universal Harmonic Module containing the matrix templates for DNA and I Ching. These systems—Tzolkin, DNA, and I Ching—are all memory- generating patterns whose codes are defined by simple number relations. To unlock the memory patterns contained in these codes is the primary task of the present moment in human history. By unlocking these memory patterns, human intelligence may arrive at an initial understanding of the construction of the Mystic Planet Body—KINAN—by A.D. 1992, the time the 260th katun is entered and the thirteenth pulsation-ray is manifest in the Sign AHAU.

THE MAYAN HARMONIC NUMERICAL SYSTEM

The Mayan numerical system is based on a binary progression that moves exponentially forward, using 20 as its base. The entire system of infinitesimal binary harmonic progressions is recorded with only three notations: a dot, indicating units; a bar, indicating five units; and a variation of a shell form, indicating zero, place, or completion. It is binary because numerically, 20 is base value 2. Precisely because it is a *vigesimal* system, base *20,* the Mayan mathematic recapitulates the universal binary progression. Thus, while in the first position, a unit equals 1; in the second, a unit equals 20; in the third, 400; and so on. In the numerical progression for the first thirteen positions, the value of a unit is as follows:

1

20

400

8000

160,000

3,200,000

64,000,000

1,280,000,000

25,600,000,000

512,000,000,000

10,240,000,000,000

204,800,000,000,000

4,096,000,000,000,000

Though in this progression we have included the zeros, in dealing with harmonics it is sufficient to indicate the base number which actually refers to a frequency that can be expressed in any given octave. The universal binary progression inherent in the Mayan system gives it a harmonic, exponential power not contained in the decimal, base 10, system now commonly in use. In the decimal system, base 1, no matter how many times it is multiplied by itself, always equals 1, whereas in the vigesimal system, 2 multiplied by itself yields the infinite binary progression.

Most often it is thought the Maya used this system to record periods or cycles of time. But because the system records a universal harmonic binary progression, the notations may also refer to the binary wave harmonic by which phenomena manifest in space. In other words, the periodicity of movements in time as well as the periodicity of manifestations in space are governed by the same universal wave harmonic operating according to the same universal binary progression. Ultimately, of course, the harmonic of space is indistinguishable from the harmonic of time.

In adopting the system to planet Earth for the purpose of computing basic cycles of time, the Maya modified the system to correspond more closely to the annual revolution of this planet around the Sun. Thus the progression used for recording terrestrial time cycles is the following:

1 : 20 : 360 : 7,200 : 144,000 : 2,880,000, etc., where base **unit 1 = 1 day**. This progression, significantly enough, corresponds to the series of the harmonics of light, where **144 = the harmonic of light**, **72 = 1/2 sine wave**, and **288 = polar light harmonic**. Harmonic 288, incidentally, is the light harmonic of Earth, 144 the harmonic of each pole.

Since the modified Mayan time-count, substituting base unit 360 for 400 in the third position, is identical with the progression of the light harmonic, the so-called calendrical counts recorded so profusely among the Mayan artifacts take on a new dimension. These counts may be read simultaneously as calendrical counts beginning from base equivalent, August 13, 3113 B.C., (= Mayan 0.0.0.0.0), as well as light harmonic calibrations.

While the universal binary progression accounts for values of 2, inclusive of the octave, the light harmonic progression is also inclusive of values of 3 and 9, 8 and 9 being the key multiples of the light harmonic, e.g., $72=8\times9$, $144=8\times9\times2$. 360, the number of degrees in a circle = 40 (8 x 5) x 9.

Along with 20 (4 x 5), the other key number, if not *THE key* number in the Mayan harmonic system, is **13**. As a prime number, 13 is the coefficient or constant of the Mayan harmonic system. Thus it is the base unit governing the sacred calendar *TZOLKIN* of 260 units, which is the product of the two coefficients of the system, **13 and 20**. The basic governing terrestrial time cycle is also computed as a cycle of thirteen baktuns. The baktun is the name given the fifth position and is a period of time slightly less than 400 years; hence a thirteen-baktun cycle is a period slightly less than 5,200 years. On the modified time-count progression, the baktun is accorded a unit value of 144,000, the value of the harmonic of light. The progression of the present thirteen, light-harmonic/baktun cycles begun 3113 B.C., concludes December 21, A.D. 2012.

The identity of light harmonics with periods of time is of special interest in this consideration of Mayan harmonic progressions. Time is the unfolding manifestation of a light harmonic. A terrestrial time sequence of thirteen such harmonics, or **great cycle** of thirteen baktuns, comprises the period for a particular manifestation to run through all of its possible permutations before being raised an octave. This means that in the current planetary scheme we shall be jumping an octave early in the next century. In a solar scale based on a progression of the wave form of the prime numbers 1-16, the 13th tone is the only one that creates a distinctly audible overtone matrix, or dimensional break. 13 is the Solar Number, or actually the prime light information wave. It represents the means for interdimensional shift.

To recapitulate: what is termed Mayan mathematics is actually a twofold system of binary progressions based on a vigesimal notation system. The primary system is the absolute universal binary progression, 2 : 4 : 8 : 16: 32 : 64 , ad infinitum. It should be noted that this progression includes base numbers for the **octave (8)**, **crystal symmetry properties (32)**, and **DNA codons (64)**. The variant of this system is the relative, temporal/terrestrial progression, **1 : 20 : 360 : 7,200 : 144,000**, etc. used in calendrical calculations, and also corresponding to the progression of light harmonics.

The mathematical system of the Maya was and still is the clearest and most efficient system for describing the universal wave harmonics governing the manifestations of all space-time matrices. The system assumes a unified field expressed through harmonic binary progressions that, being intrinsically harmonic, also describe the unified space-time matrix as a field of resonance. Since binary progression describes a universal process, the mathematical and notation systems are also universal.

Even if it did originate on this planet, the Mayan harmonic notational system could only have been obtained through the capacity of a pure resonance of mind with universal order. However, being a pure universal harmonic, the system actually describes the means for universal transmission through resonant powers operating at least at the speed of light. Complete understanding of the wave harmonics represented by the Mayan notational harmonics will unlock the gates to an order of reality, purely resonant and hence non-material, *that is so far beyond the complexities of our current material order as to be bafflingly simple.*

XAMAN	from the **North** on the right-hand side
	white and pure like the Moon in its brilliant fullness
NOHOL	from the **South** on the left-hand side
	yellow like the burnished light of the Sun setting fields ablaze
LIKIN	from the **East** where the Sun appears to rise
	red like the blood more powerful than Earth's great single sea
CHIKIN	from the **West** where the Sun appears to set
	black like the wisdom even more majestic than the night
YAXKIN	**Center** of the sky Sun's zenith
	opening where Universal beingness
	drops its plumbline joining Earth below to Heaven above
	though invisible and unreal nothing is gone
	the compass of the Earth was here before the Earth
	even before the Sun was from the place much farther beyond
	the compass spoke speaks yet the language of light

Mystic Column 225-40 N Autumn Plate Earth 40 AH

 APPENDICES

APPENDIX A. RADIAL AND DIRECTIONAL NUMBERS

The richness of the radially reciprocal understanding of the thirteen numbers is further amplified if the individual numbers in the series 1-13 (or 13-1) do not have simply a sequential but a *directional* relation to each other as well. In other words, let the first number **1** represent the East; the second number **2**, the North; the third **3**, the West, and the fourth **4**, the South; and the fifth **5**, the East again, and so forth. The series **1-13** with directional notations would now look like this:

```
1 - 2 - 3 - 4 - 5 - 6 - 7 - 8 - 9 - 10 - 11 - 12 -13
E - N - W - S - E - N - W - S - E - N - W - S - E
```

Arriving at **13**, the pulsation returns to **1**, while the directional notations continue where they left off:

```
1 - 2 - 3 - 4 - 5 - 6 - 7 - 8 - 9 - 10 - 11 - 12 -13
N - W - S - E - N - W - S - E - N - W - S - E - N  etc.
```

In order for **1** to be matched with **E** again, there will have to be **52** permutations (**13** numbers×**4** directional positions). Let us also say that the directional positions have their own cycle which consists of **5** rounds, in other words the E-N-W-S pattern must spin **5** times in sequence to complete a single cycle for a total of **20** positions—20 of course, being not only **4×5** but the sum of **7** and **13**, the two key "mystic" numbers in the series 1-13.

This being the case, a radial matrix is created in which there are a total of **260** possible permuations—the *Tzolkin*—described by the spinning of the 13 numbers each one revolving through 20 possible directional positions. If the 13 numbers are each accorded a particular tonal quality given variation by the 20 positions, then through all the possible permutations a rich harmonic description becomes possible. The **260**-unit matrix might begin to look like a multiphasic keyboard for the composition of the galactic symphony—which indeed it is!

APPENDIX B. MAYAN FACTORS & FRACTALS

To understand fractals, just remember: *a fractal is a proportion that remains constant.* For instance, a 36-degree segment of a circle will always be 36 degrees no matter how large or small the circle. Also, in this segment of a circle sufficient information is contained to allow one to construct the whole circle. The fractal principle underlies the holographic nature of things: from one fraction of a particular whole, the entire whole can be constructed.

The same principle applies to overtones. Just as a tone in one octave may be reverberated or sounded at other octaves, though the different octave tones vibrate at different frequencies, so a number or a fraction of a number set may be "sounded" at many different levels yielding similar proportional overtones. Incidentally, when a 16-tone scale is sounded, only one tone reverberates a rich matrix of overtones—the thirteenth.

For instance: **13** is a fractal of **130 (13 × 10)**, **144** is a fractal of **1,440 (144 ×10)**; that is, from the 13 we may construct the 130, or vice versa, while from the 1,440, we may derive the 144. In this case, the fractals 13 or 144 represent proportions that remain constant through a potentially infinite series.

Thus, a fractal tonality can be set up with a whole range of numbers: **26, 260, 2,600, 26,000** etc. or **52, 520, 5,200, 52,000**, etc. What is important and gives the tone to each of the numbers in a fractal series is not the quantity, which the number most certainly also denotes, but the key fractal number itself, i.e., **13, 26, 52**, etc., which creates the proportional "tone" in the series. The zeros added to a fractal series may be taken as the equivalent of higher registrations of frequencies.

Related to fractals are *factors—the numbers which provide the multiples of a given figure*, i.e. **260** is the product of the factors **13** and **20**. At the same time, **260** is a member of the *fractal* series based on **26**. **26** itself is the product of **13** and **2**. All fractals are factoral numbers which provide the basis for different series of proportional relations.

Patient reflection will show how the different numbers interpenetrate and pervade each other like different kinds of perfume. For instance, **144** would always be read as **12×12, 9×16, 18×8, 3×36**, or **72×2;** while **52** would be read as factors of **13×4** or **26×2**. Incidentally, in the Mayan system virtually all of the key fractals are factors of either **13, 4**, or **9**. Thus **260** is a factor of **13×20**; **64** is a factor of **4×16**; and **144** is a factor of **9×16**. *In this way various larger whole numbers are considered more or less harmonic according to the diversity of the factoral and fractal possibilities which they represent.*

APPENDIX C. CALENDAR HARMONICS

The 360-unit "calendar" called the *tun* represents the third positional rank of the Mayan number progression which utilizes the factor of **9**. This progression, which otherwise proceeds by multiples of **20**, could go on infinitely, but for practical purposes consists of nine orders. Read from bottom up, with the Mayan names for the respective positional places and time approximations, the nine orders are:

9. Alautun = 23,040,000,000 (or 20 kinchiltuns) 63,040,000 + years
8. Kinchiltun = 1,280,000,000 kin (or 20 calabtuns) 3,152,000 + years
7. Calabtun = 57,600,000 kin (or 20 pictuns) approx 157,600 + years
6. Pictun = 2,880,000 kin (or 20 baktuns) approx 7,900 + years
5. Baktun = 144,000 kin (or 20 katuns) approx 394 + solar years

4. Katun = 7,200 kin (or 20 tuns) approx 19 + solar years
3. Tun = 360 kin (or 18 (9 × 2) vinals) approx 1 solar year
2. Vinal = 20 kin (or 20 days)
1. Kin = 1 kin (or 1 day)

Had this progression moved purely by 20s, a tun would be the equivalent of 400 kin. Instead, the factor of 9 is introduced in the order of *vinal*, the 20-day periods. Instead of 20 vinal there are only 18. Hence, 18×20=360 kin or one tun. The rest of the progression continues by moving in multiples of 20s, but stained, as it were, by the warp caused by the introduction of the factor of 9 in the second order.

The preceding progression of nine orders is the count the Maya adopted for purposes related to computations of time. Hence, 9 is the number most closely associated with the concept of time. In any case, this progression utilizing the warp of 9 is in contrast to the Mayan "pure" count. While our positional mathematics is *decimal*, that is, advancing by 10s, the Mayan "pure" count is *vigesimal*, advancing by 20s. While our system advances 1, 10, 100, 1,000, etc, the Mayan advances in the following manner:

9th Position: one unit equals **25,6**00,000 (20×1,280,000,000)
8th Position: one unit equals **1,28**0,000,000 (20×64,000,000)
7th Position: one unit equals **64**,000,000 (20×3,200,000)
6th Position: one unit equals **3,2**00,000 (20×160,000)
5th Position: one unit equals **16**0,000 (20×8,000)
4th Position: one unit equals **8,**000 (20×400)
3rd Position: one unit equals **4**00 (20×20)
2nd Position: one unit equals **20** (20×1)
 1st Position: one unit equals **1** (1×1)

It should be noted that the fractal numbers of the Mayan pure progression—2, 4, 8, 16, 32, 64, etc.—represent the binary progression that proceeds by doubling the last sum, i.e, **2+2=4, 4+4=8, 8+8=16**, etc. This progression underlies the permutational mathematics of both DNA and the I Ching.

But to return to the "calendar" and its numbers, as noted, in the 260- and the 360-unit "calendars", we see the key numbers: **4**, **9**, and **13**. **4** is the number signifying *measure*; **9** is the number signifying *periodicity or completeness*; **13** is the number signifying the *movement immanent in all things*. The difference between **9** and **13** is, of course, **4**.

While **7**, midway between **1** and **13** is the *mystic open term* that penetrates all things, **5**, the difference between **4** and **9**, is the *number of the center* understood as the point from which things can be measured, i.e., the four directions, the seasons etc. This is because **5** is **4**, the number of measure, plus **1**, the *number of unity*.

The meaning of any number depends partially on the factors of which it is the sum. **2** (1+1) is the *number signifying polarity*, while 3 (2+1) represents the *principle of rhythm*.

6 (3x2 or 3+3) is the number of *rhythmic wholeness*, while **8** (4+4), or "measure" doubled, is the *number of the octave*, the key resonant harmonic number itself. **10** (9+1) represents the *principle of manifestation*; **11**, the *principle of dissonance*; and **12**, the *principle of dynamic stasis*.

APPENDIX D. HARMONIC NUMBERS

The principle of the harmonic number, as stated in Appendix B, is that larger whole numbers are considered more or less harmonic according to the diversity of the factoral and fractal possibilities which they represent. 936,000, representing the midpoint of the Great Cycle, is an example. Marking as it does the passage of six-and-one-half cycles of 144,000 kin or days each, the number 6.10.0.0.0 denotes **harmonic 936**, the passing of 936,000 (6.5×144,000) days or kin from the initiation of the cycle in 3113 B.C. In addition, 936,000 accommodates the key fractal 26 in that 936,000 = 2,600 tun of 360 days each. Numerologically, the date 936,000 kin (9+3+6=18=1+8) equals 9, as do all factors of 9.

The greatest harmonic number, however, is 13 66 560:

13 66 560 divided by 360 = 3796 Tun (tun = 360 kin).

13 66 560 divided by 365 = 3744 Haab (365 kin = Haab, or solar year).

The difference between 3796 Tun and 3744 Haab = 52 (13×4). 52 = a "calendar round" of 52 solar years synchronized with 73 sacred calendar cycles of 260 days each.

13 66 560 divided by 72 = 18980, the number of days in a 52-year "calendar round."

A 52-year calendar round = 52×365 or 260×73.

13 66 560 divided by 73 = 18720 = 52×360 or 260×72.

13 66 560 divided by 9, number of the Lords of Time = 15 18 40.

151,840 kin divided by 365 = 416 vague solar years (Haab).

13 66 560 divided by 260 = 5256 Tzolkin or sacred calendar cycles.

13 66 560 divided by 584, apparent days in Venus cycle = 2340 Venus years.

13 66 560 divided by 780 apparent days in a Martian cycle = 1752 Mars years.

13 66 560 divided by 2920 days = 468 Venus-solar cycles.

2920 divided by 365 = 8; divided by 584 = 5.

13 66 560 divided by 37 960 = 36 cycles of 104 years; 104 years corresponds to one conjunction of the Venus, sacred calendar, and solar cycles.

13 66 560 divided by 52 = 26 280 or 72 vague solar years.

13 66 560 divided by 12 = 1 13 880 or 312 vague solar years.

13 66 560 divided by 13 = 10 51 20 or 288 vague solar years.

13 66 560 divided by 8 = 17 08 20 or 468 vague solar years.

While we will go into detail later regarding the significance of some of these above-mentioned cycles—the calendar round and the Venus cycles in particular—it is sufficient here to merely contemplate the amazing capacity of the **harmonic 136656** to accommodate so many different factors and cyclic figures.

If we are to take the number 13 66 560 as the number of days from starting point 3113 B.C., we arrive at 9.9.16.0.0 or A.D. 631. This date is the equivalent of **3796-tun cycles** of 360 days each or **3744-haab or solar cycles** of 365 days each. The *difference* between the **3796-**tun and **3744-**solar cycles from the date 3113 B.C. is **52.** If we add **52 years**, the number of years in a *"calendar round,"* to the date 9.9.16.0.0, A.D. 631, we arrive at the date 9.12.8.13.0, or A.D. 683. The number of days elapsed from 3113 B.C., the commencement of the Great Cycle, to A.D. 683, is **1385540**, or the equivalent of **3796 vague** solar years—vague because leap-year days are not included. The number 13 85 540 also corresponds to **73 52-year calendar round cycles**. **73** is the number of 260-day Tzolkin cycles that synchronize with **52** solar years to comprise a calendar round (52×365=260×73). Thus the date A.D. 683 would correspond to a *calendar round fractal overtone.* On the other hand, 13 66 560 or A.D. 631 also corresponds to **73-tun** cycles of 52×360 units. Small wonder that Pacal Votan would be associated with the magnificent number 13 66 560!

Finally, 13 66 560 corresponds to the completion of the 36th solar-Venus cycle (each of 104 years—104×36=3744 solar years) since the commencement of the Great Cycle, 3113 B.C. As both the morning and the evening star, Venus is the planet especially associated with Quetzalcoatl-Kukulkan. For Quetzalcoatl was both Lord of Dawn, bringer of light, the morning star, and Guide of the Dead, presider over the mysteries of the dead, the evening star.

APPENDIX E. THE 52-YEAR CYCLE & DAILY CALENDAR ROUND

The Tzolkin, understood as the 260-day Sacred Calendar, when combined with the 365-day vague solar calendar or Haab, creates a cycle of 52 years. That is, the coincidence of day one of the Sacred Calendar and day one of the solar calendar occurs only once every 18,980 days or approximately 52 years. While the 260 days repeat endlessly, the 365-day Haab is divided into 18 Vinal of 20 days each with a 5-day VAYEB or clean-out period preceding the beginning of another year. Thus, a traditional Mayan date always includes a date from the 260-day cycle as well as one from the Haab, for example: 2 IK 13 ZOTZ, 13 AHAU 1 POP, etc.

52 (13×4, 26×2), 1/5 of the 260-unit Harmonic Module is clearly a key Mayan number; it also appears in the Great Seal of the United States of America (13 arrows, 13 stars, 13 stripes, 13 olive branches). Obviously, the 52-year cycle is a fractal of the 5,200-tun Great Cycle, approximately 100 52-year cycles constituting a Great Cycle. Among the later Maya, and especially the Aztecs, the 52-year cycles assumed paramount importance. At the time of the Conquest, the 52-year cycles were counted from the day 1 Reed, the Year 1 Reed, which happened to be the date Cortés landed in Mexico. This

date concluded thirteen 52-year heaven cycles and commenced nine 52-year hell cycles, which complete themselves August 16, 1987.

Part of the elegance of the 52-year cycles and the coordination of the 260-day Tzolkin with the 365-day Haab is that the beginning point of each of the 52 vague solar years in this cycle can only fall on one of four Sacred Signs in a sequence that recapitulates the counter-clockwise directional rotation. These signs and their sequence are: MULUC (East); IX (North); CAUAC (West); and KAN (South). The Mayan year currently begins on the equivalent date, July 26. July 26, 1986, was the date 7 MULUC; July 26, 1987, is the date 8 IX; July 26, 1988 is 9 CAUAC, etc. On leap years, there are six instead of five Vayeb. The Vayeb always fall on the five (or six) days prior to O POP. The first day of the Haab is always 0 POP; i.e. July 26 is always O POP. The first day of a Vinal is always O, the last day 19.

The 18 Vinal plus the Vayeb and their glyph signs are given below. From this information, along with the planet-day sign concordances given below, it is easy to construct a day-book or calendar, and, given the information in Chapter 4, to begin to work with practical, everyday Mayan "astrology."

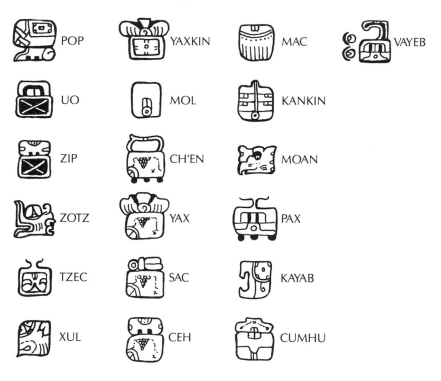

18 VINAL & VAYEB GLYPHS

CONCORDANCE OF 20-DAY SIGNS WITH PLANETS

IMIX—Solar Neptune

IK—Solar Uranus

AKBAL—Solar Saturn

KAN—Solar Jupiter

CHICCHAN—Solar A-Belt

CIMI—Solar Mars

MANIK—Solar Earth

LAMAT—Solar Venus

MULUC—Solar Mercury

OC—Galactic Mercury

CHUEN—Galactic Venus

EB—Galactic Earth

BEN—Galactic Mars

IX—Galactic A-Belt

MEN—Galactic Jupiter

CIB—Galactic Saturn

CABAN—Galactic Uranus

EDZNAB—Galactic Neptune

CAUAC—Galactic Pluto

AHAU—Solar Pluto

LIST OF YEARS, A.D. 1986-2012

1986: 7 MULUC

1987: 8 IX

1988: 9 CAUAC

1989: 10 KAN

1990: 11 MULUC

1991: 12 IX

13 AHAU Katun

1992: 13 CAUAC

1993: 1 KAN

1994: 2 MULUC

1995: 3 IX

1996: 4 CAUAC

1997: 5 KAN

1998: 6 MULUC

1999: 7 IX

2000: 8 CAUAC

2001: 9 KAN

2002: 10 MULUC

2003: 11 IX

2004: 12 CAUAC

2005: 13 KAN

2006: 1 MULUC

2007: 2 IX

2008: 3 CAUAC

2009: 4 KAN

2010: 5 MULUC

2011: 6 IX

2012: 7 CAUAC

GALACTIC SYNCHRONIZATION

BIBLIOGRAPHY

Alonzo, Gualberto Zapata. *An Overview of the Mayan World*. Mérida, 1983.

Annals of the Cakchiquels and Title of the Lords of Totonicapan. Translated by Adrian Recinos, Delia Goetz and Dionisio José Chonay. Norman: University of Oklahoma Press, 1953.

Argüelles, José. *Earth Ascending: An Illustrated Treatise on the Law Governing Whole Systems*. Boulder: Shambhala Publications, 1984.

The Transformative Vision: Reflections on the Nature and History of Human Expression. Berkeley: Shambhala Publications, 1975.

Arochi, Luis E. *La Piramide de Kukulcan: Su simbolismo solar*. Mexico City: Panorama Editorial, 1981.

Aveni, Anthony, ed. *Archeoastronomy in Pre-Columbian America*. Austin: University of Texas Press, 1975.

Skywatchers of Ancient Mexico. Austin: University of Texas Press, 1980.

Beaman, Donald G. *Return to Saqqara: Book 6, Geometric Analysis*. Boston: Donald G. Beaman, 1985.

Bentov, Isaac. *Stalking the Wild Pendulum: On the Mechanics of Consciousness*. New York: E.P. Dutton, 1977.

Bernal, Ignacio. *Official Guide: Teotihuacan*. Mexico City: INAH, 1985

Bierhorst, John. *Four Masterworks of American Indian Literature*. New York: Farrar, Strauss & Giroux, 1974.

Bernbaum, Edwin. *The Way to Shambhala*. New York: Doubleday, 1980.

The Book of Chilam Balam of Chumayel. Translated and edited by Ralph Roys. Norman: University of Oklahoma Press, 1967.

Carey, Ken (Raphael). *The Starseed Transmissions: An Extraterrestrial Report*. Kansas City: Uni Sun, 1984.

Carrasco, David. *Quetzalcoatl and the Irony of Empire: Myths and Prophecies in the Aztec Tradition*. Chicago: University of Chicago Press, 1982.

Caso, Alfonso. *Los Calendarios Prehispanicos*. Mexico City: Universidad Nacional Autonomia de Mexico, 1967.

Castaneda, Carlos. *The Fire From Within*. New York: Simon & Schuster, 1984.

The Teachings of Don Juan, A Yaqui Way of Knowledge. Berkeley: University of California Press, 1968.

Cathie, Bruce. *The Bridge to Infinity: Harmonic 371299*. Auckland, N.Z.: Quark Enterprises, 1983.

The Codex Perez and the Book of Chilam Balam of Mani, Translated by Eugene R. Craine and Reginald C. Reindorp. Norman: University of Oklahoma Press,1979.

Coe, Michael D. *The Maya*. New York: Praeger, 1966.

Coe, William R. *Tikal: A Handbook of the Ancient Maya Ruins*. Philadelphia: The University Museum of the University of Pennsylvania, 1967.

Contreras, Guillermo Garcés. *Los Codices Mayas*. Mexico City: Sep/Setentas, 1975.

Covarrubias, Miguel. *Indian Art of Mexico and Central America*. New York: Alfred A. Knopf, 1957.

Díaz-Bolio, José. *Origen de la Cronologia Maya*. Mérida: Revista de la Universidad de Yucatan, 1980.

The Rattlesnake School for Geometry, Architecture, Chronology Religion and the Arts. Mérida: Area Maya, 1984(?)

Faucett, Lawrence. *Time and Morality: Establishing a Babylonian Source for Hindu and Mayan Chronologies*. Woodland Hills, Calif.: Woodland Hills Reporter, 1956.

Frick, Thomas, ed. *The Sacred Theory of the Earth*. Berkeley: North Atlantic Books, 1986.

Gates, William. *An Outline Dictionary of Mayan Glyphs*. Baltimore: The Johns Hopkins Press, 1931.

Girard, Raphael. *Le Popul-Vuh: Histoire Culturelle des Maya Quiches*. Paris: Payot, 1954.

Grossinger, Richard, ed. *Planetary Mysteries: Megaliths, Glaciers, The Face on Mars and Aboriginal Dream-time*. Berkeley: North Atlantic Books, 1986.

Harleston, Hugh. *The Keystone: A Search for Understanding, A New Guide to the Great Pyramids of Mexico*. Bellaire, Tex. Uac-Can, 1984.

Hatcher Childress, D., ed. *The Anti-Gravity Handbook*. Stelle, Ill.: Publishers Network, 1985.

Huff, Sandy. *The Mayan Calendar Made Easy*. Safety Harbor, Fla.: 1984

Hurtak, J. J. *The Keys of Enoch: The Book of Knowledge*. Los Gatos: The Academy for Future Science, 1977.

Ivanoff, Pierre. *Monuments of Civilization: Maya*. New York: Grosset & Dunlap, 1973.

Kalachakra Initiation. Madison: Deer Park Books, 1981.

Katchongva, Dan. *From the Beginning of Life to the Day of Purification*, Translated by Danaqyumptewa. Los Angeles: The Committee for Traditional Indian Land and Life, 1972.

Krupp, Dr. E.C. *Echoes of the Ancient Skies: The Astronomy of Lost Civilizations*. New York: Harper & Row, 1983.

Landa, Friar Diego de. *Yucatan, Before and After the Conquest*. Translated by William Gates. New York: Dover Publications, 1978.

Lemusurier, Peter. *The Great Pyramid Decoded*. Longmead: Element Books, 1985.

León-Portilla, Miguel. *Pre-Columbian Literatures of Mexico*. Translated by Grace Lobanov and Miguel León-Portilla. Norman: University of Oklahoma Press, 1969.

Time and Reality in the Thought of the Maya, Translated by Charles Boiles and Fernando Horcasitas. Boston: Beacon Press, 1973.

Le Plongeon, Augustus. *Maya/Atlantis: Queen Moo and the Egyptian Sphinx*. Blauvelt, NY: Rudolf Steiner Publications, 1973.

El Libro de los Libros de Chilam Balam, Translated by Alfredo Barrera Vásquez and Sylvia Rendon. Mexico City: Fondo de Cultura Economica, 1948.

López Portillo, José, et.al. *Quetzalcoatl in Myth, Archeology and Art.* New York: Continuum Publishing Company, 1982.

Luxton, Richard, and Balam, Pedro. *Mystery of The Mayan Hieroglyphs Decoded.* New York: Harper & Row, 1982.

McKenna, Dennis J., and McKenna, Terence K. *The Invisible Landscape: Mind, Hallucinogens and the I Ching.* New York: The Seabury Press, 1977.

Marti, Samuel and Gertrude Prokosch Kurath. *Dances of Anahuac: The Choreography and Music of Pre-Cortesian Dances.* Chicago: Aldine Publishing Co., 1964.

Men, Humbatz. *Tzol Ek': Astrologia Maya.* Mexico City: Ediciones Juarez, 1983(?).

Metropolitan Museum of Art. *Before Córtes: Sculpture of Middle America.* New York: New York Graphic Society, 1970.

Morley, Sylvanus Griswold. *The Ancient Maya.* Stanford: Stanford University Press, 1956.

The Inscriptions of Peten. Washington: Carnegie Institute of Washington, 1937.

Guidebook to the Ruins of Quirigua. Washington: The Carnegie Institute, 1935.

An Introduction to the Study of Maya Hieroglyphs. New York: Dover Publications, 1975.

Nicholson, Irene. *Firefly in the Night: A Study of Ancient Mexican Symbolism and Poetry.* New York: Grove Press, 1959.

Mexican and Central American Mythology. London: Paul Hamlyn, 1967.

Ostrander, Edgar A. *Evidence that Ancient Mayan Cosmology Incorporated the Internal Functioning of the Human Brain.* Smithtown, N.Y.: Exposition Press, 1983.

Parédez, Domingo Martínez. *Parapsicologia Maya.* Mexico City: Manuel Porrua, 1981.

Piña Chan, Roman. *Chichen Itza: La Ciudad de los Brujos del Agua.* Mexico City: Fondo Cultura Economica, 1980.

Quetzalcoatl: Serpiente Enplumada. Mexico City: Fondo Cultura Economica, 1977.

Pollock, H.E.D. *Round Structures of Middle America.* Washington: The Carnegie Institute of Washington, 1936.

Popul Vuh, The Mayan Book of the Dawn of Life and the Glories of Gods and Kings. Translated by Dennis Tedlock. New York: Simon & Schuster, 1985.

Popul Vuh: The Sacred Book of the Ancient Quiche Maya. Translated by Delia Goetz and Sylvanus Morley from the Spanish of Adrian Recinos. Norman: University of Oklahoma Press, 1950.

Ramos, Ing. Alberto Escalona. "Areas y Estratos arqueologico cultural de la América Media," *Boletin de la Sociedad Mexicana de Geografia y Estadistica,* Vol LIX, nos. 1 & 2.(1944):41-66.

Reiser, Oliver. *Cosmic Humanism: A Theory of the Eight-Dimensional Cosmos Based on Integrative Principles of Science, Religion, and Art.* Cambridge: Schenkman Publishing Co., 1966.

Ritual of the Bacabs: A Book of Maya Incantations, translated and edited by Ralph L. Roys. Norman: University of Oklahoma Press, 1965.

Robertson, Donald. *Pre-Columbian Architecture*. New York: George Braziller, 1963.

Roerich, Nicholas. *Shambhala*. New York: Frederick A. Stokes Company, 1930.

Rupert, Karl. *The Caracol at Chichen Itza, Yucatan, Mexico*. Washington: The Carnegie Insitute of Washington, 1935.

Russell, Walter. *The Secret of Light*. Waynesboro, Va: The University of Science and Philosophy, 1947.

The Universal One. Waynesboro, Va.: The University of Science and Philosophy, 1926.

Santiago Robles, Federico J. *El Lenguaje de las piedras: Chinicultic, Chiapas*. San Cristobal de las Casas, 1974.

Schele, Linda, and Miller, Mary Ellen. *The Blood of Kings: Dynasty and Ritual in Maya Art*. New York: George Braziller, 1986.

Schönberger, Martin. *The I Ching and the Genetic Code: The Hidden Key to Life*. Translated by D. Q. Stephenson. New York: ASI Publishers, 1979.

Schwaller de Lubicz, R.A. *Nature Word*, Translated by Deborah Lawlor. Stockbridge Mass. The Lindisfarne Press, 1982

Sacred Science: The King of Pharaonic Theocracy, Translated by Andre and Goldian Vandenbroeck. New York: Inner Traditions, 1982.

Sejourne, Luarette. *Burning Water: Thought and Religion in Ancient Mexico*. Boulder: Shambhala Publications, 1977.

El Pensamiento Nahuatl Cifrado por los Calendarios. Mexico City: Siglo Vientiuno, 1983.

El Universo de Quetzalcoatl. Mexico City: Fondo de Cultura Económica, 1962.

Shearer, Tony. *Beneath the Moon and Under the Sun, A Poetic Appraisal of the Sacred Calendar and the Prophecies of Ancient Mexico*. Albuquerque: Sun Books, 1975.

Lord of the Dawn, Quetzalcoatl. Healdsburg: Naturegraph Press, 1971.

Sheldrake, Rupert. *A New Science of Life: The Hypothesis of Formative Causation*. London: Muller, 1982.

Sitchin, Zecharia. *The 12th Planet*. New York: Stein and Day Publishers, 1976.

Sodi, Demetrio M. *La Literatura de los Mayas*. Mexico City: Editorial Joaquin Mortiz, 1964

The Maya World. Mexico City: Minutiae Mexicana, 1976.

Sopa, Geshe Lhundub, et. al. *The Wheel of Time: The Kalachakra in Context*. Madison: Deer Park Books, 1985.

Spinden, Herbert J. *A Study of Maya Art, Its Subject Matter and Historical Development*. New York, Dover Publications, 1975.

Steiger, Brad. *Gods of Aquarius: UFOs and the Transformation of Man*. New York: Harcourt, Brace & Jovanovich, 1976.

Sten, Maria. *The Mexican Codices and Their Extraordinary History*. Mexico City: Editorial Joaquin Mortiz, 1972.

Stierlin, Henri. *Art of the Maya*. New York: Rizzoli, 1981.

Living Architecture: Mayan. New York: Grosset & Dunlap, 1964.

Stromsvik, Gustav. *Guidebook to the Ruins of Copan.* Washington: Carnegie Institute of Washington, 1947.

Stuart, George E. and Stuart, Gene S. *The Mysterious Maya.* Washington: The National Geographic Society, 1977.

Swimme, Brian. *The Universe is a Green Dragon: A Cosmic Creation Story.* Santa Fe: Bear & Co, 1984.

Talbot, Michael. *Mysticism and the New Physics.* New York: Bantam Books, 1980.

Tedlock, Barbara. *Time and The Highland Maya.* Albuquerque: University of New Mexico Press, 1982.

Thompson, J. Eric S. *A Catalog of Maya Hieroglyphs.* Norman: University of Oklahoma Press, 1962.

A Commentary on the Dresden Codex. Philadelphia: American Philosophical Society, 1972.

Maya Hieroglyphic Writing. Norman: University of Oklahoma Press, 1960.

The Rise and Fall of Maya Civilization. Norman: University of Oklahoma Press, 1954.

Thompson, William Irwin. *Blue Jade from the Morning Star: An Essay and a Cycle of Poems on Quetzalcoatl.* Stockbridge, Mass.: The Lindisfarne Press, 1983.

Tirado-González, Federico. *The Tree of Life: God, Love Creator.* Berkeley: Editorial Justa, 1986.

Tompkins, Peter. *Mysteries of the Mexican Pyramids.* New York: Harper & Row, 1976.

Secrets of the Great Pyramid. New York: Harper & Row, 1971.

Tozzer, Alfred M. *A Maya Grammar.* New York: Dover Publications, 1977.

Trungpa, Chögyam. *Shambhala: Sacred Path of the Warrior.* Boulder: Shambhala Publications, 1984.

Waters, Frank. *Mexico Mystique: The Coming Sixth World of Consciousness.* Chicago: Swallow Press, 1975.

West, John Anthony. *Serpent in the Sky: The High Wisdom of Ancient Egypt.* New York: Harper & Row, 1979.

Westheim, Paul. *The Art of Ancient Mexico,* Translated by Ursula Bernard. New York: Doubleday, 1965.

Prehispanic Mexican Art. Mexico City: Editorial Herrero, 1972.

Zukov, Gary. *The Dancing Wu Li Masters.* New York: William Morrow, 1979.

ABOUT THE AUTHOR

Artist, poet, visionary historian, and cosmic harmonist, José Argüelles, Ph.D., is recognized as a leading spokesperson for the principles of art as awakened warriorship and the role of art as a dynamic agent of planetary transformation.

Born of Mexican-American heritage on January 24, 1939, he was educated at the University of Chicago (BA, 1961; MA, 1963; Ph.D., 1969). Following completion of formal studies in the history of art, he was named Samuel H. Kress Senior Fellow and spent 1965-66 pursuing a course of free study in Paris and Europe. In his role as educator and professor, he has taught at Princeton University (1966-68); the University of California, Davis (1968-71); The Evergreen State College (1971-73); The Naropa Institute (1974-75, 1980-83); California State University, San Francisco (1974-77); The San Francisco Art Institute (1976-77); the University of Colorado, Denver (1979-83); and the Union Graduate School (1977-present), where he is currently Core Faculty and Program Coordinator, Creative Arts.

As a poet, art critic, and philosopher, Argüelles' work has appeared in many journals of art, philosophy, and leading-edge thought. His books include: *Charles Henry and the Formation of a Psychophysical Aesthetic* (1972); *Mandala* and *The Feminine, Spacious as the Sky* (with Miriam T. Argüelles, 1972 & 1977); *The Transformative Vision: Reflections on the Nature and History of Human Expression* (1975); and *Earth Ascending: An Illustrated Treatise on the Law Governing Whole Systems* (1984).

Argüelles' paintings have been exhibited around the country and reproduced in numerous books and journals. His mural activity is in evidence at the University of California, Davis (1968) and The Evergreen State College (1972). A student since 1972 of Tibetan meditation master and artist, Chögyam Trungpa, Rinpoche, Argüelles assisted Trungpa in the formulation of the principles of Dharma Art and in the staging of Dharma Art projects in Los Angeles (1980) and San Francisco (1981). Founder of the First Whole Earth Festival, Davis, California, 1970, as a transformational art activist, Argüelles went on to found the Planet Art Network in 1983 as a visionary instrument for global artistic change. Since 1983, Argüelles and his wife, Lloydine, have travelled extensively promoting "Art as a Foundation for Global Peace."

In addition to current transformationalist network activities, Argüelles is continuing his research in resonant harmonics and the principles of Cosmic Science. Residing in Boulder, Colorado, his extended family includes five children, a dog, and two cats.

CELEBRATE HARMONIC CONVERGENCE!

Harmonic Convergence, August 16 and 17, 1987, depends upon self-empowered individuals creating rituals, celebrations, and joyful events expressing their feelings of peace and harmony with the Earth and with each other. Take the initiative! Let us know of your plans. Call or write: Healing Our World (H.O.W.), P.O. Box 6111, Boulder, CO 80306, (303) 443-4328.